Omnichannel Approach to Co-Creating Customer Experiences Through Metaverse Platforms

Babita Singla
Chitkara Business School, Chitkara University, India

Kumar Shalender
Chitkara University, India

Nripendra Singh
PennWest University, USA

A volume in the Advances in Systems Analysis, Software Engineering, and High Performance Computing (ASASEHPC) Book Series

IGI Global
PUBLISHER of TIMELY KNOWLEDGE

Published in the United States of America by
IGI Global
Engineering Science Reference (an imprint of IGI Global)
701 E. Chocolate Avenue
Hershey PA, USA 17033
Tel: 717-533-8845
Fax: 717-533-8661
E-mail: cust@igi-global.com
Web site: http://www.igi-global.com

Library of Congress Cataloging-in-Publication Data

Names: Singla, Babita, 1988- editor. | Shalender, Kumar, 1984- editor. | Singh, Nripendra, 1975- editor.
Title: Omnichannel approach to co-creating customer experiences through metaverse platforms / edited by Babita Singla, Kumar Shalender, Nripendra Singh.
Description: Hershey, PA : Engineering Science Reference, [2024] | Includes bibliographical references and index. | Summary: "The primary objective of this book is to analyze, evaluate, and recommend the use of metaverse platforms across industrial sectors using the omnichannel approach"-- Provided by publisher.
Identifiers: LCCN 2023055024 (print) | LCCN 2023055025 (ebook) | ISBN 9798369318669 (hardcover) | ISBN 9798369318676 (ebook)
Subjects: LCSH: Metaverse--Economic aspects. | Customer services--Technological innovations.
Classification: LCC TK5105.8864 .O46 2024 (print) | LCC TK5105.8864 (ebook) | DDC 658.8/12--dc23/eng/20240110
LC record available at https://lccn.loc.gov/2023055024
LC ebook record available at https://lccn.loc.gov/2023055025

This book is published in the IGI Global book series Advances in Systems Analysis, Software Engineering, and High Performance Computing (ASASEHPC) (ISSN: 2327-3453; eISSN: 2327-3461)

British Cataloguing in Publication Data
A Cataloguing in Publication record for this book is available from the British Library.

For electronic access to this publication, please contact: eresources@igi-global.com.

Advances in Systems Analysis, Software Engineering, and High Performance Computing (ASASEHPC) Book Series

Vijayan Sugumaran
Oakland University, USA

ISSN:2327-3453
EISSN:2327-3461

MISSION

The theory and practice of computing applications and distributed systems has emerged as one of the key areas of research driving innovations in business, engineering, and science. The fields of software engineering, systems analysis, and high performance computing offer a wide range of applications and solutions in solving computational problems for any modern organization.

The **Advances in Systems Analysis, Software Engineering, and High Performance Computing (ASASEHPC) Book Series** brings together research in the areas of distributed computing, systems and software engineering, high performance computing, and service science. This collection of publications is useful for academics, researchers, and practitioners seeking the latest practices and knowledge in this field.

COVERAGE

- Storage Systems
- Computer System Analysis
- Computer Networking
- Enterprise Information Systems
- Network Management
- Parallel Architectures
- Distributed Cloud Computing
- Human-Computer Interaction
- Virtual Data Systems
- Metadata and Semantic Web

IGI Global is currently accepting manuscripts for publication within this series. To submit a proposal for a volume in this series, please contact our Acquisition Editors at Acquisitions@igi-global.com or visit: http://www.igi-global.com/publish/.

The Advances in Systems Analysis, Software Engineering, and High Performance Computing (ASASEHPC) Book Series (ISSN 2327-3453) is published by IGI Global, 701 E. Chocolate Avenue, Hershey, PA 17033-1240, USA, www.igi-global.com. This series is composed of titles available for purchase individually; each title is edited to be contextually exclusive from any other title within the series. For pricing and ordering information please visit http://www.igi-global.com/book-series/advances-systems-analysis-software-engineering/73689. Postmaster: Send all address changes to above address.

Titles in this Series

For a list of additional titles in this series, please visit:
http://www.igi-global.com/book-series/advances-systems-analysis-software-engineering/73689

Handbook of Research on Integrating Machine Learning Into HPC-Based Simulations and Analytics
Belgacem Ben Youssef (King Saud University, Saudi Arabia) and Mohamed Maher Ben Ismail (King Saud University, Saudi Arabia)
Engineering Science Reference • © 2024 • 400pp • H/C (ISBN: 9781668437957) • US $325.00

Machine Learning Algorithms Using Scikit and TensorFlow Environments
Puvvadi Baby Maruthi (Dayananda Sagar University, India) Smrity Prasad (Dayananda Sagar University, India) and Amit Kumar Tyagi (National Institute of Fashion Technology, New Delhi, India)
Engineering Science Reference • © 2024 • 453pp • H/C (ISBN: 9781668485316) • US $270.00

Uncertain Spatiotemporal Data Management for the Semantic Web
Luyi Bai (Northeastern University, China) and Lin Zhu (Northeastern University, China)
Engineering Science Reference • © 2024 • 500pp • H/C (ISBN: 9781668491089) • US $325.00

ODE, BVP, and 1D PDE Solvers for Scientific and Engineering Problems With MATLAB Basics
Leonid Burstein (ORT Braude College of Engineering, Israel (Retired))
Engineering Science Reference • © 2024 • 300pp • H/C (ISBN: 9781668468500) • US $245.00

Digital Technologies in Modeling and Management Insights in Education and Industry
GS Prakasha (Christ University, India) Maria Lapina (North-Caucasus Federal University, Russia) and Deepanraj Balakrishnan (Prince Mohammad Bin Fahd University, Saudi Arabia)
Information Science Reference • © 2024 • 320pp • H/C (ISBN: 9781668495766) • US $250.00

IGI Global
PUBLISHER of TIMELY KNOWLEDGE

701 East Chocolate Avenue, Hershey, PA 17033, USA
Tel: 717-533-8845 x100 • Fax: 717-533-8661
E-Mail: cust@igi-global.com • www.igi-global.com

Table of Contents

Detailed Table of Contents

The digital future is rapidly approaching, characterized by technological innovations that promise transformative changes across various facets of human existence. At the forefront of this digital transformation is the emergence of metaverse platforms—a convergence of virtual reality, augmented reality, blockchain, and artificial intelligence—reshaping the way humans interact, work, and socialize online. This chapter explores the profound implications of the technological revolution brought about by metaverse platforms on humanity and society. Through an interdisciplinary lens, this chapter delves into the multifaceted dimensions of the metaverse's impact. It examines how metaverse technologies are redefining the boundaries of human experience, enabling immersive virtual environments where individuals can work, socialize, create, and trade digital assets. In conclusion, this chapter provides a comprehensive analysis of the far-reaching implications of the technological revolution brought about by metaverse platforms in the digital future.

The presence of technologies in society is constantly increasing, and the field of education cannot remain oblivious to this situation. It must integrate new technological proposals to improve the teaching and learning processes. This chapter analyses the differences shown by university students from two different environments, specific

modernizing services provided by governments, enhancing convenience, speeding up the growth of the economy, and encouraging long-term viability. In this study, the authors explain how using the metaverse towards smart cities might spur development and enhance its implementation. They cover essential metaverse innovations, their top advantages, and smart city implementations. They demonstrate metaverse technology's applicability throughout sectors with active initiatives and cases. They also highlight and address major research hurdles that are preventing the metaverse from reaching its maximum capacity. They conclude with additional investigation objectives for developing the metaverse and smart city interconnectivity.

In the dynamic landscape of the Indian retail industry, the seamless functioning of the supply chain is paramount to ensuring product availability and minimizing out-of-stock incidents. The flexibility of the supply chain is essential to effectively address challenges within the food supply chain. This research delves into the complexities and challenges faced by retailers in India as they strive to manage their supply chains effectively and ensure a consistent flow of products to meet consumer demands. The objective of this study is to comprehensively analyze the practices, strategies, and technologies employed by retailers in India to enhance supply chain management, ultimately reducing out-of-stock incidents. With the rapid growth of e-commerce and changing consumer expectations, retailers face mounting pressure to optimize their supply chains to remain competitive and maintain customer satisfaction. The study contributes to the ongoing dialogue on the role of supply chain management in ensuring the success and sustainability of retail businesses in India's rapidly evolving market.

Preface

Welcome to *Omnichannel Approach to Co-Creating Customer Experiences Through Metaverse Platforms*, an edited reference book that delves into the transformative intersection of metaverse platforms and omnichannel business models. As editors, we are pleased to present a comprehensive exploration of this dynamic landscape, bringing together insights from esteemed contributors to offer a panoramic view of the metaverse's impact on the retail industry.

The essence of this edited volume lies in its multidimensional approach, traversing the realms of marketing, finance, human resources, supply chain, and economics. We aim to provide a roadmap for seamlessly embedding metaverse platforms into omnichannel business models across various product categories and service domains. The book unfolds with a holistic perspective, illuminating the potential benefits metaverse adoption can bring to stakeholders throughout the omnichannel value chain.

Omnichannel Approach to Co-Creating Customer Experiences Through Metaverse Platforms aspires to be a beacon for scholars, practitioners, and policymakers alike. We invite our readers to conceptualize and integrate virtual platforms into business models, unlocking the potential of the digital revolution. By disseminating knowledge for immersive and empowered customer engagement, this title strives to create a win-win scenario for industry stakeholders, including customers and policymakers.

ORGANIZATION OF THE BOOK

Chapter 1: This chapter serves as a foundational exploration of the digital future, focusing on the transformative role of metaverse platforms. It investigates the profound implications of metaverse technologies on human experience, examining how virtual reality, augmented reality, blockchain, and artificial intelligence converge to reshape online interactions. The interdisciplinary lens employed offers readers a comprehensive analysis of the far-reaching implications of the metaverse's technological revolution.

Chapter 2: Delving into the realm of education, this chapter analyzes the motivations behind the use of educational technologies among university students. The study compares students from rural and urban environments, exploring their preferences in accessing knowledge. By examining the role of technology in the learning process, the chapter provides insights into how students, particularly future teachers, engage with and are motivated by technology.

Chapter 3: This research analysis focuses on the economic implications of virtual goods and digital assets within the metaverse. Exploring the metaverse as a marketplace, the chapter investigates factors influencing demand, pricing mechanisms, and the impact of scarcity and blockchain on virtual asset valuation. Additionally, it examines the intersection of the metaverse's digital economy with the traditional world economy, shedding light on virtual jobs, income streams, and challenges associated with taxation.

Chapter 4: This chapter explores the relationship between brand experience and brand equity in the context of the online shopping industry. Highlighting the importance of adopting a long-term, ethical, and collaborative strategy, it discusses how brands can navigate the metaverse space. The article emphasizes the positive influence of sensory, affective, behavioral, and intellectual dimensions of brand experience on various aspects of brand equity.

Chapter 5: This chapter explores the trend of ordering food online and its impact on the gig economy. Discussing the advantages and disadvantages of online meal delivery services, the chapter highlights the role of technological integration in enhancing consumer satisfaction. It concludes by emphasizing the influence of social, economic, and individual factors on food delivery platforms.

Chapter 6: Examining the growing popularity of omnichannel retail, this chapter identifies critical elements influencing effective strategies. It delves into customer behavior, preferences, and the role of technology, data analytics, and personalized marketing in creating individualized retail experiences. The chapter provides practical ideas for creating flexible omnichannel frameworks through case studies and industry best practices.

Chapter 7: This chapter explores the impact of the metaverse on the retail sector, highlighting how immersive and interactive experiences reshape the conventional shopping environment. It emphasizes the importance of a careful evaluation of ethical and practical ramifications for a successful and lasting integration of the metaverse in the retail industry.

Chapter 8: Focusing on the creator's economy within the metaverse, this chapter discusses the benefits for creators, brands, and retailers. It explores how creators can leverage the metaverse for unique shopping experiences, brands can reach new audiences, and retailers can adopt comprehensive retailing strategies. The chapter underscores the importance of collaboration and integration across physical and virtual worlds.

Chapter 9: This chapter explores the potential of using the metaverse to enhance smart cities. Examining essential metaverse innovations and their benefits, it discusses smart city implementations and addresses research challenges. The chapter concludes with further research objectives for developing metaverse and smart city interconnectivity.

Chapter 10: Focusing on the Indian retail industry, this chapter examines the challenges and complexities faced by retailers in managing their supply chains. It aims to comprehensively analyze practices, strategies, and technologies employed to enhance supply chain management, ultimately reducing out-of-stock incidents. The study contributes to the ongoing dialogue on the role of supply chain management in ensuring the success and sustainability of retail businesses in India.

Chapter 11: This chapter investigates the substantial influence of artificial intelligence on the adoption of digital technologies in India. It explores how AI technology facilitates advancements in various domains, contributing to financial inclusion, healthcare accessibility, and socioeconomic progress. The study also addresses challenges and ethical concerns associated with the utilization of artificial intelligence within the framework of digital technology adoption in India.

We extend our gratitude to the contributors for their invaluable insights and to the readers for joining us on this intellectual journey. May this book inspire innovative thinking and practical strategies as we navigate the exciting intersection of the digital world and retail evolution.

Babita Singla
Chitkara Business School, Chitkara University, Punjab, India

Kumar Shalender
Chitkara Business School, Chitkara University, India

Nripendra Singh
Pennsylvania Western University, USA

Chapter 1
Implications of the Technological Revolution on Human Life in the Digital Future:
A Metaverse Perspective

V. Suganya
https://orcid.org/0000-0001-5301-8317
SRM Institute of Science and Technology, Vadapalani, India

M. Kalaivani
SRM Institute of Science and Technology, Vadapalani, India

ABSTRACT

The digital future is rapidly approaching, characterized by technological innovations that promise transformative changes across various facets of human existence. At the forefront of this digital transformation is the emergence of metaverse platforms—a convergence of virtual reality, augmented reality, blockchain, and artificial intelligence—reshaping the way humans interact, work, and socialize online. This chapter explores the profound implications of the technological revolution brought about by metaverse platforms on humanity and society. Through an interdisciplinary lens, this chapter delves into the multifaceted dimensions of the metaverse's impact. It examines how metaverse technologies are redefining the boundaries of human experience, enabling immersive virtual environments where individuals can work, socialize, create, and trade digital assets. In conclusion, this chapter provides a comprehensive analysis of the far-reaching implications of the technological revolution brought about by metaverse platforms in the digital future.

DOI: 10.4018/979-8-3693-1866-9.ch001

INTRODUCTION

In the annals of human history, a handful of technological revolutions have left an indelible mark, reshaping the way we live, work, and connect with one another. From the advent of the printing press to the harnessing of electricity and the rise of the internet, each revolution has ushered in a new era defined by unprecedented possibilities and unforeseen challenges. As we stand at the precipice of the 21st century, the burgeoning metaverse is poised to spearhead yet another transformation, heralding the dawn of the digital future.

The metaverse, a term coined by science fiction author Neal Stephenson, has rapidly evolved from a realm of speculative fiction to a tangible and expanding digital universe. It represents a convergence of virtual reality (VR), augmented reality (AR), artificial intelligence (AI), blockchain technology, and spatial computing, offering a rich tapestry of immersive experiences and interconnected digital worlds. Within this vast digital expanse, people can gather, collaborate, trade, and explore in ways hitherto unimagined.

As the metaverse emerges as a formidable force in the technological landscape, it casts a spotlight on the profound implications it holds for human life. This analysis seeks to unravel the multifaceted consequences of the technological revolution brought forth by the metaverse, offering a perspective that spans the domains of society, economy, culture, and individual existence.

The research on "Implications of the Technological Revolution on Human Life in the Digital Future: A Metaverse Perspective" has several objectives aimed at comprehensively understanding and analyzing the impact of the metaverse on various aspects of human life. These objectives provide a clear roadmap for the research:

OBJECTIVES OF THE STUDY

- To gain a deep understanding of the metaverse, including its technologies, platforms, and the ways in which it is currently being utilized.
- To analyse its influence on social interactions, relationships, and the formation of communities within digital spaces.
- To analyse its role in creating virtual economies, virtual employment opportunities, and its impact on traditional economic systems.
- To analyse and assess how the metaverse impacts individuals on personal, psychological, and physical levels.

- To Identify Opportunities and Challenges: Identify the opportunities and challenges that the metaverse presents to individuals, businesses, governments, and society as a whole
- To provide recommendations based on the research findings, offer informed recommendations for individuals, organizations, policymakers, and society at large.
- To Contribute to the body of knowledge about the metaverse's impact on human life

LITERATURE REVIEW

In October 2021, Facebook changed its name to Meta, which means after and beyond. As a result, the term "Metaverse" entered the general public. In a similar vein, Metaverse, when combined with a three-dimensional virtual reality Metaverse, might be the next internet. Web 3.0, the upcoming version of the internet, is another idea that is gaining popularity. Lasile Shannon, Nokia's head of trend scouting, discussed the importance of the Metaverse. According to her, "The spatial internet is the culmination of everything that AR and VR is developing today" (CryptoStars, 2022, para. Additionally, Mark Zuckerberg refers to the Metaverse as "an embodied internet" since, in his opinion, the internet has developed into a more embodied experience (Kelly, 2021, para. 2). All of this suggests that Metaverse may be the next major virtual location where people congregate to interact, shop, sell, work, and have fun. Everything will start out as an alternative to social media and end up embracing the internet as we know it. Large corporations are attempting to take control of the Metaverse by incorporating virtual experiences into their current goods. According to a Bloomberg Intelligence analysis, digital reality will be worth $2 trillion by 2030 due to its promising economic possibilities. (2022, Moro Visconti). With these numbers, it is simple to understand why major technology companies envision Metaverse as the Internet of the future. Numerous businesses are working hard to set the bar high while fast achieving their goal of creating the best Metaverse. Numerous examples indicate how Facebook has evolved into a Meta. The leader of Facebook, Mark Zuckerberg, is the one who is putting the most money into the Metaverse because he announced that Facebook would change its name to Meta and that Facebook is now concentrating on the Metaverse. He asserts, "I think we are basically moving from being a company that puts Facebook first to being a company that puts Metaverse first" (Heath, 2021, para. 1). The business is making a $10 billion investment in the Metaverse's future. Other tech behemoths have been drawn into the frenzy as a result, with some vowing to contribute to the new business. Microsoft Mesh Company is one illustration of this (MSFT, 2021). According to Microsoft Mesh, it is a mixed reality concept that enables presence and experience sharing across all devices.

Microsoft thinks that businesses interested in using this new platform to offer products or services will have a chance. Alibaba and other fashion and business firms, in addition to tech giants like Amazon, have invested close to $1,6 million in the business. Companies like Burberry, Dolce & Gabbana, Louis Vuitton, and Amarossa will be able to promote their products in a way that is more effective than the ways they do it now. (2022 Ciaravino) It would also enable entertainment firms like Walmart and Disney to offer their goods and services through immersive marketing campaigns by acting as a virtual window for incoming consumers to experience the reality of purchased stuff. This would enable people to buy things more quickly. (Hernandez,2022) Companies that want to make sure that their characters are accessible everywhere in the world so that people may enjoy them wherever they go have potential in the metaverse. However, Metaverse also has significant legal and regulatory ramifications, much like the ones that tech behemoths are now dealing with in the market. These ramifications revolve on a global debate over the subjects of user privacy, data rights, and rules. The next challenge for these problems could be the metaverse. According to data acquired by Hootsuite, 3.48 billion people, or 45% of the world's population, are connected to social media while we are taking care of protection-related issues via social media (Hootsuite Inc., 2020). Social media collects a ton of personal information, far more than we might intuitively think we are doing.

There are currently few regulations from the government regarding data sharing and privacy issues. This opens a door for a tech company to leverage a user's private information to acquire insight into the personal information used to understand people and then try to take advantage of the situation for their own personal gain. The APWG Phishing Activity Trends Report (Surwade, 2020) indicates that phishing activities began to increase in 2021 starting about 2020. An individual's information is mined through Botnets1, which are networks of computerized accounts used for online entertainment. Generally speaking, these problems won't go away, and in the recently suggested Metaverse, everything except more copies of these difficulties will likely be there.

Figure 1. Conceptual framework for the study

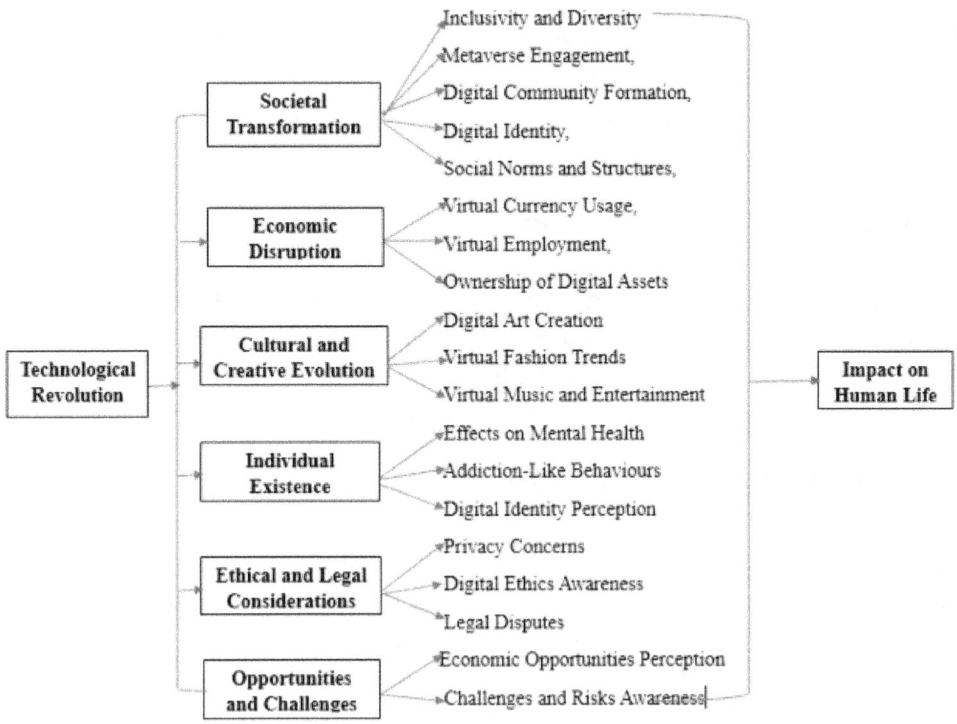

Challenges Of Human Life Due to Metaverse Platforms

The metaverse, while holding great promise, also presents several significant challenges to human life. These challenges are a reflection of the transformative nature of this technology and its potential impact on various aspects of society.

Digital Addiction and Escapism

Spending excessive time in the metaverse can lead to digital addiction, with individuals becoming engrossed in virtual worlds at the expense of real-life activities and relationships.

The metaverse can offer an enticing escape from real-world problems, potentially leading to disengagement from reality.

Privacy and Security Concerns

Users in the metaverse share a vast amount of personal information and data, which can be vulnerable to breaches, hacking, or misuse.

The potential for surveillance and tracking within the metaverse raises privacy concerns.

Mental Health Implications

The immersive nature of the metaverse can have psychological effects, including social isolation, anxiety, and depression.

Real-world issues like cyberbullying and harassment can persist in the virtual realm, impacting users' mental well-being.

Digital Divide and Inequality

Access to the metaverse requires specific hardware and a stable internet connection, which may exacerbate existing inequalities, particularly for those in underserved or economically disadvantaged regions.

Economic disparities can be reinforced as users with more resources can access and benefit from the metaverse to a greater extent.

Identity and Authenticity Issues

The ability to create and control digital avatars can raise questions about identity and authenticity in the metaverse. It becomes difficult to discern real from fake.

This can lead to issues like catfishing, impersonation, and a loss of trust.

Legal and Ethical Challenges

The metaverse is a complex space in terms of regulation and governance, posing legal and ethical challenges. Issues related to jurisdiction, intellectual property, and digital rights can be hard to address effectively.

The use of AI and automation in the metaverse may raise ethical questions regarding data handling, algorithmic bias, and transparency.

Environmental Impact

Running the servers and infrastructure required to maintain the metaverse can consume significant amounts of energy, contributing to environmental concerns, especially if not managed sustainably.

Education and Skills Gap

While the metaverse offers immersive educational possibilities, it can also lead to a digital skills gap. Those who lack the necessary skills to navigate and create within the metaverse may face challenges in the job market.

Monopoly and Concentration of Power

The metaverse industry is currently dominated by a few major corporations. This concentration of power can stifle competition and innovation, raising concerns about a lack of diversity and choice.

Real-world Impact on Economy and Work

As people spend more time in the metaverse, real-world productivity and work-life balance can be affected, leading to concerns about burnout and blurred boundaries between work and leisure.

In conclusion, the implications of the technological revolution, particularly in the context of the metaverse, are vast and transformative for human life in the digital future. While the metaverse holds great promise for immersive experiences, economic opportunities, and creative expression, it also brings with it a host of challenges and considerations.

CONCLUSION

The metaverse's impact on human life spans various dimensions, including social interaction, work, education, entertainment, identity, mental health, regulation, and environmental sustainability. It promises to reshape the way we connect, learn, work, and play, offering novel opportunities while also introducing potential pitfalls.

To fully harness the benefits of the metaverse while mitigating its challenges, it is imperative for individuals, businesses, governments, and society as a whole to collaborate in setting ethical standards, ensuring digital inclusivity, safeguarding privacy, and addressing mental health concerns. Regulation and oversight will play a critical role in establishing a framework that promotes fairness, security, and responsible use of the metaverse.

The digital future, with the metaverse at its forefront, presents both exciting possibilities and complex dilemmas. Striking the right balance will be an ongoing journey as we navigate this new era of technology, always striving to maximize its potential for human progress, creativity, and connection while safeguarding the well-being and rights of individuals in the ever-evolving landscape of the metaverse.

REFERENCES

Aleksandar, A. (2022). *Alibaba Cloud accused of violating China's cybersecurity law*. Academic Press.

Apptuts, E. (2022). *Microsoft Mesh: Microsoft's gambit into the metaverse, AppTuts.net -Aplicativos Android, iPhone, iPad, Mac OSX e Windows*. Available at: https://www.apptuts.net/en/tutorial/android/microsoft-mesh-gambit-metaverse/

Barré, R., & David, B. (2004, May). Participative and coherent scenario building: An input/output balance model: The case of the French national futuris operation. In *Proceedings of the EUUS Scientific Seminar: New Technology Foresight, Forecasting & Assessment Methods in Seville, Spain* (pp. 3-14). Academic Press.

BBC. (2016). *France Data Authority criticises Windows 10 over privacy*. BBC News. Available at: https://www.bbc.com/news/technology-36854909

Bella, S. (2019, November 4). *Book Review: The Age of Surveillance Capitalism: The Fight for a Human Future at the New Frontier of Power by Shoshana Zuboff | LSE Review of Books*. LSE Review of Books. Available at: https://blogs.lse.ac.uk/lsereviewofbooks/2019/11/04/book-review-the-age-of-surveillancecapitalism-the-fight-for-the-future-at-the-new-frontier-of-power-by-shoshana-zuboff/

Berkhout, F., & Hertin, J. (2002). Foresight futures scenarios: Developing and applying a participative strategic planning tool. *Greener Management International, 2002*(37), 37–52. doi:10.9774/GLEAF.3062.2002.sp.00005

Bodoni, S. (2021). *Amazon gets record $888 million EU Fine Over Data violations.* ACEDS. Available at: https://aceds.org/stephanie-bodoni-amazon-gets-record-888-million-eu-fineover-data-violations

Burgos, J. (2022). *Alibaba shares jump as Chinese e-commerce giant posts record transactions, Forbes*. Forbes Magazine.

Carpenter, D. (2021). *Digital Marketing, the metaverse, and web 3.0, Digital Marketing Agency based in Seattle, Connection Mode*l. Available at:https://www.connectionmodel.com/blog/digital-marketing-the-metaverse-and-web-3.0

Chalmers, D. (2003). *The matrix as metaphysics*. Available at:https://www.consc.net/papers/matrix.pdf

Chalmers, D. J. (2022). Reality+: Virtual worlds and the problems of philosophy. Penguin UK.

Ciaravino, C. (2022). *Fashion Brands arrive in the metaverse.* The Cryptonomist. Available at: https://cryptonomist.ch/2022/07/20/fashion-brands-arrive-in-the-metaverse/?amp=1

CNN. (2022). *Meta fast facts.* CNN. Cable News Network. Available at: https://edition.cnn.com/2014/02/11/world/facebook-fast-facts/index.html

Conklin, W. A., & McLeod, A. (2009). Introducing the information technology security essential body of knowledge framework. *Journal of Information Privacy and Security*, *5*(2), 27–41. doi:10.1080/15536548.2009.10855862

Cryptostars. (2022). *The metaverse is coming*. Available at: https://blog.cryptostars.is/themetaverse-is-coming-c0c8de3b5a99

Dave, A. (2020). *Meta partners with Balenciaga, Prada, and Thom Browne and launches Digital Fashion Marketplace, The Block.* The Block.

Decker, K. (2022) *Into the metaverse: How digital twins can change the Business Landscape.* Entrepreneur. Entrepreneur. Available at: https://www.entrepreneur.com/article/425444

Di Pietro, R., & Cresci, S. (2021, December). Metaverse: Security and Privacy Issues. In *2021 Third IEEE International Conference on Trust, Privacy and Security in Intelligent Systems and Applications (TPS-ISA)* (pp. 281-288). IEEE.

Digital Watch Observatory. (n.d.). Available at: https://dig.watch/updates/alibaba-cloud-accusedviolating-chinas-cybersecurity-law

Donath, J. (2007). Signals in social supernets. *Journal of Computer-Mediated Communication, 13*(1), 231–251. doi:10.1111/j.1083-6101.2007.00394.x

Duan, H., Li, J., Fan, S., Lin, Z., Wu, X., & Cai, W. (2021, October). Metaverse for social good: A university campus prototype. In *Proceedings of the 29th ACM International Conference on Multimedia* (pp. 153-161). 10.1145/3474085.3479238

Fahey, L., & Randall, R. M. (Eds.). (1997). *Learning from the future: Competitive foresight scenarios*. John Wiley & Sons.

Fink, C. (2021). Facebook releases Blockbuster app for remote work, Forbes. *Forbes Magazine*. Available at: https://www.forbes.com/sites/charliefink/2021/08/19/facebook-releasesblockbuster-app-for-remote-work/?sh=4346462652fd

Frankenfield, J. (2022). Digital currency types, characteristics, Pros & Cons, future uses. *Investopedia*. Available at: https://www.investopedia.com/terms/d/digitalcurrency.asp

Fu, Z. (2022). *Alibaba takes a step further into the metaverse by launching a new shopping venue*. PingWest. Available at: https://en.pingwest.com/a/10257

Gross, R., & Acquisti, A. (2005, November). Information revelation and privacy in online social networks. In *Proceedings of the 2005 ACM workshop on Privacy in the electronic society* (pp. 71-80). 10.1145/1102199.1102214

Harari, Y. N. (2018). *Why Technology Favors Tyranny, The Atlantic*. Atlantic Media Company. Available at: https://www.theatlantic.com/magazine/archive/2018/10/yuval-noah-hararitechnology-tyranny/568330/

Heath, A. (2021). *Mark Zuckerberg on why Facebook is rebranding to Meta, The Verge*. The Verge. Available at: https://www.theverge.com/22749919/mark-zuckerberg-facebookmeta-company-rebrand

Hernandez, O. (2022). *Web3 watch: Disney and Walmart Target Young Audiences in the metaverse*. Blockworks. Available at: https://blockworks.co/web3-watch-disney-andwalmart-target-young-audiences-in-the-metaverse

Hootsuite Inc. (2020). *More than half of the people on Earth now use social media*. Available at: https://www.hootsuite.com/newsroom/press-releases/more-than-half-of-the-people-onearth-now-use-social-media

Jaloza, L. B. (2022). *Connect 2021: Our vision for the metaverse*. Tech at Meta. Available at:https://tech.fb.com/ar-vr/2021/10/connect-2021-our-vision-for-the-metaverse/

Johnson, B. (2010). Privacy no longer a social norm, says Facebook founder. *The Guardian*. https://www.theguardian.com/technology/2010/jan/11/facebook-privacy

Jordannovet. (2022). *Mark Zuckerberg envisions a billion people in the metaverse spending hundreds of dollars each, CNBC*. CNBC. Available at: https://www.cnbc.com/2022/06/22/mark-zuckerberg-envisions-1-billion-people-in-themetaverse.html

Kastrenakes, J., & Heath, A. (2021). *Facebook is spending at least $10 billion this year on its metaverse division, The Verge*. The Verge. Available at: https://www.theverge.com/2021/10/25/22745381/facebook-reality-labs-10-billionmetaverse

Kelly, N. M. (2018). "Works like Magic": Metaphor, Meaning, and the GUI in Snow Crash. *Science Fiction Studies*, *45*(1), 69–90. doi:10.5621/sciefictstud.45.1.0069

Kelly, S. M. (2021). *Facebook changes its company name to Meta | CNN business*. CNN.

Kosow, H., & Gassner, R. (2008). *Methods of future and scenario analysis: Overview, assessment, and selection criteria*. Deutsches Institut für Entwicklungspolitik.

Kosow, H., & Gaßner, R. (2008). *Methods of future and scenario analysis: overview, assessment, and selection criteria* (Vol. 39). DEU.

Kramer, S. (2022). Council post: Metaverse privacy concerns: Are we thinking about our data? *Forbes Magazine*. Available at: https://www.forbes.com/sites/forbestechcouncil/2022/06/01/metaverse-privacy-concerns are- we-thinking-about-our-data/

Laidler, J. (2019). *Harvard professor says surveillance capitalism is undermining democracy*. Academic Press.

Lord, J. (2022). *Franklin Templeton Launches Metaverse ETF in Europe*. Available at: https://www.etfstrategy.com/franklin-templeton-launches-metaverse-etf-in-europe-10339/

McKinsey & Company. (2022). *Value creation in the metaverse*. McKinsey & Company. Available at: https://www.mckinsey.com/capabilities/growth-marketing-and sales/ourinsights/value-creation-in-the-metaverse

Meggsauer. (2022). *Jeff Bezos keeps a 16-year-old framed magazine as a 'reminder' that Amazon's most profitable service was once just a 'risky bet', CNBC*. CNBC. Available at: https://www.cnbc.com/2022/05/20/why-jeff-bezos-keeps-a-reminder-that-aws-was-oncejust-a-risky-bet.html

Microsoft Center. (2022). *Microsoft to acquire Activision Blizzard to bring the joy and community of gaming to everyone, across every device, Stories*. Available at: https://news.microsoft.com/2022/01/18/microsoft-to-acquire-activision-blizzard-to-bringthe-joy-and-community-of-gaming-to-everyone-across-every-device

Mietzner, D., & Reger, G. (2005). Advantages and disadvantages of scenario approaches for strategic foresight. *International Journal Technology Intelligence and Planning*, *1*(2), 220–239. doi:10.1504/IJTIP.2005.006516

Mileva, G. (2022). *Understanding the metaverse through real-world examples*. Influencer Marketing Hub. Available at: https://influencermarketinghub.com/metaverse-examples/

Moro Visconti, R. (2022) From physical reality to the internet and the metaverse: A Multilayer Network valuation. SSRN *Electronic Journal*, 101–133. doi:10.2139/ssrn.4054674

MSFT. (2021). *Introducing Microsoft Mesh: Here can be anywhere*. Available at: https://www.microsoft.com/en-us/mesh

Murphy, H. (2022). Facebook owner Meta Targets Finance with 'Zuck Bucks' and creator coins, subscribe to read. *Financial Times*. Available at: https://www.ft.com/content/50fbe9ba-32c8-4caf-a34e-234031019371

Needle, D. (2022). *The metaverse explained: Everything you need to know, WhatIs.com*. TechTarget. Available at: https://www.techtarget.com/whatis/feature/The-metaverseexplained-Everything-you-need-to-know

Neilson, R. E., & Wagner, C. J. (2000). Strategic scenario planning at CA International. *Knowledge Management Review*, *12*, 4–21.

News Network. (n.d.). Available at: https://www.cnn.com/2021/10/28/tech/facebook-markzuckerberg-keynote-announcements/index.html

Novak, T. (2012). Quality of virtual life. Transformative consumer research for personal and collective well-being. *Revista Fronteiras*, 225–246.

O'Flaherty, K. (2022). *The Data Game: What Amazon knows about you and how to stop it, The Guardian.* Guardian News and Media. Available at: https://www.theguardian.com/technology/2022/feb/27/the-data-game-what-amazonknows-about-you-and-how-to-stop-it

Pandaily. (2022). *Taobao to launch metaverse shopping for 618 E-commerce festival.* Pandaily. Available at: https://pandaily.com/taobao-to-launch-metaverse-shopping-for-618-ecommerce-festival/

Parton, S. (2018). *The rise of dataism: A threat to freedom or a scientific revolution?* Singularity Hub. Available at: https://singularityhub.com/2018/09/30/the-rise-of-dataism-a-threat-tofreedom-or-a-scientific-revolution/

Peters, J. (2022). *Meta is reportedly making 'zuck bucks', The Verge*. The Verge. Available at: https://www.theverge.com/2022/4/6/23013896/meta-facebook-zuck-bucks-financefinancial-services-products

Pietro, D. R. (2022). *The metaverse: Technology, privacy and security risks, and the road ahead, The Metaverse: Technology, Privacy and Security Risks.* Available at: https://www.hbku.edu.qa/en/news/CSE-AI-MTPSR

Pladson, K. (2021). *In 2021, Big Tech may have finally gotten too big – DW – 12/28/2021.* Deutsche Welle. Available at: https://www.dw.com/en/in-2021-big-tech-may-have-finallygotten-too-big/a-60211242

Purdy, M. (2022). How the metaverse could change work. *Harvard Business Review*. Available at: https://hbr.org/2022/04/how-the-metaverse-could-change-work

PYMNTS. (2022). *Meta opens its metaverse platform to payments, Meta Opens Its Metaverse Platform to Payments.* PYMNTS.com. Available at: https://www.pymnts.com/metaverse/2022/meta-opens-its-metaverse-platform to payments -and-it-doesnt-come-cheap/

Ramirez, R., Mukherjee, M., Vezzoli, S., & Kramer, A. M. (2015). Scenarios as a scholarly methodology to produce "interesting research". *Futures*, *71*, 70–87. doi:10.1016/j.futures.2015.06.006

Ratan, R., & Meshi, D. (2022). The metaverse is money and crypto is king – why you'll be on a blockchain when you're virtual-world hopping. *The Conversation*. Available at: https://theconversation.com/the-metaverse-is-money-and-crypto-is-king-why-youll-be on a-blockchain-when-youre-virtual-world-hopping-171659

Ryufath Soepeno. (2021). *Metaverse A Potential Threat to Humanity and Ethics. GCOM1304: Final-term essay*. Sampoerna University.

Shankar, V. (2022). How bezos and Amazon changed the world. *The Conversation*. Available at: https://theconversation.com/how-bezos-and-amazon-changed-the-world-154546

Shin, D. H. (2010). The effects of trust, security and privacy in social networking: A security-based approach to understand the pattern of adoption. *Interacting with Computers*, *22*(5), 428–438. doi:10.1016/j.intcom.2010.05.001

Stephenson, N. (1992). *Snow Crash*. Random House Worlds.

Stokel-Walker, C. (2021). Why has Facebook changed its name to Meta and what is the metaverse? *New Scientist*. Available at: https://www.newscientist.com/article/2295438-why-has-facebook-changed-its-name-to-meta-and-what-is-the-metaverse/

Surwade, A. U. (2020). Phishing e-mail is an increasing menace. *International Journal of Information Technology : an Official Journal of Bharati Vidyapeeth's Institute of Computer Applications and Management*, *12*(2), 611–617. doi:10.1007/s41870-019-00407-6

Tahseen, I. (2011). *Facebook's setting changes confuse users: Study.* Available at: https://www.indiansinkuwait.com/news/Facebook-s-setting-changes-confuseusers-Study

Thornhill, J. (2022). Reality+ - looking forward to life in the metaverse, subscribe to read, Financial Times. *Financial Times*. Available at: https://www.ft.com/content/e9d4875c06ab-44bc-8d93-4655b80b88b8

WEF. (2020). *Read Yuval Harari's blistering warning to Davos in full.* World Economic Forum. Available at: https://www.weforum.org/agenda/2020/01/yuval-hararis-warning-davosspeech-future-predications/

Wilson, K. B., Karg, A., & Ghaderi, H. (2022). Prospecting non-fungible tokens in the digital economy: Stakeholders and ecosystem, risk and opportunity. *Business Horizons*, *65*(5), 657–670. doi:10.1016/j.bushor.2021.10.007

Wright, G., Cairns, G., & Bradfield, R. (2013). Scenario methodology: New developments in theory and practice: Introduction to the Special Issue. *Technological Forecasting and Social Change*, *80*(4), 561–565. doi:10.1016/j.techfore.2012.11.011

Yimu, J., & Shangdong, L. (2020). *Threats from botnets*. Computer Security Threats. [Preprint], doi:10.5772/intechopen.88927

Zuboff, S. (2015). Big other: Surveillance capitalism and the prospects of an information civilization. *Journal of Information Technology*, *30*(1), 75–89. doi:10.1057/jit.2015.5

Zuboff, S. (2019, January). Surveillance capitalism and the challenge of collective action. *New Labor Forum*, *28*(1), 10–29. doi:10.1177/1095796018819461

Zuboff, S. (2020). *The age of surveillance capitalism: The fight for a human future at the New Frontier of Power*. Public Affairs.

Chapter 2
Motivation for the Use of Technologies in Different University Contexts

Oscar Navarro-Martinez
https://orcid.org/0000-0002-3176-6194
University of Castilla-La Mancha, Spain

Juana Maria Anguita-Acero
https://orcid.org/0000-0002-8390-857X
National University of Distance Education, Spain

Francisco Javier Sanchez-Verdejo Pérez
https://orcid.org/0000-0003-1112-5995
University of Castilla-La Mancha, Spain

ABSTRACT

The presence of technologies in society is constantly increasing, and the field of education cannot remain oblivious to this situation. It must integrate new technological proposals to improve the teaching and learning processes. This chapter analyses the differences shown by university students from two different environments, specific students from small towns located in rural settings and students from Madrid, the capital of Spain. Data were collected from a sample of 312 primary education teacher degree students; 221 were women and 91 were men. Motivation for the use of educational technologies is examined by their preferences regarding access to knowledge, taking into account the context in which they live and their gender. It can be concluded that university students and future teachers generally have a great motivation toward the use of technology in their learning process. However, students do it more intensely since they perceive information more visually. There is also a greater preference for students who live in an urban environment.

DOI: 10.4018/979-8-3693-1866-9.ch002

INTRODUCTION

Technologies can be motivating resources which students relate to leisure activities, but which can provide another approach to addressing education. It is important to bear in mind the diversity of students in a classroom, depending on the preference they have to learn following each one's tendency to assimilate content visually or verbally. Based on these possibilities, it is important to determine which is the best way to access more meaningful learning for students and thus achieve higher academic performance.

One of the resources traditionally used by teachers to attain their objectives by students' needs is motivation, considered a natural source of learning. In the field of education, motivation is geared at having students perform certain activities due to the satisfaction the latter produce in them, rather than the results or consequences of the activities. Through motivation, students are encouraged to participate while having fun or feeling personally challenged, and not simply as a reaction to external rewards or pressure (Ryan and Stiller, 1991). When psychological needs are satisfied, intrinsic motivation may increase and have a positive effect on classroom activity. It is thus considered to be of major importance in the field of education (Ryan and Deci, 2000).

The need to understand the nature of motivation was highlighted by Vázquez and Manassero (2000), who studied in depth different aspects related to this concept, including its evolution, the instruments used to measure it and the assessment of its dimensions. At present, there is no unanimous consensus regarding the meaning of the concept of learning, and thus can be considered from different points of view. Related initially to data expectations and competencies (Atkinson, 1976), later the theory of Social-Cognitive Learning proposed that motivation influenced individuals' concept of self-efficacy (Bandura, 1986).

From the point of view of students, it is important to distinguish between extrinsic and intrinsic motivation. Extrinsic motivation refers to the initial situation in which external aspects have a positive effect on students that enables improving the teaching-learning process (Ausubel, 1968). On the other hand, intrinsic motivation takes place when students identify the goals related to motivation with learning, as this implies an interest on their part to develop and improve their abilities (García and Doménech, 1997). Therefore, learning goals are different from performance or performance goals (Elliott and Dweck, 1988).

For digital natives, it is important to have ICTs incorporated into learning methodologies and access to knowledge to feel motivated (Hernández, 2017). The use of different devices, such as a personal computer, a tablet or a mobile phone, can thus be identified as an intrinsic motivational factor towards learning (García and Doménech, 1997).

Since the use of these devices can enhance the acquisition of digital skills, incorporating computer applications in the classroom will favour the entire teaching-learning process (Area, Cepeda, González, and Sanabria, 2010). It also enables the use of strategies such as learning by discovery through the Internet or games (Aguaded and Tirado, 2010).

The theoretical framework and the different tools used in this research study are presented below, followed by the results obtained and their interpretation. The paper ends with a discussion of the results and conclusions.

THEORETICAL FRAMEWORK

Human motivation is a complex field deeply rooted in academic disciplines such as psychology, sociology, and education, among others. Motivation can be understood as the result of the interaction between the individual and the situation. Despite the different definitions concerning motivation, there seems to be a common ground concerning the individuals' engagement in certain activities provided those activities satisfy their needs (Sansone and Harackiewicz, 2000; Kian & Yusoff, 2015).

The term motivation seems to derive from the word motive, which refers to a mental state that activates and directs human behaviour, helping us accomplish goals. Motivation is not always conscious, as Freud put it simply when showing unconscious motivation in his theories of human behaviour. Motivation occurs within people's minds. And we would add that within our hearts. Also, motivation can be classified as intrinsic and extrinsic (Osemeke & Adegboyega, 2017).

One can find different bibliographical references which deal with motivation in different educational stages, including university studies.

Research on motivation has attracted academic interest over the last decades. Undoubtedly, motivation has a positive impact on both students as well as professors. Motivation directly links to performance, serving as a catalyser involved in any task, and in this case, education (Wenzel & Wigfield, 2009; Anderman & Heather, 2011, pp. 219–241; Sekhar, Patwardhan & Singh, 2013).

In general terms, motivation can be considered either a feeling or a personal state. Its main characteristics can be arranged considering its origin, which can be varied, its subjective character, and the fact that it needs the involvement of a person, who needs it since there are several degrees of motivation. And it is also necessary to count on the person's desire to be motivated (Chekola, 1974).

When referring to needs, it must be stated that the need or belief of need arises from any individual's wishes. And it was Abraham Maslow who developed the Motivation Theory (1954), establishing a hierarchy of human beings' needs. He devised it ranging from the most basic and ending in the highest level. Later on, the Theory of the Need for Achievement was explained by David McClelland (1958), and such a consideration stemmed from the previously referred approach. Considering this, motivation is governed by three types of needs: the need for power, the need for achievement and the need for affiliation (Osemeke & Adegboyega, 2017). Notwithstanding, we must reckon that no other elements were considered by these two authors, such as the idea of maturity or individual needs.

Motivation may be described as a driving force that helps individuals to continue with a certain activity. Depending on the implication, it can be extrinsic or intrinsic motivation (Ryan and Deci, 2000). Individuals are intrinsically motivated when they aim to find enjoyment, interest, the satisfaction of curiosity, self-expression, and/or personal challenge in their work. Intrinsic Motivations derive from emotions and feelings attached to the task individuals are about to face. On the other hand, extrinsic motivation includes anything coming from an outside source (Osemeke & Adegboyega, 2017).

Regarding these two types of motivation, Grant and Dweck (2003) state that trying to achieve certain goals positively influences an individual's intrinsic motivation, especially when faced with prolonged challenges. Likewise, McInerney, Marsh and Yeung (2003) say that setting goals previously contribute to spurring intrinsic motivation, directing efforts, consequently, towards achieving the desired results. When referring to education, teachers should always try to make motivation inherent in their students to achieve a favourable development of the teaching and learning process.

Regarding one of the objectives of this work, which focuses on the study of intrinsic motivation in university students, Ryan and Deci's Intrinsic Motivation Inventory (IMI) has been used for analysis purposes. The IMI is a multidimensional measuring instrument that values participants' subjective experience concerning a specific activity; in this case, the predisposition of university students to use Information and Communication Technologies. The IMI questionnaire consists of six subscales, although only three will be used in this research, the three that are the most relevant to the data collected in this study.

Interest/Enjoyment is considered an intrinsic motivation measure *per se*, and it is often considered more than others. Pressure/Tension is a negative predictor of motivation, which provides us with indicators showing that an individual's results should be reversed. Finally, the Value/Usefulness subscale assesses internalization and self-regulation regarding the activity that students consider valuable and useful for themselves (McAuley, Duncan, and Tammen, 1987).

In the educational field, the intrinsic motivation of university students must be favoured, not only to access their learning. It is especially relevant for future teachers. They experience it themselves and they will be able to transmit it to their students in the future (González et al., 2020).

Traditionally, and mainly in the past centuries, it was long considered that all students learn in the same way. However (and we would add, fortunately) this homogenization of the educational process has been questioned by different authors and theories, among which the Theory of Multiple Intelligences stands out. The Theory of Multiple Intelligences, developed by psychologist Howard Gardner in the late 1970s and early 1980s, claims that individuals possess eight or more intelligence (Gardner, 2006). Gardner's different styles of learning theory opened the leading path to personalize the abilities and qualities of each student (Davis, et al., 2011).

Learning style is an approach concerning the description of some behaviours and attitudes that determine the preferred mode of learning (Honey and Mumford, 2006). Keefe (1987) considers that the psychological, affective and cognitive characteristics of behaviour serve as stable indicators of how students perceive, respond and interact with the learning environment (Coffield et al., 2004a; Coffield et al., 2004b). Those two advocate learning style models state that students learn int different ways. Therefore, all adult students do not learn the same way and also teachers should accommodate the learning needs of most or all students. Thus, since adult students learn in different ways, higher education teachers should increase the repertoire of learning activities to embrace as wide as possible to achieve more effective learning (Hawk and Shah, 2007).

In the research carried out in this study, we have opted for the Felder and Silverman Learning Styles Inventory (The Index of Learning Styles, ILS), since it is one of the most widespread models, consisting of forty-four items (Felder and Silverman, 1988). However, in our case, only the questions that allow us to know if the students have a preference towards Visual or Verbal learning have been used.

One can find several styles or models that the human being has when it comes to perceiving information. One of them, and one that is becoming more and more relevant, is the visual one. These people show a predilection for accessing knowledge through the greatest possible visual stimulation through videos, blackboards, information boards, screens, etc (Dunn, 1984).

Visually accessing knowledge allows a direct interaction to be generated between the perception of information and the learning itself. In this way, metacognitive processes are strengthened, and thus, more significant learning is achieved (Ausubel et al., 1991).

Concerning the verbal language when the information is displayed, the Visual and Verbal dichotomy arises. Persons with a visual profile find it easier to perceive the world around them and recreate it. In addition, they prefer to receive information visually through images, movies, graphics, etc. On the other hand, when the verbal option predominates, there is a greater preference for a style with explanations, whether oral or written (Navarro, 2018).

If one looks at previous experiences, verbal learning has a preponderant position in comparison with other forms such as verbal one. There is the possibility of accompanying this instruction with multimedia elements, which greatly improves the entire process (Caro & Monroy, 2008). Therefore, when technologies are used, the competence of students can be favoured from remarkably diverse fields (Carrascal et al., 2019).

There is a direct relationship between the visual learning style and better handling and development in a virtual environment. There is a high percentage of students who achieve better objectives and results in instruction when they are adapted to their preferences, and these were visual access to information (Brennan & Macnutt, 2006).

The preference for highly visual or verbal elements will condition certain aspects such as the pedagogical method that can be used, the characteristics of the media that are used, as well as the specific teaching strategies that are used, whether they are games or simulations for learning, visual and panel discussion, brainstorming or questions for the Verbal (Franzoni et al., 2008).

METHODS

The main purpose of this study is to find out the levels of motivation towards the use of technologies that university students may have in different educational contexts. Thus, it will be necessary to analyse how the individuals who are enrolled in the Primary School Teacher Degree programme show greater preference for the use of technologies depending on whether they live and operate in a rural or an urban environment. To that end, it is also important to consider whether students' access to knowledge and their tendency to do so, is based on a more visual or verbal mode. Based on this general approach, the study's specific objectives are the following:

- To determine the motivation of future primary school teachers for the use of technology.
- To find out the differences in accessing knowledge depending on the gender of future teachers.
- To review the relationship between the style of visual and verbal learning, and the motivation of students enrolled in Primary School Teacher programmes.
- To describe the main variables of intrinsic motivation for the use of technologies by future teachers.

For the data collection phase, part of the Intrinsic Motivation Inventory (IMI) developed by Deci and Ryan (1985) was used. With this tool, which can be fragmented into different dimensions, it is possible to determine people's intrinsic motivation. In this study, a simplified version of the tool was applied, taking into account three of the dimensions (Interest-Enjoyment, Pressure-Tension and Value-Usefulness), which were used as dependent variables. In addition, the visual and verbal learning styles were used as dependent variables. For these purposes, a simplified part of Felder and Silverman's Inventory of Learning Styles (Felder and Silverman, 1988) was also used. Both questionnaires were filled out on the Internet using different devices, preferably cell phones, which are very accessible to all students. The independent variables that were considered were the university students' gender and the environment in which they usually lived, either rural or urban.

The study was carried out with students enrolled in the Primary School Teacher Degree programme at two Spanish universities. The total sample comprised 312 individuals, 91 men and 221 women. 163 of them were students at the Rey Juan Carlos University in the region of Madrid, who had generally lived in an urban environment. The other 149 were students at the University of Castilla-La Mancha and had lived in smaller towns before beginning their university studies.

Bearing in mind the variables mentioned above and the basis of the study, the following hypotheses were formulated:

$\mathbf{H_{1.0}}$: There is no relationship between intrinsic motivation and visual and verbal learning styles.

$\mathbf{H_{1.1}}$: There is a relationship between intrinsic motivation and visual and verbal learning styles.

$\mathbf{H_{2.0}}$: There are no differences in the motivation for the use of technologies and the environment in which students live.

$\mathbf{H_{2.1}}$: There are differences in the motivation for the use of technologies and the environment in which students live.

$\mathbf{H_{3.0}}$: There are no differences in the motivation for the use of technologies and students' gender.

$\mathbf{H_{3.1}}$: There are differences in the motivation for the use of technologies and students' gender.

$\mathbf{H_{4.0}}$: There is no relationship between the visual and verbal learning styles and students' gender.

$\mathbf{H_{4.1}}$: There is a relationship between the visual and verbal learning styles and students' gender.

To process the data obtained from the two questionnaires administered to the students, the results were exported to the Statistical Package for the Social Sciences (SPSS).

Different statistics were used depending on whether the variables were measured with nominal, ordinal or interval scales. The Spearman correlation was used to analyse the relationship between the variables, the Chi-Square test to find out if there were significant differences between the variables, and the Student's t-test to assess whether there were differences in means.

RESULTS

The results of this study are provided below, together with the relationships that exist between the different variables that were taken into account in the research. The differences that appear in the motivation of university students for the use of the information and communication technologies depending on students' gender and environment in which they study are specified. In addition, the preferences for the learning that is more focused on visual or verbal aspects according to gender are shown. However, this last variable has not revealed any differences depending on the environment. University students from rural and urban environments have similar motivations, irrespective of whether they are in urban or rural environments.

Table 1 shows the relationship that exists between the three dimensions of intrinsic motivation that are analysed in this study, and the preference for a learning style that is more visual or verbal. Some of the results were predictable. For example, there is a negative correlation between the preference for learning in a visual and a verbal manner, in addition to an exceedingly high level of significance of - 0.225 (p = 008). These results were to be expected as they are variables with opposite characteristics.

Table 1. Correlation (Spearman) among the dimensions of intrinsic motivation and visual or verbal learning style

	Interest / Enjoyment	Pressure / Tension	Value / Usefulness	Visual	Verbal
Interest / Enjoyment	1	-.318**	.677**	.455**	-.235**
	.	.000	.000	.000	.003
Pressure / Tension		1	-.163*	-.244**	.067
		.	.043	.002	.408
Value / Usefulness			1	.270**	-.154
			.	.001	.054
Visual				1	-.222**
				.	.005
Verbal					1
					.

** Correlation is significant at the level 0.01 (bilateral).
* Correlation is significant at the level 0.05 (bilateral).

In respect to the variables that show a greater motivation for the use of technologies, a positive correlation between them is also observed. There is a correlation between three dimensions that were analysed. The relation is positive, except in the case of pressure when it comes to use them. However, since it is an inverse variable, the positive correlation between them can be confirmed. Moreover, in nearly all cases the significance levels are very high, obtaining a value of $p < 0.01$.

In respect to the relationship between the dimensions of the visual and verbal learning teaching styles and motivation, in most cases there exists a correlation between them. On the one hand, university students who have a preference for visual learning also show greater motivation for the use of technologies, always with a high level of significance, taking into account the negative value of the Pressure/Tension dimension. Values of 0.455 (p < 0.001), - 0.244 (p = 0.002) and 0.270 (p = 0.001) are obtained for the dimensions of Interest, Pressure and Usefulness, respectively. In the case of students who prefer a more verbal type of learning, a significant value is only obtained in the case of the variable Interest of the motivation dimensions, with a value of - 0,235 (p = 0.003). No significant differences are seen in the other two cases. It is thus not possible to confirm that students with a preference for verbal learning perceive greater usefulness or pressure for using technologies.

Figure 1. Dimensions of motivation according to environment

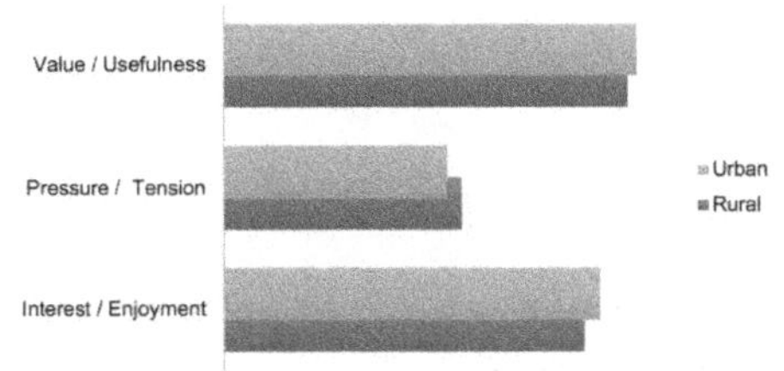

Figure 1 shows the difference of means between the three dimensions of intrinsic motivation analysed, depending on the environment in which the university students live. The results are quite similar, without major differences, although there is a clear tendency. Students who live in an urban environment show greater interest for the use of technologies; significant differences are confirmed with a value of t = - 1.414 (p = 0.037). Likewise, these students from urban areas feel less pressure than those who live in a rural environment; differences with a high level of significance are also confirmed, with a value of t = 1.359 (p = 0.003). On the other hand, there is also a tendency for students in the urban environment to consider that the technologies provide usefulness and value, without however showing statistically significant differences.

Figure 2. Dimensions of motivation according to gender

Figure 3. Preference for visual or verbal learning according to gender

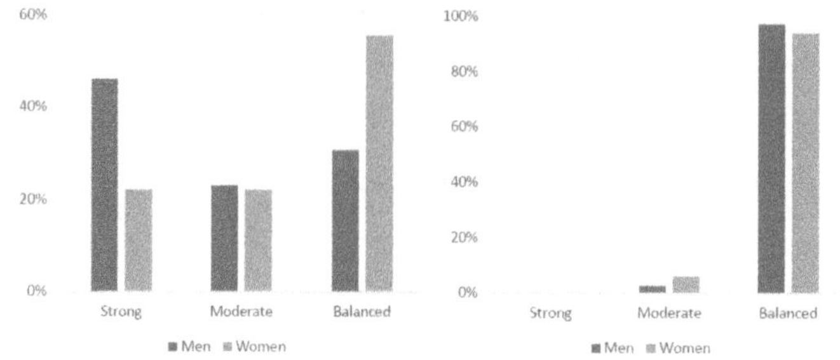

Figure 3 shows the preference university students have for a visual type of learning. There is a clear difference in favour of men. Nearly one half of them have a strong preference, as compared to one fifth of women. There is a large degree of similarity when the preference is moderate, entailing approximately one fifth of both genders. In addition, it can be confirmed that these differences are statistically significant, moreover with a very high level of significance, obtaining a Chi-Square value of 9.590 ($p = 0.008$).

However, students' preference for verbal learning is very similar in both genders, with a very low preference in both cases. In addition, although a greater tendency is seen in the case of women, it does not reach a sufficiently significant level; hence the results for men and women are considered to be similar.

DISCUSSION AND CONCLUSION

Having analysed the results, this section assesses whether the hypotheses proposed can be accepted. It also presents the study's main conclusions.

Given the negative correlation obtained between visual and verbal learning, it is clear that when students show preference for one style in particular, they do not show preference for any other, from that point of view their approach to learning is quite different. These results between the three dimensions of intrinsic motivation used in this study, namely interest, pressure and usefulness, were also to be expected.

In the case of the relationship of the variables of the three dimensions of intrinsic motivation that are analysed and students' preference for more visual or verbal learning, no ample differences were observed. On the one hand, students who have a visual preference feel strongly motivated to use technologies. They show greater interest and feel less pressure for learning, and in addition find that the content learned is more useful. However, in the case of students who have a greater preference for verbal learning, greater interest is seen for the use of technologies, but not in other dimensions. In consequence, Hypothesis $\mathbf{H}_{1.1}$, which proposed that there is a relationship between intrinsic motivation and visual and verbal learning styles, can be partially accepted.

In general, students who live and study in an urban environment show greater intrinsic motivation in respect to the use of technologies. The tendency is clear in all dimensions, particularly in the interest and pressure for their use. In these last two cases, statistically significant differences were obtained. In consequence, Hypothesis $\mathbf{H}_{2.1}$, which proposed that there are differences in the motivation for the use of technologies and the environment in which students live, can be accepted.

Men students showed greater motivation than women when it came to using technologies. There is a clear tendency, but in particular they present greater interest and feel less pressure when they are using said technologies. Perhaps this is conditioned by the fact that men have a greater and stronger predisposition to access to visual learning. In consequence, Hypothesis $\mathbf{H}_{3.1}$, which proposed that there are differences in the motivation for the use of technologies and students' gender, is accepted.

In general, most of the students, without taking into account gender, have a preference for a visual type of learning. The predisposition to learn in a verbal manner is barely more than 5% in the case of women and below that figure for men. There is a clear tendency towards accessing knowledge in a visual manner, especially in the case of men, who show a greater preference in respect to women when there is a strong predisposition. In consequence, Hypothesis $\mathbf{H}_{4.1}$, which proposes that there is a relationship between the visual and verbal learning style and students' gender, is accepted.

It is thus possible to conclude that university students, regardless of their preference for a learning style, feel great motivation for the use of technologies in their learning process. However, this tendency is more intense in the case of students who have a preference and ease for perceiving information in a visual manner. There is also greater motivation in the case of students who live in an urban environment. Perhaps this is due to the fact that the presence of technologies is greater in an urban context, and that said experience leads to a closer relationship with technologies. This tendency may also be the result of the considerable advance of technologies at all levels over the last three decades and that students are exposed to all sorts of digital screens from a very young age (Szymkowiak et al., 2021), which is in line with the results of this study. Moreover, there is greater preference on the part of men, which may be due to the fact that they have greater spatial perception, directly related to a more visual type of learning (Heo & Toomey, 2020).

REFERENCES

Aguaded, J. I., & Tirado, R. (2010). Ordenadores en los pupitres: Informática y telemática en el proceso de enseñanza-aprendizaje en los centros TIC de Andalucía. *Pixel-Bit. Revista de Medios y Educación*, *36*, 5–28.

Anderman, E., & Dawson, H. S. (2011). Learning with motivation. In R. E. Mayer & P. A. Alexander (Eds.), *Handbook of research on learning and instruction* (pp. 219–241). Routledge.

Área, M., Cepeda, O., González, D. and Sanabria, A. (2010). Un análisis de las actividades didácticas con TIC en aulas de educación secundaria. *Un análisis de las actividades didácticas con TIC en aulas de educación secundaria*, *38*, 187-199.

Atkinson, J. W. (1976). *An introduction to motivation*. Van Nostrand.

Ausubel, D. P. (1968). *Educational psychology: A cognitive view*. Holt, Rinehart and Winston.

Ausubel, D. P., Novak, J. D., & Hanesian, H. (1991). *Psicologia educativa: Un punto de vista cognoscitivo*. Trillas.

Bandura, A. (1986). From thought to action: Mechanisms of personal agency. *The Journal of Psychology*, *15*, 1–17.

Brennan, M., & Macnutt, L. (2006). *Learning Styles and Learning to Program: An Experiment in Adapting Online Resources to Match a Student's Learning Style*. Institute Of Technology Blanchardstown.

Caro, E. O., & Monroy, M. N. (2008). *Relación de los ambientes hipertextuales de aprendizaje gráfico y sonoro, con los estilos de aprendizaje verbal y visual*. Avances en Sistemas e Informática.

Carrascal, S., Magro, M., Anguita, J., & Espada, M. (2019). Acquisition of Competences for Sustainable Development through Visual Thinking. A Study in Rural Schools in Mixco, Guatemala. *Sustainability (Basel)*, *11*(8), 1–18. doi:10.3390/su11082317

Chekola, M. G. (1974). *The concept of happiness*. University of Michigan.

Coffield, F. J., Moseley, D. V., Hall, E., & Ecclestone, K. (2004a). *Learning styles and pedagogy in post-16 learning: A systematic and critical review.* Learning and Skills Research Centre.

Coffield, F. J., Moseley, D. V., Hall, E., & Ecclestone, K. (2004b). *Learning styles: What research has to say to practice.* Learning and Skills Research Centre.

Davis, K., Christodoulou, J., Seider, S., & Gardner, H. (2011). The theory of multiple intelligences. In R. J. Sternberg & S. B. Kaufman (Eds.), *Cambridge Handbook of Intelligence* (pp. 485–503). Cambridge University Press. doi:10.1017/CBO9780511977244.025

Deci, E. L., & Ryan, R. M. (1985). *Intrinsic motivation and self-determination in human behavior.* Plenum. doi:10.1007/978-1-4899-2271-7

Dunn, R. (1984). Learning style: State of the science. *Theory into Practice, 23*(1), 10–19. doi:10.1080/00405848409543084

Dweck, C. S., & Leggett, E. L. (1988). A social cognitive approach to motivation and personality. *Psychological Review, 95*(2), 256–273. doi:10.1037/0033-295X.95.2.256

Elliott, E. S., & Dweck, C. S. (1988). Goals: An approach to motivation and achievement. *Journal of Personality and Social Psychology, 54*(1), 5–12. doi:10.1037/0022-3514.54.1.5 PMID:3346808

Felder, R. M., & Silverman, L. K. (1988). Learning and Teaching Styles in Engineering Education. *Engineering Education, 78*(7), 674–681.

Franzoni, A. L., Assar, S., Defude, B., & Rojas, J. (2008). Student Learning Styles Adaptation Method Based on Teaching Strategies and Electronic Media. *2008 Eighth IEEE International Conference on Advanced Learning Technologies*, 778-782. https://doi.org/10.1109/ICALT.2008.149

García, F. J., & Doménech, F. (1997). Motivación, aprendizaje y rendimiento escolar. *Revista Electrónica de Motivación y Emoción, 1*, 1-8. http://reme.uji.es/articulos/pa0001/texto.html

Gardner, H. (2006). *Multiple intelligences: New horizons.* Basic Books.

González, Á. L., Navarro, Ó., Sánchez-Verdejo, F. J., & Muelas, Á. (2020). Psychological Well-Being and Intrinsic Motivation: Relationship in Students Who Begin University Studies at the School of Education in Ciudad Real. *Frontiers in Psychology, 11*(2054), 1–10. doi:10.3389/fpsyg.2020.02054 PMID:33013520

Hawk, T. F., & Shah, A. J. (2007). Using Learning Style Instruments to Enhance Student Learning. *Decision Sciences Journal of Innovative Education, 5*(1), 1–19. doi:10.1111/j.1540-4609.2007.00125.x

Heo, M., & Toomey, N. (2020). Learning with multimedia: The effects of gender, type of multimedia learning resources, and spatial ability. *Computers & Education, 146*, 1–12. doi:10.1016/j.compedu.2019.103747

Hernández, A. (2017). Enseñar E/LE a la primera generación de nativos digitales. *Foro de profesores de E/LE, 13*, 165-176.

Kian, T. S., & Yusoff, W. F. W. (2015). Intrinsic-Extrinsic motivation revisited: Exploring their definitions. *International Journal of Management Sciences, 6*(3), 136–140.

Maslow, A. H. (1954). *Motivation and personality*. Harper & Row Publishers Inc.

McAuley, E., Duncan, T., & Tammen, V. V. (1987). Psychometric properties of the Intrinsic Motivation Inventory in a competitive sport setting: A confirmatory factor analysis. *Research Quarterly for Exercise and Sport, 60*(1), 48–58. doi:10.1080/02701367.1989.10607413 PMID:2489825

McClelland, D. C. (1958). Methods of measuring human motivation. In J. W. Atkinson (Ed.), *Motives in fantasy, action, and society* (pp. 7–42). D. Van Nostrand Company Inc.

McInerney, D. M., Marsh, H. W., & Yeung, A. S. (2003). Toward a hierarchical goal theory model of school motivation. *Journal of Applied Measurement, 4*, 335–357. PMID:14523254

Osemeke, M., & Adegboyega, S. (2017). Critical Review and Comparison between Maslow, Herzberg and McClelland's Theory of Needs. *FUNAI Journal of Accounting, 1*(1), 161–173.

Ryan, R. M., & Deci, E. L. (2000). Self-determination theory and the facilitation of intrinsic motivation, social development, and well-being. *The American Psychologist, 55*(1), 68–78. doi:10.1037/0003-066X.55.1.68 PMID:11392867

Sansone, C., & Harackiewicz, J. M. (2000). *Intrinsic and extrinsic motivation: The search for optimal motivation and performance*. Academic Press.

Sekhar, C., Patwardhan, M., & Singh, R. K. (2013). A literature review on motivation. *Glob Bus Perspect, 1*(4), 471–487. doi:10.1007/s40196-013-0028-1

Szymkowiak, A., Melović, B., Dabić, M., Jeganathan, K., & Kundi, G. S. (2021). Information technology and Gen Z: The role of teachers, the internet, and technology in the education of young people. *Technology in Society, 65*, 1–10. doi:10.1016/j.techsoc.2021.101565

Vázquez, Á., & Manassero, M. A. (2000). Análisis empírico de dos escalas de motivación escolar. *Revista Electrónica de Motivación y Emoción, 3*, 5–6.

Wenzel, K. R., & Wigfield, A. (Eds.). (2009). *Handbook of motivation at school*. Routledge. doi:10.4324/9780203879498

Chapter 3
Economic Implications of Virtual Goods and Digital Assets in the Scope of Metaverse:
An Analysis

V. Suganya
https://orcid.org/0000-0001-5301-8317
SRM Institute of Science and Technology, Vadapalani, India

V. Sasirekha
SRM Institute of Science and Technology, Vadapalani, India

ABSTRACT

The advent of the metaverse has ushered in a new era of digital interaction, fundamentally reshaping the global economy. This research analysis delves into the economic implications of virtual goods and digital assets within the metaverse, shedding light on the complex dynamics that underpin this emerging digital economy. First the authors explore the metaverse as a thriving marketplace for virtual goods, investigating the factors driving demand and pricing mechanisms for these intangible assets. They analyse the impact of scarcity, digital scarcity, and blockchain-based ownership systems on the valuation and trade of virtual assets. Second, the research investigates the interplay between the metaverse's digital economy and the traditional world economy. They examine the emergence of virtual jobs, income streams, and the taxation challenges associated with this new form of work. Third, this study scrutinizes the role of virtual assets and metaverse platforms in reshaping advertising, marketing, and branding strategies.

DOI: 10.4018/979-8-3693-1866-9.ch003

INTRODUCTION

The advent of the metaverse represents a groundbreaking frontier in the digital landscape, promising to redefine our interactions, experiences, and economies. At the core of this transformative shift lies the proliferation of virtual goods and digital assets, which have become integral to the metaverse's intricate fabric. This research embarks on a comprehensive analysis of the economic implications associated with virtual goods and digital assets within the expansive scope of the metaverse.

The metaverse is a concept that was once the stuff of science fiction but is now rapidly materializing as a shared virtual space where individuals converge to engage, socialize, and conduct business. Within this digital realm, virtual goods and digital assets have evolved into pivotal elements, ushering in a novel and dynamic digital economy. From virtual real estate and in-game assets to digital collectibles and blockchain-based tokens, the metaverse has forged a new paradigm for economic activities.

This research endeavor seeks to unveil the intricate web of economic consequences that these virtual entities bring to the fore. It underscores the importance of comprehending the potential impacts on various economic dimensions, including ownership and property rights, monetization and entrepreneurship, the role of marketplaces and platforms, the integration of cryptocurrencies and blockchain, changes in labour and employment landscapes, considerations of social and economic inclusion, and the challenges of regulation and taxation.

As we embark on this exploration, it becomes clear that the economic implications of virtual goods and digital assets within the metaverse are profoundly transformative. This research serves as a beacon, illuminating the path to understanding how the metaverse is reshaping our economic landscape, and offering insights into how individuals, businesses, and governments can harness this digital frontier's potential for prosperity, innovation, and equitable participation. By comprehensively analysing this intricate tapestry, we gain a deeper understanding of the metaverse's capacity to revolutionize our economies, redefine industries, and influence the lives of people on a global scale.

OBJECTIVES OF THE STUDY

- To investigate how virtual goods and digital assets in the metaverse challenge conventional notions of ownership and property rights.
- To explore their implications on intellectual property, digital property rights, and legal frameworks.

- To examine the diverse monetization avenues within the metaverse, including virtual commerce, content creation, and virtual events, and evaluate how these strategies impact individuals, content creators, and businesses.
- To assess the role and influence of virtual marketplaces and platforms as intermediaries for virtual asset exchange, including their impact on economic activities and regulatory oversight.
- To investigate the integration of cryptocurrencies, blockchain technology, and NFTs within the metaverse.
- To analyze their impact on financial systems, investment opportunities, and cross-border transactions.
- To explore the emergence of virtual job markets and the digital gig economy within the metaverse.
- To assess how these dynamics are reshaping employment opportunities and income generation.
- To Study the potential for virtual goods and digital assets to bridge or exacerbate societal disparities, including issues related to access, affordability, and participation in the metaverse economy.
- To evaluate the complex regulatory and taxation issues surrounding virtual assets within the metaverse, with a focus on implications for government revenue, consumer protection, and market stability.
- To Offer policy recommendations for governments and regulatory bodies to adapt to the changing economic landscape of the metaverse, promoting innovation, economic stability, and consumer protection.
- To Anticipate potential future trends and developments in the metaverse's economic ecosystem, considering how they may impact individuals, businesses, and government agencies.
- To Contribute to the body of knowledge by providing valuable insights and data on the economic implications of virtual goods and digital assets in the metaverse, which can be used for both academic research and practical decision-making.

LITERATURE REVIEW

The metaverse has been conceptualized and defined in a number of ways by literary works. Morgado describes it as "a plethora of interconnected world" (Morgado, 2008), while Herrman and Browning (2021) define it as "a fully realized digital world that exists beyond the analogue one in which we live." Platforms Meta, Inc. Put more succinctly, Bosworth and Clegg (2021) define the "metaverse" as a collection of virtual locations that you can construct and explore with others who aren't in the same physical location as you.

According to several definitions, the term "metaverse" refers to a persistent, interactive, and collaborative parallel reality that is produced by combining virtual worlds into which individuals can connect, work, and play with one another using personal avatars. The perceived immersion is increased by virtual technologies due to the inhabitants' and avatars' realistic personalities. They enable users to freely engage with virtual items and intelligent agents as well as to communicate with one another. Typically, they are networked and placed with intelligent agents (Shen et al., 2021). An infinite number of users can experience these worlds synchronously and persistently in multiple forms (Ball, n.d.; Hollensen et al., 2022).

Hyper spatiotemporality, sociality, and multitechnology are characteristics of the metaverse that are shared (Ning et al., 2021). As part of an economic system built on blockchain, it incorporates a number of emerging technologies, such as augmented reality (AR), virtual reality (VR), and mixed reality (MR) (multi-technology). The metaverse permits the dissolution of temporal and spatial bounds (hyper spatiotemporality), embracing sociality, legality, and cultural systems in a virtual environment (Ning et al., 2021).

Figure 1. Conceptual framework for the study

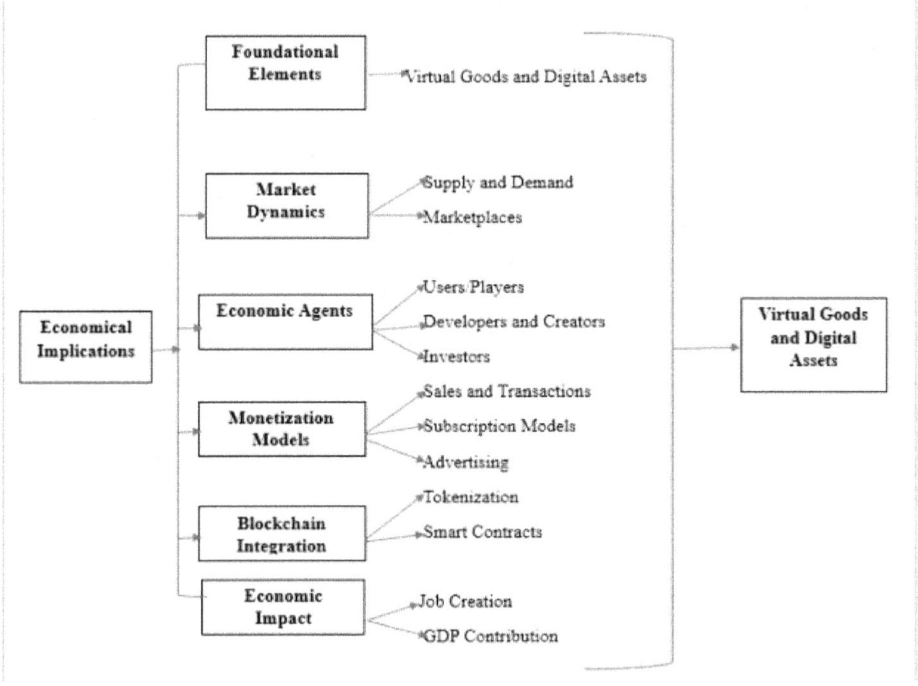

Metaverse changes are often linked to shifts in consumer and company behavior (Gursoy et al., 2022; Han et al., 2022). Scholarly research focuses on consumers' journeys, buying behaviors, value propositions and perceived values, as well as consumption patterns (Han et al., 2022). People have the ability to engage with the metaverse landscape while living through immersive experiences. While customers are driven to fulfill their functional demands in the virtual world by utilitarian incentives, hedonic motives encourage them to engage in virtual experiences for fun and pleasure (Gursoy et al., 2022). Another important factor influencing individuals' engagement with the metaverse is their desire to escape reality (Han et al., 2022). ICTs, especially virtual worlds, facilitate escapism by supporting those who wish to "leave" their current reality on an emotional and cognitive level (Henning & Vorderer, 2001).

THE ECONOMIC POTENTIAL OF THE METAVERSE

When it comes to the creation and uptake of metaverse technologies, Asia Pacific leads the globe. According to an independent analysis conducted by Deloitte Centre for the Edge last year, by 2035 the metaverse might have an annual impact on regional GDP of between US$0.8 and 1.4 trillion. People are already using virtual platforms for networking, studying, shopping, gaming, and accessing social services. Japan, Taiwan, and Korea all have thriving VR business ecosystems. A number of regional governments, such as those in South Korea and Japan, have included the metaverse into their economic strategies.

There is a thriving creative economy and they are setting the standard for augmented reality technology in developing countries like Thailand, India, and Indonesia where VR technology is not yet widely used. In Asia Pacific, the metaverse is opening up new ways to work, new marketplaces, and new business prospects. Creators are at the vanguard of bringing this future closer.

The metaverse still has a lot of potential to stimulate global economic growth and creativity. Reaching its full potential will require keeping the metaverse ecosystem relatively open while making sure users are properly protected while interacting with immersive experiences. It will take the sustained participation and cooperation of tech firms, governments, scholars, and civil society organizations around the world to achieve this.

CONCLUSION

In conclusion, the economic implications of virtual goods and digital assets in the metaverse represent a transformative shift in how we perceive, interact with, and derive value from virtual environments. This analysis has unveiled a multifaceted landscape where virtual goods and digital assets are not mere components of online gaming but integral elements shaping a burgeoning metaverse economy.

The metaverse has given rise to a novel economic paradigm, where virtual goods are not confined to in-game experiences but extend to real-world economic activities. The market dynamics within the metaverse mirror traditional economic principles of supply and demand, with the scarcity and desirability of virtual goods determining their economic value. The emergence of decentralized marketplaces, enabled by blockchain technology and non-fungible tokens (NFTs), has added a layer of transparency, security, and ownership, fundamentally altering how we transact and establish value in the digital realm.

Key economic agents, including users, developers, and investors, play pivotal roles in shaping the metaverse economy. As users actively engage in the metaverse, creating demand for virtual goods, developers and creators become essential suppliers, driving innovation and content creation. Investors, recognizing the economic potential of the metaverse, contribute to the growth of the ecosystem, further fuelling economic activities. Monetization models within the metaverse, ranging from direct sales and subscriptions to advertising, reflect the diverse ways in which economic value is generated. Additionally, the regulatory landscape, encompassing intellectual property rights, consumer protection, and taxation, is evolving to address the complexities of virtual asset transactions.

The metaverse's economic impact extends beyond virtual realms, influencing job creation, GDP contribution, and cultural expression. While the metaverse offers unprecedented opportunities, challenges such as environmental considerations and regulatory frameworks require careful navigation. In essence, the economic implications of virtual goods and digital assets in the metaverse underscore a paradigm shift, where the virtual and real economies intertwine. As this digital frontier continues to evolve, understanding and adapting to the economic dynamics of the metaverse will be crucial for stakeholders across industries, ushering in an era where the boundaries between physical and virtual economies blur, and new economic possibilities emerge.

REFERENCES

Ball, M. (n.d.-a). *Framework for the Metaverse*. Available online: https://www.matthewball.vc/all/forwardtothemetaverseprimer

Ball, M. (n.d.-b). *The Metaverse: What It Is, Where to Find It, Who Will Build It, and Fortnite*. Available online: https://www.matthewball.vc/all/themetaverse

Bosworth, A., & Clegg, N. (2021). *Building the Metaverse Responsibly*. Available online: https://about.fb.com/news/2021/09/building-the-metaverse-responsibly/

Gursoy, D., Malodia, S., & Dhir, A. (2022). The metaverse in the hospitality and tourism industry: An overview of current trends and future research directions. *Journal of Hospitality Marketing & Management*, *31*(5), 527–534. doi:10.1080/19368623.2022.2072504

Han, D. I. D., Bergs, Y., & Moorhouse, N. (2022). Virtual reality consumer experience escapes: Preparing for the metaverse. *Virtual Reality (Waltham Cross)*, *26*(4), 1443–1458. doi:10.1007/s10055-022-00641-7

Henning, B., & Vorderer, P. (2001). Psychological escapism: Predicting the amount of television viewing by need for cognition. *Journal of Communication*, *51*(1), 100–120. doi:10.1111/j.1460-2466.2001.tb02874.x

Herrman, J., & Browning, K. (2021, Oct. 29). Are we in the metaverse yet? *The New York Times.*

Hollensen, S., Kotler, P., & Opresnik, M. O. (2022). Metaverse—The new marketing universe. *The Journal of Business Strategy*.

Morgado, L. (2008). Interconnecting virtual worlds. *Journal of Virtual Worlds Research*, 1.

Ning, H., Wang, H., Lin, Y., Wang, W., Dhelim, S., Farha, F., & Daneshmand, M. (2021). *A Survey on Metaverse: The State-of-the-art, Technologies, Applications, and Challenges*. arXiv:2111.09673.

Shen, B., Tan, W., Guo, J., Zhao, L., & Qin, P. (2021). How to Promote User Purchase in Metaverse? A Systematic Literature Review on Consumer Behavior Research and Virtual Commerce Application Design. *Applied Sciences (Basel, Switzerland)*, *11*(23), 11087. doi:10.3390/app112311087

Chapter 4
Effective Brand Building in Metaverse Platform:
Consumer-Based Brand Equity in a Virtual World (CBBE)

S. Catherine
https://orcid.org/0009-0007-2403-0879
SRM Institute of Science and Technology, India

V. Kiruthiga
SRM Institute of Science and Technology, India

Suresh N. V.
ASET College of Science and Technology, India

Reena Gabriel
SRM Institute of Science and Technology, India

ABSTRACT

Brand equity is one of the prime and strategic assets for most contemporary business organizations. Companies are focusing on novel and innovative ways in order to build brand equity. Brand experience is one such construct that can be used by marketing managers in building and managing brand equity. Only a few studies have explored the relationship between brand experience and brand equity, particularly in the online shopping industry. The fear of missing out on opportunities in the metaverse is a driving force for many brands. It is essential to approach this emerging space with a long-term, ethical, and collaborative strategy. The long-term impact of consumers and managers need to explore opportunities aligning with their business. Brands are living entities that drive business organizations in modern times. This

DOI: 10.4018/979-8-3693-1866-9.ch004

chapter explains about the four dimensions of brand experience (sensory, affective, behavioural, and intellectual) have a positive influence on all four dimensions of brand equity (brand awareness, brand association, perceived quality, brand loyalty).

INTRODUCTION

Brands are living entities that drive modern corporate organisations. A brand can be described as a customer's subjective and abstract appraisal of a brand. Smith & Milligan, (2002), brands provide an immense value to the businesses, as they provide them with a dependable and continuous revenue stream which is difficult to imitate by competition.

Although branding originally evolved as a means for differentiating products in the competition (Cowley, 1991), in contemporary times, brands convey different meanings for their consumers, and consumers may develop feelings. Marketing research has also revealed that consumers no longer demand products or services but they desire experiences (Morrison & Crane, 2007). The sensory impressions, emotions/feelings, cognitions, and behavioural reactions produced by brand-associated stimuli that are a component of a brand's design, character, communications, packaging, and environment are referred to as brand experiences. The concept of brand experience has gotten a lot of attention in marketing over the last decade, thanks to research showing its favourable impact on numerous brand aspects. The impact of experiential marketing on customer behaviour, brand personality, brand relation, and brand attitude has been studied. The purpose of this study is to fill a substantial gap in the literature by investigating the relationship between individual variables of consumer experience and brand equity in the online shopping sector. This research study was undertaken to study causal relationship between consumer experience and brand equity of online shopping portals in the state of Tamilnadu in India.

The following segment will begin with a literature review which will discuss Consumer experience and brand equity.

LITERATURE REVIEW

Consumer Brand Experience

Holbrook and Hirschman (1982) consumption includes stimulating a consumer's innermost feelings and thoughts which form the experience content.

Feelings, imaginations and pleasure play a significant role in influencing consumer's decisions. This position marks a contrast to earlier theories which emphasized customer's interest in only functional attributes in an offering. Pine and Gilmore (1998) further put forward the concept of customer experience, and more importantly, the 'experience economy' which marked the transition from service economy and drastic change in consumer behaviour.

Real experiences are quite contrary to services because purchasing services implies buying a bundle of intangible activities, whereas buying experiences means consumers pay for spending time and pleasure in return for memorable events provided by the company. Schmitt (1999) considered that consumers consider functional attributes, quality and a good brand image inherently present in an offering. As such, they desire product offerings and marketing communications that astonish their senses, sway their hearts and stimulate their minds, with which they can feel associated and can integrate or assimilate into their lifestyle.

Thus, consumer experiences are as a result of stimuli provided by the marketers. Experience was identified as a key attribute in deciphering consumer behaviour (Addis & Holbrook, 2001).

Brand experience comprises four dimensions, namely sensory, affective, intellectual and behavioural experiences (Brakus, Schmitt, & Zarantonello, 2009).

Brand Equity

Brand equity is defined as the differentiation between a branded and an unbranded product from the perspective of consumer choices. High levels of brand equity lead not only to good stock returns (Aaker & Jacobson, 1994), but also to purchase intentions and better consumer preferences (Cobb-Walgren, Ruble, & Donthu, 1995). Most of the studies on consumer-based brand equity (CBBE) consider it as a complex measure (Keller & Lehmann, 2006). Brand equity as defined by Aaker (1991) includes five categories of brand assets or liabilities (brand associations, perceived quality, brand awareness, brand loyalty and brand assets, such as channel relationships, trademarks and patents) which are linked with a name or symbol of a brand that adds to or deducts from the value offered by a product/service. The first four components are related to the consumer, and the last dimension is concerned with the financial value of assets such as patents and trademarks. This research has considered only the first four components of brand equity given by Aaker (1991) as part of CBBE. Brand awareness is an important element of brand equity. Brand awareness can be defined as the likelihood that a consumer could discriminate and recall that a brand pertains to a particular brand class (Aaker, 2009). Brand awareness consists of brand recall and brand recognition (Hoeffler and Keller, 2002). Brand awareness is an assurance of brand's commitment and quality which leads to brand familiarity and inclusion of brand in customer's consideration set during buying (Aaker, 1991). In Aaker's (1991) model of brand equity, brand awareness is followed by brand association, because a consumer can form associations with a brand after he/she becomes aware of the brand (Washburn & Plank, 2002). Aaker (2009) defines brand association as 'anything linked in memory to a brand'. The level and nature of an abstract determines the brand associations (Keller, 1993). Brand loyalty is also defined as the inclination to be loyal towards a brand as demonstrated by the consumer's intention to purchase the brand as a primary choice (Yoo & Donthun, 2001). The ultimate goal of brand management is customer's brand loyalty (Chi, Yeh, & Yang, 2009). When a brand is considered by the consumers as their primary choice, it shows their intentions to buy that brand (Keller, 1998). Consumers who are more confident about a particular brand in comparison to its substitutes are actually more loyal and ready to pay a greater price for that brand.

OBJECTIVE OF THE STUDY

The past decade has witnessed studies in brand experience which focussed on the creation of unique consumer brand experiences in order to build strong brands (Keller & Lehmann, 2006). But, the literature shows only some studies that have described the significance of brand experience in influencing and building brand equity (Zarantonello & Schmitt, 2010). This also requires studying the brand experiences in other developing nations. Thus, study focusses on online shopping industry, as it is one of the fastest growing businesses (services) worldwide and is the future of shopping worldwide. The e-commerce sales in India are expected to surpass the United States by the year 2034 to become the world's second biggest e-commerce market (IBEF, 2020). The concept of experiences in shopping is getting a lot of attention in recent times with a focus on experiential characteristics while shopping for goods and services. This elicits the need to study influence of brand experience on brand equity with respect to online shopping portals.

THEORETICAL FRAMEWORK

Consumer Brand Experience and Brand Awareness

In services (Berry, 2000), personalised customer-firm engagement results in positive experiences that generate strong perceptions, which in turn favourably influence brand awareness (Rossiter & Piercy, 1997). A customer's firsthand experience with a brand will initiate to aid in the customers recall of that brand. Brand recalls and brand identity (Hoch, 2002). are influenced by the memory of a client encounter. Berry (2000) It was hypothesised that service experiences increased both brand awareness and recall.

Brand Experience and Brand Association

Direct experiences are important in building associations in customers' minds about brand benefits and features. Strong brand associations come from increased customer interactions with brand communication. Positive service experiences foster strong associations, resulting in brand uniqueness. Service experience is an important factor in developing brand associations. The repercussions of tangible attributes connected with a product are driven by utilitarian and cognitive criterion, resulting in brand quality perception. Quality evaluation considers experience and (Srinivasan & Till, 2002).

Brand Experience and Brand Loyalty

The long-term brand experiences stored in the consumer's mind are likely to influence satisfaction and loyalty among consumers (Mittal & Kamakura, 2001). Positive brand experience is critical in developing strong and long-lasting brand loyalty (Mascarenhas, Kesavan, & Bernacchi, 2006). A study by Brakus, Schmitt, and Zarantonello (2009) postulated brand experiences influence future-directed consumer loyalty. There is also enough evidence in literature suggesting that brand experience is an important antecedent of customer loyalty and satisfaction (Schmitt, 1999). The conceptual model proposed by authors is given below (Figure 1).

Figure 1. Conceptual framework

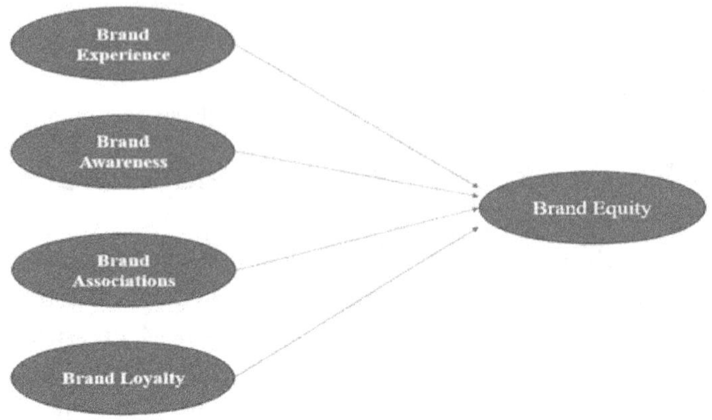

METHODOLOGY

Research Design

For this study, a quantitative research design using a structured questionnaire was used. An extensive assessment of the literature aided in the development of a self-administered questionnaire, which was pretested during the pilot project. For the research project, both primary and secondary data were gathered. The survey method was used to collect data in both the early and final phases of the investigation. The sampling frame included students from the state's nine universities. The justification for selecting university students was that they are representative of online customers due to their familiarity with e-commerce and computers. For the independent variable (Brand Experience), the study adopted five-point Likert scale from the study of Brakus, Schmitt, and Zarantonello (2009). For the dependent variable (Brand equity), the study adopted five-point Likert scale.

Data

The sample size of 114 for the final study was determined on the basis of the formula given by Krejcie and Morgan (1970). The questionnaire was distributed to 200 respondents, but only 120 functional responses were used in the research study. The sampling method adopted for the final study was Probability sampling.

Data Analysis

The total number of respondents considered for the final study was 114. The percentage of male respondents in the sample were 56.82 per cent and 43.17 per cent were female. Overall, 52.85 per cent students were pursuing post-graduation, followed by 36.47 per cent pursuing graduation, 3.22 per cent pursuing MPhil and 7.44 per cent pursuing PhD. The age group of 96.27 per cent students were 18–29 years, 3.72 per cent belonged to age group of 30–39 years and no respondents were in the age group of 40–49 years and above 50 years. Overall, 33.99 per cent of the respondents have chosen Amazon as their favourite e-commerce brand, followed by Flipkart (23.57 per cent), Snapdeal (19.10 per cent) and 23.32 per cent of the respondents have selected the other option. Additionally, 69.23 per cent of the total respondents shop 1 to 5 times a year, followed by 21.83 per cent who shop 5 to 10 times a year, 7.69 per cent shop 10–15 times a year and 1.24 per cent shop more than 15 times a year. Also, 70.23 per cent spend less than ₹10, 000 yearly, 21.58 per cent spend between ₹10,000 and ₹20,000 yearly, 5.21 per cent spend between ₹20,000 and 50,000 yearly and 2.23 per cent spend above ₹50,000 yearly.

Scale Reliability

The reliability of the instrument for both endogenous and exogenous variables in pilot study was assessed using Cronbach Alpha. The values of 'Cronbach Alpha' calculated using SPSS 20.0 are above the minimum acceptable level of 0.70 in social sciences research (Hair, Anderson, Tatham, & Black, 1998).

The results obtained showed that the hypotheses H1a, H2a, H3a and H4a are statistically supported which means sensory experience positively impacts the brand awareness ($\beta = 0.431$ and t value = 2.847), brand association ($\beta = 0.392$ and t value = 3.049), and brand loyalty ($\beta = 0.330$ and t value = 0.745).

The hypotheses H1b, H2b, H3b and H4b are statistically supported as indicated by the results which means affective experience positively impacts the brand awareness ($\beta = 0.312$ and t value = 0.221), brand association ($\beta = 0.434$ and t value = 4.668), perceived quality ($\beta = 0.309$ and t value = 0.658) and brand loyalty ($\beta = 0.451$ and t value = 2.779).

Results show the hypotheses H1c, H2c, H3c and H4c are statistically supported which means behavioural experience positively impacts the brand awareness ($\beta = 0.500$ and t value = 9.825), brand association ($\beta = 0.160$ and t value = 0.993), perceived quality ($\beta = 0.392$ and t value = 7.133) and brand loyalty ($\beta = 0.260$ and t value = 1.032).

Results showed that the hypotheses H1d, H2d, H3d and H4d are statistically supported which means the intellectual experiences positively impacts the brand awareness (β = 0.133 and t value = 0.122), brand association (β = 0.185 and t value = 2.953), perceived quality (β = 0.194 and t value = 1.867) and brand loyalty (β = 0.226 and t value = 3.740).

DISCUSSIONS

Managing a company's brand equity is critical from both a marketing and a strategic standpoint. The study's findings demonstrated that sensory experience had a favourable influence on brand awareness, brand association, perceived quality, and brand loyalty. As a result, internet shopping platforms must actively focus on offering consumer experiences that affect and gratify their senses. Online retailers can improve their sensory experiences in a variety of ways to influence and improve various aspects of CBBE. To improve their consumers' sensory experiences, online shopping portals can improve their online aesthetics, website navigation, routinely update product information, and make their adverts more appealing.

According to the study, behavioural experience has a favourable influence on the four dimensions of brand equity, namely brand awareness, brand association, perceived quality, and brand loyalty. Purchase, consumption, and suggesting online shopping portals to other users are all depicted as behavioural experiences. This experience, as expressed through customer conduct, has an impact on brand equity. As a result, the relevance of behavioural experiences in developing brand equity for online purchasing brands/portals is critical. Online shopping portals should provide incentives to their consumers in the form of better products, more product options, pleasing services, and discounts so that they will buy from their online shopping portals on a regular basis and recommend the brand to other users.

CONCLUSION

Modern consumers seek fulfilment from sources other than a product or service. They want remarkable experiences as part of every offering made to them. Because traditional marketing activity focuses just on functional brand advantages, which is costly and time-consuming, the current study has demonstrated that brand equity can be positively influenced through the experiential approach. Thus, brand experience may be used to create brand success in the online buying marketplace in an efficient and cost-effective manner. The new research approach has enhanced marketing research by giving valuable insights into brand experience and brand equity in the online retail sector. This research has provided academics with the ability to apply structural models to determine how multiple characteristics of experiences influence specific variables of brand equity. This study provides empirical evidence indicating that brand experience is a significant predictor of brand equity. The four elements of brand experience chosen for the study have a positive link with the four dimensions of online shopping site brand equity.

REFERENCES

Aaker, D. (1991). *Managing brand equity: Capitalizing on the value of a brand name*. The Free Press.

Addis, M., & Holbrook, M. B. (2001). On the conceptual link between mass customisation and experiential consumption: An explosion of subjectivity. *Journal of Consumer Behaviour*, *1*(1), 50–66. doi:10.1002/cb.53

Brakus, J. J., Schmitt, B. H., & Zarantonello, L. (2009). Brand experience: What is it? How is it measured? Does it affect loyalty? *Journal of Marketing*, *73*(3), 52–68. doi:10.1509/jmkg.73.3.052

Cowley, D. (1991). *Understanding brands by ten people who do*. Kogan Page.

Haeckel, S. H., Carbone, L. P., & Berry, L. L. (2003). How to lead the customer experience. *Marketing Management*, *12*(1), 18–18.

Hoeffler, S., & Keller, K. L. (2002). Building brand equity through corporate societal marketing. *Journal of Public Policy & Marketing*, *21*(1), 78–89. doi:10.1509/jppm.21.1.78.17600

Holbrook, M. B., & Hirschman, E. C. (1982). The experiential aspects of consumption: Consumer fantasies, feelings, and fun. *The Journal of Consumer Research*, *9*(2), 132–140. doi:10.1086/208906

IBEF. (2018). *E-commerce industry in India*. Retrieved from https://www.ibef.org/industry/ecommerce.aspx

Keller, K. L. (1993). Conceptualizing, measuring and managing customer-based brand equity. *Journal of Marketing*, *57*(1), 1–22. doi:10.1177/002224299305700101

Keller, K. L. (1998). *Strategic brand management building, measuring, and managing brand equity*. Prentice Hall.

Keller, K. L. (2003). *Strategic brand management: Building, measuring and managing brand equity* (4th ed.). Prentice-Hall.

Khan, I., & Rahman, Z. (2015). A review and future directions of brand experience research. *International Strategic Management Review*, *3*(1–2), 1–14. doi:10.1016/j.ism.2015.09.003

Mittal, V., & Kamakura, W. A. (2001). Satisfaction, repurchase intent, and repurchase behavior: Investigating the moderating effect of customer characteristics. *JMR, Journal of Marketing Research*, *38*(1), 131–142. doi:10.1509/jmkr.38.1.131.18832

Pine, B. J., & Gilmore, J. H. (1999). *The experience economy*. Harvard Business Press.

Pine, J. B. II, & Gilmore, J. H. (1998). Welcome to the experience economy. *Harvard Business Review*, *76*(4), 97–105. PMID:10181589

Pitta, D. A., & Franzak, F. J. (2008). Foundations for building share of heart in global brands. *Journal of Product and Brand Management*, *17*(2), 64–72. doi:10.1108/10610420810864676

Rust, R. T., Zeithaml, V. A., & Lemon, K. N. (2000). *Driving customer equity: How customer lifetime value is reshaping corporate strategy*. Free Press.

Smith, S., & Milligan, A. (2002). *Uncommon practice: People who deliver a great brand experience*. Pearson Education.

Tong, X., & Hawley, J. M. (2009). Measuring customer-based brand equity: Empirical evidence from the sportswear market in China. *Journal of Product and Brand Management*, *18*(4), 262–271. doi:10.1108/10610420910972783

Zarantonello, L., & Schmitt, B. H. (2013). The impact of event marketing on brand equity: The mediating roles of brand experience and brand attitude. *International Journal of Advertising*, *32*(2), 255–280. doi:10.2501/IJA-32-2-255-280

Chapter 5
Food Items Moving From Restaurants to Online Platforms in the Developing Gig Economy:
Is It Bliss?

K. Shanthi
https://orcid.org/0009-0000-2496-4128
SRM Institute of Science and Technology, Vadapalani, India

V. Suganya
SRM Institute of Science and Technology, Vadapalani, India

ABSTRACT

The newest trend is to order food online while lounging at home rather than dining out. Additionally, they browse the different food options when ordering an online meal. Gig workers profit from the opportunities for employment, independence, and flexibility that this rapidly expanding gig economy provides. Giving people the freedom to choose from various food items makes trying new things enjoyable, but it also has some drawbacks. Technological integration makes real-time ordering and online payment processing possible, which raises consumer happiness. This chapter discusses the advantages and disadvantages of online meal delivery services. It will conclude by emphasizing the influence of social, economic, and individual factors on food delivery platforms.

DOI: 10.4018/979-8-3693-1866-9.ch005

1. INTRODUCTION

The gig economy has fundamentally altered how we work, live, and eat. The food industry has changed dramatically in the past few years as more food items are distributed online rather than through physical restaurants. Some have welcomed this shift as a positive development that offers consumers and gig economy members opportunities, convenience, and variety. As with any significant societal change, there are serious concerns about how it will affect conventional companies, the rights and welfare of gig workers, and the quality of food. In this inquiry, we will delve into the complexities of this phenomenon, examining its potential benefits and drawbacks and how it is transforming the food industry in developing nations.

The final section of this chapter will explain how social, economic, and individual issues affect the use of food delivery services. Using consumer data, adapting to the evolving needs of Generation Z, evaluating economic impacts, and leveraging social influence are all significant contributions to food delivery systems. Understanding consumer behavior, in addition to cultural and economic norms, is heavily emphasized. Platforms can segment their target audience, offer a range of menu options, and offer reasonably priced food substitutes. Policymakers should consider how food delivery platforms affect society and the economy when drafting legislation to support fair competition and welfare.

2. REVIEW OF LITERATURE

2.1 Food Delivery Platforms

Food delivery platforms are web or mobile apps that link customers with nearby eateries and make it easier for them to receive food orders at home or work. These platforms have transformed how people order and consume food, which is growing in popularity. Online Food changes how people buy, cook, and eat, impacting how people and their food connect. There has been much discussion about how these developments have affected interpersonal connections and whether or not online commercial networking improves or worsens family time and community contacts (Li et al., 2020). According to Allah Pitchay et al. (2022), price-saving orientation, time-saving orientation, quality of information, and social influence significantly impact people's attitudes regarding online meal delivery services and their intentions to use the applications.

2.2 Demographics of Clients Using Food Delivery Platforms

Food delivery service usage online was associated with male identification, ethnic minority membership, younger age, better educational attainment, and having children under eighteen. Consumers of online meal delivery services are similar in their sociodemographic characteristics across national borders. The strength of the associations varied, however. The observed differences between nations may be attributed to a variety of factors, including international variations in regulations related to purchasing food prepared outside the home, time limitations that prevent cooking meals at home, and the range and number of food facilities available for online food delivery services (Keeble et al., 2020). Over the past ten years, the proportion of people accessing and purchasing the Internet has steadily increased across all generations. The majority of online shoppers belonged to Generation Y and Generation Z. Due to their small markets, Gen Xers and Baby Boomers are viewed as secondary targets. These age groups include consumers who lack purchasing power or are too old to comprehend internet shopping and new technologies (Sangeeta et al., 2020).

2.3 Reason for Using Food Delivery Platforms

The rise in new deliveries can be explained through two sources of client demand. The first one can be used as a restaurant substitute. Thanks to innovative food delivery services, customers may dine at home and enjoy the same high-quality meals they would receive at a nice restaurant (Carsten et al., 2016). Online food delivery platforms leverage various marketing strategies to enhance user experiences and increase consumers' intentions to purchase food. If the user has a positive experience, the software will urge them to use it whenever they desire a satisfying meal. Previous studies have found that factors affecting the utilitarian value of online purchasing include ease of use, affordability, a large selection, accessibility to information, and personalized goods or services (Horta et al., 2022). The impact of previous experiences, the influence of other parties, and customers' subjective expectations will all have a positive and considerable impact on their utilitarian worth and hedonic value. Because of this, platform operators have to be careful while building their brand and explaining to customers how they handle problems to avoid giving them the wrong idea, which could encourage the spread of additional negative reviews. The intention to purchase meals via delivery systems is also positively and considerably influenced by hedonistic and utilitarian objectives. Utilitarian and hedonistic values mediate attitudes, subjective norms, perceived behavioral control, and customers' desire to purchase food delivery platforms (Chen et al., 2020).

The Theory of Reasoned Action holds that an individual's intentions shape her actual action. Her attitudes about behavior and subjective norms around the behavior are the two antecedent aspects that impact her behavioral intention. Behavioral intention measures "how far individuals are willing to go to accomplish the activity" as well as "how extensively they intend to exert to perform the act". Intentions have an advantageous influence on people's act, enabling them to carry out their intended behaviors. A person's assessment of conduct is conveyed in their opinions toward it (Rustagi & Prakash, 2022). They are determined by her prevailing assumptions about the advantages and disadvantages of the conduct. It has been demonstrated that attitude directly affects buying intentions and can even reduce the correlation between visibility and intention to buy. Therefore, marketers should educate consumers about the benefits of regulators to encourage a positive attitude toward using these platforms. Agency developers might do more in this regard then only employ advertisements and other methods of increasing brand awareness. Developers might, for example, include features in this agency interface that highlight the restaurant's distinctive attributes, including its local business status, most popular dishes, or personnel background details to bolster the perceived authenticity of the experience or service. Such information could positively influence people's views (Tandon et al., 2021).

2.4 Benefits of Using Food Delivery Platforms

Customers no longer need to leave the house to buy food from their favorite eateries thanks to online food delivery companies. Those who like to stay at home or work and don't want to cook will find this very appealing. These platforms frequently offer a large selection of eateries, cuisines, and menu items, enabling patrons to sample and discover new cuisines. Online ordering allows consumers to rapidly explore menus, place orders, and pay from the comfort of their computers or cellphones, saving a significant amount of time. The primary advantages of food delivery platforms include the simplicity with which an order can be placed at any time and from any location, the range of payment options available, including digital wallets and net banking, the capacity to look for a nearby restaurant, the capacity to save time, seller discounts, free delivery, secure transactions, and comprehensive service information (Surendhranatha et al., 2020). Online food delivery services give restaurants access to a wider consumer base, which could boost revenue and brand awareness. Customers may choose foods more easily with the help of these platforms, which frequently offer digital menus with pictures and explanations.

2.5 Drawbacks of Using Food Delivery Platforms

Online platforms with capital monopolies are always looking to maximize profits. Small, medium, and micro businesses on the platform may find it more difficult to live due to the platform's profit-seeking tactics of high commissions and promotion fees. This may force them to turn to illegal production in order to cut costs, which significantly raises the risks associated with food safety in online meal delivery. The people surveyed acknowledged that takeaway meals linked with health risks may be accessed through online meal delivery services. Those surveyed did not necessarily purchase healthy food from online food delivery services, even though they were aware of the possibility. From the standpoint of public health, research suggests that, if current sociocultural values are ignored, the effectiveness of interventions meant to encourage healthier online food purchases through online food delivery services may be constrained. Improving the nutritional value of food that is sold online without necessarily drawing attention to the modifications might be one method to get around this (Keeble et al., 2022).

Food quality can occasionally be harmed throughout the delivery procedure. If you order food online instead of at the restaurant, it can come cold, mushy, or less fresh. Some restaurants only provide a small selection of their menu for online orders, which could not include all that is served to dine-in patrons. Delivery windows are subject to change, and you might have to wait longer to get your food during busy times. Additionally, there's a chance that orders will be canceled or delayed because of problems with the platform's system or delivery drivers. A few users have complained about surprise fees and price differences between the restaurant's menu and the app. Conflicts and confusion may result from this.

3. THE INFLUENCE OF INDIVIDUAL, SOCIAL, AND ECONOMIC ASPECTS ON THE USAGE OF FOOD DELIVERY PLATFORMS

Under the direction of earlier research investigations, a conceptual framework covering the individual, societal, and economic aspects of food delivery platforms is constructed (Figure 1). Under each dimension, subcategories are identified for added clarity. Individual characteristics include age, income, and preferences for junk food or healthful food; societal dimensions include breaking traditions, food choices; and economic dimensions include revenue growth and prospects for gig labor.

3.1 Individual Aspects

Regarding the individual dimension. The use of food delivery platforms is influenced by factors such as age, income, and preferences for junk food or nutritious cuisine. Young people make up the bulk of consumers of digital food delivery apps. Food delivery services are mostly used by millennials, who spend a greater percentage of their income than any other group. Younger and working-class clients are more likely to use online food delivery services. Men are more likely than women to buy food online. Married customers were more likely to place online food orders than single customers (Surendhranatha et al., 2020).

3.2 Social Aspects

The custom of preparing meals at home and occasionally dining out has been replaced by ordering food anytime it's needed. In public gatherings, people share how they tried a new dish from a new restaurant, which encourages others to try new foods as well. Another approach is to choose culinary items from a long list that is posted on websites. Social impact is another aspect that affects behavior and the intention to use new technologies. The process via which friends, family, coworkers, and other people convince someone to investigate new technology is known as social influence (Muangmee et al., 2021).

3.3 Economic Aspects

The gig economy is expanding so quickly that there are more chances for gig work and the country's economy is strengthening as a result. The food delivery services ensure both the long-term profitability of their business ventures and their total GDP contribution (Muangmee et al., 2021).

Figure 1. Influence of individual, social, and economic aspects on the usage of food delivery platforms

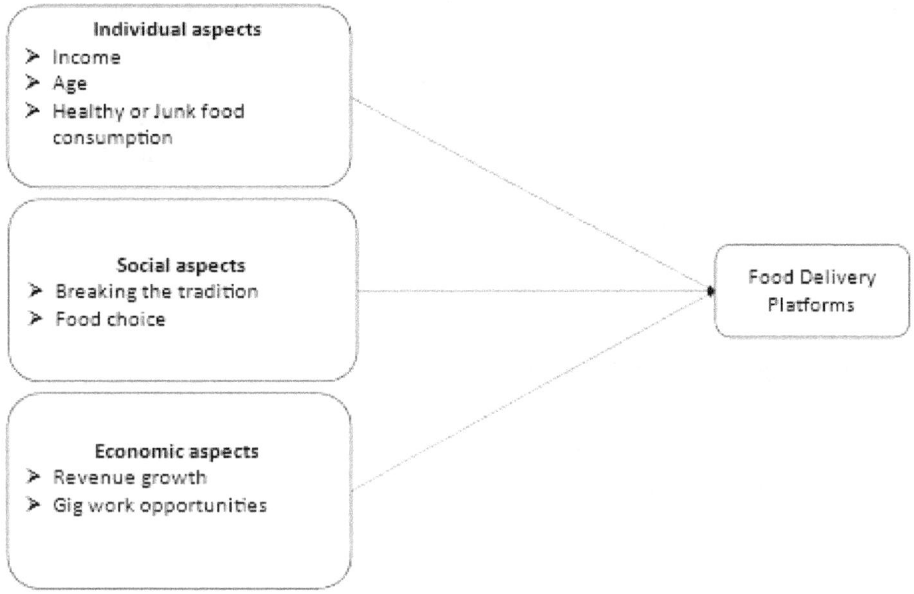

3.4 Other Elements

Food delivery platforms are influenced by various factors, including lifestyle, tech-savviness, personal preferences, age and generation, health and mobility, peer influence, cultural norms, food sharing, and social events. Lifestyle factors include busy individuals who value convenience and have limited time for cooking or dining out. Tech-savvy individuals are more comfortable with mobile apps and online ordering. Personal preferences include dietary restrictions and the availability of a variety of cuisine.

Generational factors, such as Millennials and Gen Z, are more inclined to use food delivery apps due to their accustomedness to digital solutions. Health and mobility also play a role in the adoption of food delivery platforms. Social factors include peer influence, cultural norms, food sharing, and social events.

Economic factors include income levels, cost and discounts, unemployment and economic uncertainty, urban vs. rural areas, and market competition. Higher-income individuals may use food delivery more frequently due to convenience and willingness to pay for the service, while lower-income individuals may use it less frequently due to cost concerns. Cost and discounts can also influence usage.

Unemployment and economic uncertainty can reduce peoples' usage during economic downturns or periods of unemployment. Urban areas often have more access to restaurants and delivery services, while rural areas may be less commonly used. Market competition among food delivery platforms can also affect usage, leading to better deals and options for users.

In order to properly focus their goods and satisfy client expectations, food delivery platforms and enterprises must have a thorough understanding of these elements. These elements should be taken into account by researchers and policymakers when examining how food delivery affects the economy and society.

4. MANAGERIAL IMPLICATIONS

Four managerial implications are identified based on the above conceptual framework. These include using consumer data to develop food delivery platforms, adapting to the changing needs of Generation Z, leveraging social influence to spread the use of food delivery platforms, and analyzing the economic impact of food delivery platforms by policy makers and utilizing it for eradicating unemployment and improving the economy as a whole.

Acquiring knowledge of the factors impacting the utilization of food delivery services may aid in comprehending customer behavior. Platform administrators may look more closely at how different demographic groups respond to these factors and why they choose to use a certain meal delivery service over another. This might make it easier to understand how eating habits and food tastes are changing. The effect that Gen Z and Millennials have had on the uptake of food delivery services highlights the need of doing generational studies on the uptake of technology and changes in lifestyle. By hinting that future generations will continue to rely on digital solutions for their nutritional needs, it emphasizes the need for businesses to adapt to shifting customer desires.

The significance of food sharing, cultural norms, and social gatherings in the use of food delivery services highlights the impact of social dynamics and culture on consumer decisions. Food delivery platform administrators can look at how food delivery services fit into cultural norms and influence social dynamics and food-sharing traditions. According to the economic factors affecting food delivery platforms, these services have the capacity to influence the economy in addition to being influenced by it. Examining the relationship between food delivery platforms and economic indicators might give policymakers and the government insight into how these platforms could promote employment and regional economic development.

Food delivery platforms can effectively segment their target audience by tailoring their offerings, marketing strategies, and user experiences to cater to different consumer segments. They can also diversify their menu options to accommodate dietary restrictions, catering to health-conscious customers, vegetarians, and those with specific food allergies. Geographic expansion can be strategically considered, with urban areas having higher demand due to greater restaurant density. During economic downturns, platforms can introduce cost-effective meal options, discounts, and promotions to maintain customer loyalty. They can also explore initiatives that contribute to local employment and support small-scale restaurants. Data-driven decision-making is crucial for optimizing operations and improving customer satisfaction. Policymakers should consider the multifaceted impact of food delivery platforms on society and the economy, designing regulations and policies to ensure fair competition, protect consumer rights, promote healthy food delivery practices, and consider the welfare of workers in the gig economy.

5. CONCLUSION

Food delivery platforms are influenced by individual characteristics such as age, income, and preferences for junk food or healthy cuisine. Young people, particularly millennials, are the primary consumers of digital food delivery apps. Men are more likely to buy food online than women, and married customers are more likely to place online food orders. Social aspects include the shift from home-cooked meals to ordering food anytime, with social influencing behavior and the intention to use new technologies. The gig economy is expanding rapidly, providing more opportunities for gig work and strengthening the country's economy. Food delivery services ensure long-term profitability and contribute to the country's GDP. Overall, the growth of food delivery platforms is influenced by various factors, including individual, societal, and economic aspects.

To put it briefly, the rise of food delivery services is a reflection of how our society is constantly evolving and how accessibility and technology are becoming more and more integrated into our daily lives. It does, however, have several drawbacks, including difficulties with worker protection and environmental protection. As these platforms continue to grow, a balance must be achieved between technological innovation, individual preferences, and the well-being of those employed in the gig economy to build a prosperous and inclusive future. Gaining insight into the interplay of lifestyle, generational, economic, and societal factors enable businesses to enhance customer service and contribute positively to economic growth and society.

REFERENCES

Allah Pitchay, A., Ganesan, Y., Zulkifli, N. S., & Khaliq, A. (2022). Determinants of customers' intention to use online food delivery application through smartphone in Malaysia. *British Food Journal, 124*(3), 732–753. doi:10.1108/BFJ-01-2021-0075

Chen, H. S., Liang, C. H., Liao, S. Y., & Kuo, H. Y. (2020). Consumer attitudes and purchase intentions toward food delivery platform services. *Sustainability (Basel), 12*(23), 1–18. doi:10.3390/su122310177

Hirschberg, Rajko, Schumacher, & M. W. (2016). *The changing market for food delivery*. doi:10.1109/FIE.1994.580625

Horta, P. M., Matos, J. D. P., & Mendes, L. L. (2022). Food promoted on an online food delivery platform in a Brazilian metropolis during the coronavirus disease (COVID-19) pandemic: A longitudinal analysis. *Public Health Nutrition, 25*(5), 1336–1345. doi:10.1017/S1368980022000489 PMID:35232512

Keeble, M., Adams, J., & Burgoine, T. (2022). Investigating experiences of frequent online food delivery service use: A qualitative study in UK adults. *BMC Public Health, 22*(1), 1–14. doi:10.1186/s12889-022-13721-9 PMID:35842625

Keeble, M., Adams, J., Sacks, G., Vanderlee, L., White, C. M., Hammond, D., & Burgoine, T. (2020). Use of online food delivery services to order food prepared away-from-home and associated sociodemographic characteristics: A cross-sectional, multi-country analysis. *International Journal of Environmental Research and Public Health, 17*(14), 1–17. doi:10.3390/ijerph17145190 PMID:32709148

Li, C., Mirosa, M., & Bremer, P. (2020). Review of online food delivery platforms and their impacts on sustainability. *Sustainability (Basel), 12*(14), 1–17. doi:10.3390/su12145528

Mehrolia & Alagarsamy Subburaj. (2020). Customers response to online food delivery services during COVID-19 outbreak. *Int J Consumer Studies.*

Muangmee, C., Kot, S., Meekaewkunchorn, N., Kassakorn, N., & Khalid, B. (2021). Factors determining the behavioral intention of using food delivery apps during covid-19 pandemics. *Journal of Theoretical and Applied Electronic Commerce Research, 16*(5), 1297–1310. doi:10.3390/jtaer16050073

Rustagi, P., & Prakash, A. (2022). Review on Consumer'S Attitude & Purchase Behavioral Intention Towards Green Food Products. *International Journal of Health Sciences, 6*(May), 9257–9273. doi:10.53730/ijhs.v6nS1.7092

Surendhranatha Reddy, C., & Aradhya, D. G. B. (2020). Driving Forces for the Success of Food Ordering and Delivery Apps: A Descriptive Study. *International Journal of Engineering and Management Research, 10*(02), 131–134. doi:10.31033/ijemr.10.2.15

Tandon, A., Kaur, P., Bhatt, Y., Mäntymäki, M., & Dhir, A. (2021). Why do people purchase from food delivery apps? A consumer value perspective. *Journal of Retailing and Consumer Services, 63*(September). doi:10.1016/j.jretconser.2021.102667

Chapter 6
Omnichannel Retailing:
A Comprehensive Exploration of Integration, Customer Engagement, and Market Share in Today's Retail

Sanjay Taneja
https://orcid.org/0000-0002-3632-4053
Graphic Era University (Deemed), India

Rishi Prakash Shukla
https://orcid.org/0000-0003-0854-7302
Chandigarh University, India

ABSTRACT

The chapter examines how omnichannel retail is becoming a popular tactic used by modern merchants to successfully target customers and capture a sizable portion of the market. The chapter identifies the critical elements influencing effective omnichannel strategies by examining customer behavior and preferences. It emphasizes the significance of technology, data analytics, and personalized marketing in creating individualized experiences. Additionally, it looks at how in-store technology, social media integration, and mobile commerce may increase consumer involvement and loyalty. The chapter provides useful ideas for creating flexible omnichannel frameworks across a range of retail industries through case studies and industry best practices. In the end, it emphasizes how crucial it is to tackle omnichannel retail holistically in order for merchants to forge stronger bonds with their target customers and take up a healthy market share in a cutthroat retail environment.

DOI: 10.4018/979-8-3693-1866-9.ch006

INTRODUCTION

The term "omnichannel retail" describes a company strategy that offers clients a completely integrated online and physical buying experience across several channels or platforms. Customers can engage with a retailer across a variety of touchpoints, including websites, mobile applications, social media, and physical stores, in an effort to establish a smooth and consistent customer journey. Delivering a unified and seamless experience—where customers can easily switch across channels while receiving consistent product information, price, and customer service—is the main goal of an omnichannel retail strategy (Abadie et al. 2011). In order to maximize customer happiness and loyalty, it is important to cater to the demands and preferences of the consumer while offering ease and flexibility throughout the whole buying experience.

Evolution and Importance of Omnichannel Strategy

Technology breakthroughs and shifting customer behavior have had a significant impact on the development of the omnichannel approach. Traditional retail used to be primarily centered on physical storefronts and offered few ways for consumers to engage with brands. But as e-commerce has grown and people use digital devices more frequently, they have come to anticipate a more streamlined and customized purchasing experience. In response to the changing needs of contemporary consumers, merchants have developed and implemented omnichannel strategies (Angrist et al. 2008) . A number of crucial criteria make the implementation of an omnichannel strategy imperative:

Improved customer experience: Omnichannel retail gives consumers a consistent and tailored experience by enabling them to interact with a business across a variety of channels. This method satisfies a variety of consumer inclinations and habits, which boosts client happiness and loyalty.

Increased brand exposure and reach: Retailers may reach a larger audience and engage with more people by creating a presence across a variety of media. By capturing potential consumers at several touchpoints and increasing brand awareness, this enhanced visibility promotes better brand recognition and customer acquisition.

Smooth integration of online and offline channels: Omnichannel strategies help merchants combine their online and offline businesses to give customers a unified online and offline buying experience. Customers' convenience and flexibility are enhanced by this connection, which makes options like buy online, pick up in-store (BOPIS) and return online purchases in-store possible.

Analytics and insights fuelled by data: Omnichannel retailing produces enormous volumes of data from several touchpoints with customers. Retailers may use this information to learn important things about the tastes, behavior, and purchasing habits of their customers. These information may be applied to enhance overall business operations, tailor consumer interactions, and optimize marketing efforts.

Competitive advantage: Retailers may get a market advantage by putting into practice an efficient omnichannel strategy. Retailers may set themselves apart from the competition and become customers' first choice by providing a simple and convenient purchasing experience.

Overview of the Changing Retail Landscape

Over time, the retail industry has seen substantial changes due to a variety of factors, including shifting customer tastes, market dynamics, and technology improvements. An outline of some of the major changes that have affected the retail sector is provided below:

The E-commerce Revolution: As e-commerce has grown, the retail environment has seen a significant transformation, offering consumers increased accessibility and convenience. Consumer purchasing patterns have changed as a result of the substantial expansion of online shopping platforms and their broad selection of goods and services (Avery et al. 2012).

Omnichannel Retailing: To give customers a smooth shopping experience, retailers are embracing omnichannel tactics, which combine online and physical channels. With this strategy, customers may communicate with companies via a variety of channels, including as websites, mobile applications, and physical storefronts.

Customization and Client Experience: Shopkeepers are emphasizing customized client experiences in an effort to meet unique needs and raise customer satisfaction levels. Retailers may provide customized goods and services by using AI and data analytics to better understand customer behavior.

Sustainability and Ethical Consumption: As environmental concerns get more attention, customers are looking for items that are sourced ethically and sustainably. In response to the expectations of environmentally concerned consumers, retailers are developing transparent supply chains, marketing eco-friendly items, and embracing sustainable practices.

Experiential Retail: A lot of stores are stressing the value of offering distinctive and engaging in-store experiences in order to draw in and keep customers. This include interesting activities, events, and interactive displays that entice customers to spend longer time in physical stores.

Digital Payment Solutions: Using electronic funds transfers' solutions has improved client convenience and security by streamlining the shopping process. The increasing use of mobile payment alternatives, contactless purchases, and cryptocurrencies has further influenced how customers interact with shops.

Data-Driven Retail: To obtain important insights into customer behavior, market trends, and inventory management, retailers are utilizing big data and analytics. Retailers may make well-informed decisions regarding product offers, pricing schemes, and marketing efforts with the aid of this data-driven strategy.

Supply Chain Challenges: The COVID-19 pandemic and other disruptions to global supply chains have brought attention to the need for robust and flexible supply chain management. In order to reduce risks and guarantee that items are delivered on time to satisfy consumer demand, retailers are looking at novel tactics.

THEORETICAL FRAMEWORK OF OMNICHANNEL RETAIL

Understanding Consumer Behaviour in the Digital Era

The extensive use of digital technology and the internet has resulted in substantial changes in consumer behaviour in the digital age. Businesses must comprehend these developments in order to interact with and serve their target audience in an efficient manner (Bakos 1997). The following are some salient features of modern digital-era consumer behaviour:

Online Research: Before making a purchase, consumers now conduct in-depth research on goods and services online. On social media and review sites, they read reviews, evaluate costs, and look for peer recommendations.

Multi-Channel Shopping: Websites, social media, and mobile applications are just a few of the channels that customers frequently use to purchase. Customers anticipate an integrated and smooth experience using all of these channels.

Personalization: Based on their browsing history, past interactions, and preferences, customers anticipate individualized experiences. Companies can use AI and data analytics to customize products and marketing materials for specific customers.

Social Media Influence: Consumer behavior is greatly influenced by social media. When making judgments on what to buy, consumers frequently turn to social media influencers and peer recommendations.

Mobile Dominance: As smartphone usage rises, mobile commerce has taken center stage. Customers anticipate a flawless online and mobile buying experience from websites and applications that are easy to use.

Fast Gratification: The advent of digital technology has led to a culture in which customers want convenient and speedy services, such same-day delivery, fast customer assistance, and one-click purchasing.

Openness and Trust: When interacting with businesses, customers seek authenticity and openness. People are inclined to believe in brands that are forthright with their beliefs, procedures, and product details.

Exploring the Significance of Seamless Customer Experience

In today's corporate environment, a smooth customer experience is crucial since it has a direct influence on customer happiness, loyalty, and brand perception (Bang et al. 1997). It describes the seamless, integrated, and consistent experience that consumers have with a brand throughout all of their interactions and touchpoints. This is why it's so important to have a smooth client experience:

Enhanced Customer Satisfaction: Smooth interactions with various channels and touchpoints result in happier customers. Customers are more likely to feel appreciated and understood when they can move through the many phases of their relationship with a company with ease.

Enhanced Customer Loyalty: Repeat business and loyalty are stimulated by a flawless customer experience. Consumers who often have outstanding experiences from businesses are more likely to remain loyal to them since they feel more at ease and secure interacting with the brand over and again.

Enhanced Customer Retention: Organizations may lower customer attrition and boost retention rates by eliminating consumer effort and guaranteeing a seamless shopping experience from start to finish. Loyal and content consumers are less likely to move to rival brands.

Positive Brand Perception: A flawless consumer experience contributes to a favorable brand impression. When consumers regularly enjoy a hassle-free, integrated experience across several touchpoints, they view a company as dependable, trustworthy, and customer-centric.

Competitive Advantage: Companies that put a high priority on smooth customer interactions stand out in the marketplace. In a time when consumers have high expectations, companies who succeed in creating a seamless experience for their customers are more likely to differentiate themselves from rivals.

Role of Technology in Enabling Omnichannel Strategies

The implementation of successful omnichannel strategies, which center on delivering a smooth and integrated consumer experience across several channels and touchpoints, is made possible in large part by technology. The following are some ways that technology makes omnichannel strategy execution easier:

Consumer Data Integration: Thanks to advancements in technology, companies are now able to gather and combine consumer data from a variety of sources, such as social media, in-person and online interactions, and customer service touchpoints. Businesses are able to tailor interactions and services across channels thanks to the integrated data that contributes to the creation of a comprehensive consumer perspective.

Customer Relationship Management (CRM) Systems: CRM systems assist companies in tracking consumer preferences, behaviors, and past purchases across various channels by managing and analyzing customer interactions and data. This data is necessary to provide targeted and customized experiences.

Cloud Computing: Cloud computing technology gives organizations the scale and flexibility they need to handle data and apps across several channels (Blackburn,2005). It makes information accessible in real time and guarantees coherence and consistency in client interactions across all channels.

Data Analytics and AI: These two technologies enable companies to extract useful information from consumer data, enabling them to predict demands and tailor interactions. Chatbots and virtual assistants driven by AI may offer real-time customer care, improving the omnichannel experience as a whole.

Inventory Management Systems: Businesses may synchronize inventory data across several channels with the help of technology, guaranteeing that customers receive correct information about the availability and characteristics of products. Stockouts are less likely thanks to this connection, which also guarantees a unified online and offline buying experience.

MULTIPLE FORMATS IN OMNICHANNEL RETAIL

Physical Store Integration in the Digital Sphere

Physical stores are essential to an omnichannel retail strategy because they provide a smooth shopping experience for customers (Brynjolfsson et al. 2009). Brick and mortar shops may use technology to improve consumer interaction and optimize operations by integrating with the digital world. This combination may consist of:

Interactive kiosks and digital displays within stores that provide shoppers access to the whole product inventory, online reviews, and suggestions.

Click-and-collect services bridge the gap between online and offline shopping by enabling customers to buy things online and pick them up at a real store.

Integration of online and offline technologies to give customers real-time access to information about product availability across all channels.

Giving clients the choice to utilize digital wallets and accepting digital payment methods

E-commerce Platforms and their Role in Omnichannel Strategy

The foundation of omnichannel strategy are e-commerce platforms, which provide customers the flexibility to purchase whenever and from anywhere. They allow companies to:

To duplicate the in-store purchasing experience, provide a thorough product catalog with in-depth descriptions and high-quality photos (Cachon, 2013).

Enable a safe and easy checkout experience by offering a variety of payment alternatives and secure payment channels to facilitate seamless online transactions.

Implement targeted promos, recommendations, and customized product suggestions as well as other personalized marketing methods based on consumer data and behavior.

To accommodate a range of consumer choices, provide effective order management and fulfillment with alternatives for curbside pickup, same-day delivery, and home delivery.

Mobile Applications and Their Impact on Customer Engagement

In an omnichannel retail setting, mobile apps are essential for increasing consumer engagement and revenue (Coughlan AT et al. 2006). Businesses are able to:

Customers should be able to easily explore items, make purchases, and follow orders from their mobile devices with an easy-to-use interface.

To provide customers with tailored offers, promotions, and pertinent information based on their interests and proximity to physical stores, use location-based services and push notifications.

Promote a consistent and linked buying experience by facilitating easy interaction with various digital channels. This will allow customers to move between the mobile app, website, and physical store with ease.

To encourage consumer interaction and cultivate enduring relationships with the business, provide loyalty programs and prizes via mobile applications.

EFFECTIVE TARGETING IN OMNICHANNEL RETAIL

Personalization Strategies for Improved Customer Engagement

Adjusting product recommendations and promotions according to the unique tastes, past purchases, and cross-channel browsing habits of each individual client.

Putting into practice customized marketing strategies that speak to the needs and interests of certain customers via targeted SMS, push alerts, and emails (Davis S, et al. 1995).

Constructing dynamically adjusted landing pages and website content that are tailored to each individual customer's preferences and prior interactions.

Delivering individualized customer care experiences to increase client happiness and loyalty, such as customized product support, advice, and help.

Data-Driven Approaches for Targeted Marketing Campaigns

Obtaining insights into the behavior and preferences of customers by gathering and evaluating consumer data from a variety of touchpoints, including as social media activity, past purchases, and online interactions (Eppen et al. 1979).

Using psychographic, behavioral, and demographic data to segment customers in order to develop marketing strategies that are appealing to particular client segments.

Businesses may proactively provide relevant products and services before customers actively seek them out by using predictive analytics to anticipate customer requirements and preferences.

Optimizing marketing campaigns and determining the best practices for various client groups via the use of A/B testing and other data-driven studies.

Utilizing Customer Analytics for Enhanced Product Recommendations

Businesses are able to generate data-driven product suggestions and bundle offerings by analyzing consumer data to identify purchasing patterns, product affinities, and cross-selling potential (Forman et al. 2009).

Putting collaborative filtering and recommendation algorithms into practice to provide product recommendations based on past purchases, user preferences, and offline and online activity.

Utilizing real-time data to dynamically modify promotions and product suggestions in response to a customer's past contacts with the business and current browsing habits.

Businesses are able to satisfy consumer expectations by customizing suggestions and improving product offerings through the continual monitoring and analysis of customer feedback and reviews to detect trends and preferences.

ENHANCING MARKET SHARE THROUGH OMNICHANNEL STRATEGIES

Competitor Analysis and Comparative Market Positioning

Carrying out in-depth competition study to pinpoint the major companies in the industry, comprehend their advantages and disadvantages, and ascertain their omnichannel tactics (Forman et al. 1979).

Evaluating the competitive environment to find holes and chances that may be used to obtain a competitive advantage, including finding underutilized markets or untapped distribution avenues.

Examining consumer preferences and market trends to predict changes in consumer behavior and keep a step ahead of rivals by implementing cutting-edge omnichannel strategies.

Defining a distinct comparative market positioning strategy that emphasizes the advantages of the omnichannel approach and draws attention to the business's distinct value propositions and differentiators from those of its rivals.

Leveraging Customer Insights for Competitive Advantage

Gathering and examining client data from various channels and touch points to learn about their preferences, habits, and trouble areas (Gallino S et al. 2014).

Identifying areas for improvement and adjusting the omnichannel approach to better satisfy the requirements and expectations of the consumer base through the use of customer evaluations and feedback.

Putting customer journey mapping into practice to comprehend the entire client experience and find ways to improve satisfaction and engagement.

Creating specialized marketing and advertising strategies based on consumer data to increase client loyalty, acquisition, and retention.

Case Studies of Successful Market Penetration Through Omnichannel Integration

Examining case studies of businesses that have effectively used omnichannel tactics to increase revenue, increase market share, and enhance consumer engagement.

Examining the efficient ways in which these businesses used their online and physical platforms to provide a unified and smooth consumer experience.

Becoming aware of the particular omnichannel strategies and tools that prosperous companies use to increase client loyalty and engagement.

Analyzing the obstacles these businesses encountered while putting their omnichannel strategy into practice and the methods they used to get over them.

LITERATURE REVIEW

Omnichannel retail is defined by the integration of physical stores, e-commerce platforms, and mobile applications to provide a unified shopping experience. Shifting consumer behavior towards personalized and convenient shopping experiences necessitates data-driven insights for effective marketing strategies. A seamless customer experience across all touchpoints is vital for building strong customer relationships and enhancing brand perception. The critical role of technology, including AI, data analytics, and CRM systems, in facilitating personalized experiences and optimizing operations is highlighted

(Gensler S et al. 2012). Businesses face challenges in implementing successful omnichannel strategies, necessitating the adoption of innovative technologies and comprehensive planning. Emerging trends such as AR, VR, sustainability, and blockchain integration offer opportunities for future growth and enhanced transparency in the retail landscape (Ghose A et al., 2006).

METHODOLOGY FOR IMPLEMENTING OMNICHANNEL RETAIL

Research Design and Data Collection Techniques

To determine the target client categories, comprehend their preferences, and evaluate the competitive environment, do in-depth market research.

To get information about consumer behavior, expectations, and purchasing habits, combine qualitative and quantitative research techniques like focus groups, interviews, surveys, and data analytics.

Utilize data analytics and customer relationship management (CRM) systems to gather and examine consumer information from a variety of touchpoints, such as online and offline encounters.

To continually improve the omnichannel approach based on real-time consumer data and feedback, use user testing and feedback systems.

Analysis of Consumer Preferences and Behavior Patterns

Examine consumer information to find patterns, inclinations, and purchasing patterns through various channels and interactions.

By using segmentation techniques, you may group clients according to their psychographic, behavioral, and demographic characteristics, which will allow you to tailor your marketing campaigns and products.

To find out how well various marketing campaigns, deals, and product suggestions affect consumer engagement and sales, run A/B tests and evaluate the outcomes.

To improve the entire purchasing experience and raise customer happiness, identify parts of the current customer journey that need improvement and consumer pain points.

Examination of Technology Integration and Infrastructure Requirements

Determine the gaps and needs for a smooth integration across all channels, including online platforms and physical stores, by evaluating the current technological infrastructure.

Examine several platforms and software options that help with inventory management, order fulfillment across numerous channels, data integration, and customer involvement.

Put in place strong data security protocols and compliance guidelines to guarantee that client information is protected and that industry rules are followed.

Invest in adaptable and scalable technology solutions that can change with the demands of your customers and the pace of technological development in the retail sector.

Figure 1. Model framework for successful omnichannel integration

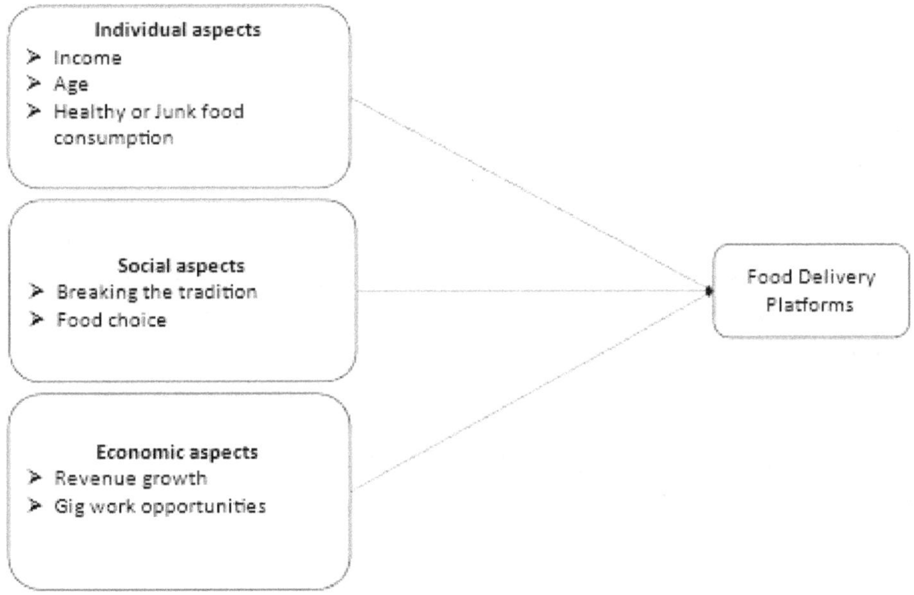

MODEL FRAMEWORK FOR SUCCESSFUL OMNICHANNEL INTEGRATION

Developing a Comprehensive Customer Journey Map

Determine the points of contact with customers through a variety of channels, including as websites, retail locations, mobile apps, and customer support exchanges.

Draw out the customer journey, taking into mind the many phases and possible interactions, from early awareness and consideration to the ultimate purchase and post-purchase assistance.

Examine consumer habits, requirements, and complaints at every point of contact to find areas that may be optimized and improved.

Use engagement techniques that are tailored to the individual client segments and their distinct travel pathways.

Integration of Inventory Management Systems for Seamless Operations

To guarantee accurate and up-to-date information about product availability and stock levels in real time, integrate inventory management systems with all channels.

Install a centralized system for managing inventory to facilitate order fulfillment, product restocking, and online and offline sales channel coordination.

To reduce stockouts, steer clear of overstocking, and maximize inventory turnover rates, use automated inventory tracking and replenishment systems.

Allow for flexible fulfillment alternatives to give customers more delivery options and improve their buying experience, such as ship from store and click-and-collect services.

Aligning Marketing Strategies With Unified Brand Messaging

Create a single, coherent brand message that appeals to the target market via all media while preserving the company's voice, values, and aesthetics.

Develop integrated marketing programs that target clients at different points in the customer journey by utilizing a variety of channels, such as social media, email marketing, and targeted advertising.

Use customer insights and segmentation to inform tailored and pertinent messages to various consumer segments by using data-driven marketing tactics.

Track and evaluate the effectiveness of marketing efforts across various channels, and adjust tactics according to the knowledge acquired to maximize consumer involvement and conversion rates.

CHALLENGES AND FUTURE TRENDS IN OMNICHANNEL RETAIL

Overcoming Operational and Technological Hurdles

Combining current technology with historical systems to provide smooth data transfer and channel-to-channel connectivity.

Coordinating intricate supply chains and logistics to enable effective order fulfillment, particularly when click-and-collect and same-day delivery options are offered.

Preserving data security and privacy across a range of digital touchpoints in order to safeguard client information and stop possible data breaches.

Equipping staff members with the knowledge and skills necessary to handle omnichannel operations, such as order fulfillment, inventory control, and customer support.

Anticipating Shifts in Consumer Preferences and Market Dynamics

Adjusting to shifting cultural norms, developing trends, and technology developments that may have an impact on customer behavior and preferences (Forman, 2009).

Recognizing and meeting the rising consumer demand for ethical and sustainable business practices, which has a big influence on supply chain management and product offers.

Keeping an eye on market developments and exercising flexibility to modify business plans and product offerings in reaction to shifting competition and market conditions.

predicting how external variables, such as world events, alterations in the economy, and changes in regulations, would affect consumer purchasing patterns and retail operations.

Embracing Innovations for Sustained Growth and Adaptability

Highlighting the application of machine learning and artificial intelligence (AI) to improve supply chain management, improve consumer customization, and expedite operational efficiency (Guide V., D., R., 2006).

Utilizing virtual and augmented reality (VR) technology to give customers engaging and interactive online and in-store shopping experiences.

Putting money into predictive modeling and sophisticated data analytics technologies will help you better estimate demand, improve pricing tactics, and anticipate client wants.

Investigating the use of blockchain technology to safe-guard transactions, enhance supply chain transparency, and foster consumer confidence in terms of product legitimacy and sourcing methods.

CONCLUSION

We have emphasized the revolutionary power of omnichannel retail in the digital age throughout this conversation. We have underlined how crucial it is to comprehend customer behavior, make use of technology, and put into practice practical tactics in order to improve customer satisfaction and spur company development. The importance of customization, data-driven insights, and seamless integration across several channels to satisfy changing customer expectations and preferences are some of the key findings.

Summary of Recommendations for Implementing Effective Omnichannel Strategies

Businesses should concentrate on creating thorough customer journey maps, integrating inventory management systems, and coordinating marketing efforts with cohesive brand message in order to successfully deploy omnichannel strategies. To create a smooth and uniform experience across all touchpoints, it is imperative to prioritize operational efficiency, embrace technological integration, and leverage consumer data. In order for companies to remain competitive and relevant in the changing retail scene, they need also prioritize data security, keep an eye on market trends, and invest in cutting-edge technology.

Significance of Omnichannel Integration for Sustainable Market Share Growth

Sustainable market share development requires omnichannel integration because it helps companies to cultivate strong customer connections, increase customer loyalty, and promote brand advocacy. Businesses may expand customer happiness, boost retention rates, and gain a competitive edge in the market by offering a smooth and customized client experience. The attainment of long-term sustainable growth and the maintenance of a robust market position are contingent upon the capacity to adjust to evolving customer tastes and technical improvements.

REFERENCES

Abadie, A., Diamond, A., & Hainmueller, J. (2011). Synth: An r package for synthetic control methods in comparative case studies. *Journal of Statistical Software*, *42*(13). Advance online publication. doi:10.18637/jss.v042.i13

Angrist, J. D., & Pischke, J. S. (2008). Mostly Harmless Econometrics: An Empiricist's Companion. Princeton University Press.

Avery, J., Steenburgh, T. J., Deighton, J., & Caravella, M. (2012). Adding bricks to clicks: Predicting the patterns of cross-channel elasticities over time. *Journal of Marketing*, *76*(3), 96–111. doi:10.1509/jm.09.0081

Bakos, J. Y. (1997). Reducing buyer search costs: Implications for electronic marketplaces. *Management Science*, *43*(12), 1676–1692. doi:10.1287/mnsc.43.12.1676

Bang, H., & Robins, J. M. (2005). Doubly robust estimation in missing data and causal inference models. *Biometrics, 61*(4), 962–972.

Blackburn, J. D., Guide, V. D. R. Jr, Souza, G. C., & Van Wassenhove, L. N. (2004). Reverse supply chains for commercial returns. *California Management Review*, *46*(2), 6–22. doi:10.2307/41166207

Brynjolfsson, E., Hu, Y. J., & Rahman, M. S. (2009). Battle of the retail channels: How product selection and geography drive cross-channel competition. *Management Science*, *55*(11), 1755–1765. doi:10.1287/mnsc.1090.1062

Cachon, G., Gallino, S., & Olivares, M. (2013). *Does adding inventory increase sales? Evidence of a scarcity effect in us automobile dealerships*. Working Paper.

Coughlan, A. T., Anderson, E., Stern, L. W., & Ansary, A. I. (2006). *Marketing channels*. Pearson/Prentice Hall.

Davis, S., Gerstner, E., & Hagerty, M. (1995). Money back guarantees in retailing: Matching products to consumer tastes. *Journal of Retailing*, *71*(1), 7–22. doi:10.1016/0022-4359(95)90010-1

Eppen, G. D. (1979). Noteeffects of centralization on expected costs in a multi-location newsboy problem. *Management Science*, *25*(5), 498–501. doi:10.1287/mnsc.25.5.498

Forman, C., Ghose, A., & Goldfarb, A. (2009). Competition between local and electronic markets: How the benefit of buying online depends on where you live. *Management Science*, *55*(1), 47–57. doi:10.1287/mnsc.1080.0932

Gallino, S., & Moreno, A. (2014). Integration of online and offline channels in retail: The impact of sharing reliable inventory availability information. *Management Science*, *60*(6), 1434–1451. doi:10.1287/mnsc.2014.1951

Gensler, S., Leeflang, P., & Skiera, B. (2012). Impact of online channel use on customer revenues and costs to serve: Considering product portfolios and self-selection. *International Journal of Research in Marketing*, *29*(2), 192–201. doi:10.1016/j.ijresmar.2011.09.004

Ghose, A., Smith, M. D., & Telang, R. (2006). Internet exchanges for used books: An empirical analysis of product cannibalization and welfare impact. *Information Systems Research*, *17*(1), 3–19. doi:10.1287/isre.1050.0072

Guide, V. D. R. Jr, Souza, G. C., Van Wassenhove, L. N., & Blackburn, J. D. (2006). Time value of commercial product returns. *Management Science*, *52*(8), 1200–1214. doi:10.1287/mnsc.1060.0522

Chapter 7
An Epitome Shift in Consumer Experience:
The Impact of Metaverse on the Retail Sector

V. Kiruthiga
SRM Institute of Science and Technology, India

S. Catherine
https://orcid.org/0009-0007-2403-0879
SRM Institute of Science and Technology, India

ABSTRACT

The retail industry is just one of several sectors affected by the fast-developing metaverse, a virtual reality environment that combines the real world and the internet. The immersive and interactive experiences that the metaverse introduces reshape the conventional shopping environment. In summary, the metaverse is bringing about a new age for the retail sector and changing both how consumers purchase and how retailers run their businesses. A successful and long-lasting integration of the metaverse in the retail sector requires careful evaluation of the ethical and practical ramifications. Adopting these technical breakthroughs can put merchants at the forefront of the changing consumer landscape.

DOI: 10.4018/979-8-3693-1866-9.ch007

INTRODUCTION

The rise of the metaverse stands out as a revolutionary force in the constantly changing technological landscape, promising to change how we view, interact with, and interact with the digital world. The metaverse has evolved beyond its science fiction roots as we stand at the nexus of reality and virtuality, becoming a physical and dynamic space with significant ramifications for numerous businesses. Retail, a field closely linked to the pulse of consumer behavior and technological trends, is one such industry primed for a paradigm transformation.

The metaverse appears as a colorful thread in the tapestry of technological progress, woven across the fabric of our digital existence and testing the limits of traditional consumer engagement. The metaverse beckons as we approach a transformative period, offering to alter not only how we view reality but also how we conduct the age-old activity of trade. In this study, the dramatic effects of the metaverse on the retail industry are explored. The COVID-19 pandemic has been a major factor in hastening the metaverse's development. Owing to the limitations on mobility, the internet world swiftly rose to prominence. As new technological items started to appear, many companies tried to quickly adapt.

The idea of the metaverse has become a transforming force in the dynamic fabric of technological growth, providing a link between the real and the virtual worlds. The metaverse is not just a trendy term; it represents a deep paradigm shift that has the ability to transform key facets of our daily lives as we navigate the wide terrain of digital innovation. Retail is one industry that is leading the way in this transformation because it places a premium on the customer experience and is experiencing a seismic shift in how the physical and digital worlds interact.

The metaverse, which combines immersive technologies such as augmented reality (AR), virtual reality (VR), and others, is fundamentally a collaborative virtual shared world. By providing users with a complete world that goes beyond the flat internet interfaces, it exceeds the constraints of conventional online encounters. Users can interact with one other, virtual items, and environments in the metaverse in real time, which creates a presence and immersion that was before unthinkable.

The phrase "metaverse," which was originally associated with science fiction, has moved beyond its theoretical context to become a real-world location. It stands for a collective virtual environment that combines actual and virtual worlds and is smoothly connected by the internet. Beyond the limitations of conventional online spaces, the metaverse encourages users to take part in an immersive, shared experience where the lines between the real world and the virtual world are blurred, creating new opportunities for interaction and creation.

At its core, the metaverse is a collective digital place where users can communicate, collaborate, and create in ways that go beyond what is possible in conventional online settings. The metaverse, which includes virtual and augmented realities, is a space where the lines between fantasy and reality are blurred, creating a new level of human experience. We set out on a journey into a world where innovation and customer expectations merge as we investigate the enormous effects of the metaverse on the retail industry.

The resilient and adaptable retail industry is going through a seismic transformation as it embraces the metaverse. This change involves reinventing the entire consumer process, not simply building virtual storefronts. The metaverse is ushering in a new era where the distinctions between the physical and digital purchasing environments are becoming progressively blurred. Examples include immersive shopping experiences, virtual try-ons, and interactive product displays.

The retail industry, a mainstay of economic activity, was early to understand how the metaverse could change how consumers shop. The metaverse provides a canvas for merchants to paint completely new and inventive storylines, ranging from virtual stores and immersive shopping experiences to individualized avatars participating in digital commerce. Retailers are faced with both obstacles and previously unheard-of chances to fascinate and engage their audience as consumers spend more and more time in this virtual world.

The metaverse ushers in a paradigm shift that goes well beyond the simple digitalization of storefronts in the retail industry, where the success of a business depends on the quality of the customer experience. With a blank canvas where imagination and technology may converge to create unheard-of purchasing experiences, it challenges merchants to reinvent the entire consumer journey. The metaverse offers merchants a sandbox to innovate and enthrall in previously unimagined ways, from virtual showrooms and interactive product trials to individualized avatars engaged in commerce.

The nature of commerce is changing as the metaverse blurs the distinctions between physical and digital locations. Investigating this change offers insightful information about the direction of digital commerce. New business models can be created by taking into account how transactions take place in the metaverse and how users interact with virtual goods and services. There are difficulties in integrating metaverse technologies into the retail industry.

This study can give light on the challenges that merchants confront, whether those challenges are due to technology, regulations, or consumer acceptability. For effective solutions to be developed, it is essential to comprehend these difficulties.

Beyond the retail industry, the metaverse has an impact on broader sociological and economic developments. One can develop a comprehensive grasp of how the metaverse is changing consumer behavior, cultural norms, and economic systems by researching its influence. Retail success is closely related to customer involvement and satisfaction. Retailers have a special chance to improve customer experiences in the metaverse through individualized and immersive interactions. Insights on techniques that can foster a more consumer-centric retail environment, which will boost client loyalty and pleasure, can be gained by studying this shift.

With insights that can help retailers make strategic decisions, encourage innovation, and ensure a seamless integration of metaverse technology into the retail environment, this study acts as a compass for those navigating the undiscovered metaverse. The study on how the metaverse affects the retail industry is more than just a theoretical investigation; it also has real-world ramifications for companies, customers, and society at large. The integration of the metaverse into the retail environment is approached with foresight, responsibility, and a dedication to improving customer experiences. It assists decision-makers in negotiating the difficulties of this disruptive shift.

LITERATURE REVIEW

Technologies for augmented and virtual reality are crucial in determining how consumers perceive the metaverse. The integration of AR and VR in the retail industry is the subject of scholarly studies in this section (Tussyadiah. et.al 2018). New methods of product interaction, such as virtual try-ons and interactive displays, are made possible by the metaverse. Researchers are starting to look into how these functionalities affect consumer choice (Fiore, A et al 2004).

A unique channel for businesses to interact with customers has been identified as the metaverse, a communal virtual realm. According to Johnson et al. (2021), the metaverse has the potential to transform conventional online buying experiences into immersive, individualized retail experiences. For shops looking to build meaningful relationships with customers, understanding consumer behavior within the metaverse is essential. Williams and Chen (2022) examine the aspects that affect consumers' engagement and decision-making as they move about virtual retail venues.

Lee and Wang (2018) address the potential for the metaverse to provide individualized retail experiences and look at how personalization in virtual settings might increase client pleasure and loyalty. Smith and Brown (2021) examine the elements driving consumer adoption of the metaverse and the difficulties businesses encounter in implementing metaverse-based purchasing experiences.

AR has begun to be extensively incorporated into marketing strategies, goals, and techniques. As a result, various phrases are created expressly for that industry to address the perspectives of customers and businesses. From the standpoint of the consumer, the term AR experiential marketing (AREM) is now frequently employed. AREM is mostly utilized to stimulate customers during the consideration stage of their purchasing process. This is due to the fact that before making purchases, buyers often weigh their options and accessible alternatives. Therefore, augmented reality (AR) plays a significant role in that stage by allowing consumers to experience the product before they decide to buy it, initiating their buying intentions, and ensuring their confidence in their decisions (Bulearca and Tamarjan, 2010).

With Facebook's renaming as Meta Platforms and the release of its ambition to build a space where people can work, play, and connect with others in immersive, online experiences, the metaverse has attracted significant interest. The term "metaverse" is not one that has been agreed upon by all (Golf-Papez et al., 2022), leaving the idea rather divided.

The term "Metaverse" was first used in Neal Stephenson's science fiction book Snow Crash in 1992. The name "metaverse," which combines the prefix "meta" (which means beyond) and the prefix "universe," refers to the extension of the physical internet of things into a 3D shared space and virtual world. Users communicate with one another through three-dimensional human representations known as avatars in cyberspace, according to Stephenson, in this vast virtual environment that combines the real physical and digital worlds (Lik-Hang et al. 2021). It brings together virtual worlds, augmented reality, and the internet all at once.

ATTRIBUTES CONTRIBUTING TO METAVERSE IN RETAIL INDUSTRY

Retailers may design realistic 3D environments that resemble physical storefronts thanks to the metaverse. Beyond the conventional online shopping interfaces, customers may explore and traverse these virtual places, which improves the purchasing experience. Immersion areas give customers a sense of presence and investigation, much like actual companies do, which improves the shopping experience. Artificial intelligence (AI) algorithms examine client information, including as prior purchases, interests, and behavior, to offer tailored product recommendations and shopping experiences. By creating a customized shopping experience, personalization raises the possibility that shoppers may discover goods that suit their tastes. This in turn improves client loyalty and satisfaction.

With the help of augmented and virtual reality technologies, buyers can virtually try on items or see how they would appear in their own spaces. Fig.1 displays the attributes of metaverse in fretail. This makes buying decisions more informed. By addressing fit, style, and aesthetic issues, virtual try-ons improve the online purchasing experience by decreasing the chance of returns and raising customer satisfaction. Artificial intelligence (AI)-powered virtual shopping assistants improve the whole shopping experience by offering customers real-time assistance and direction. Virtual assistants who work in real-time enhance customer service by assisting users in finding what they're looking for, getting answers to their questions, and navigating online stores more skillfully. Retailers may now access a global audience through the metaverse, delivering goods and experiences to customers all over the world, by overcoming geographic barriers. A more inclusive and diversified consumer base is fostered by increased accessibility, which guarantees that customers from various regions can engage in the metaverse retail experience.

Customers can have a seamless online and in-store shopping experience when real stores and the metaverse are seamlessly integrated. Customers may freely transition between virtual and in-store shopping experiences thanks to this integration, which makes the retail ecosystem more comprehensive and linked.

With the introduction of numerous features that enhance the shopping experience, the metaverse is changing the retail scene. By creating immersive 3D worlds in the metaverse, retailers are able to go beyond typical online shopping and offer customers engaging and interactive virtual stores. Concerns about fit and style can be addressed by virtually trying on things thanks to augmented and virtual reality technologies. AI-powered personalized shopping experiences provide recommendations that are specifically suited to each customer's tastes and behavior. The metaverse is a fertile ground for social commerce, as it provides communal shopping experiences where users may communicate, exchange recommendations, and make decisions in real time. Blockchain technology establishes digital ownership and adds value to virtual assets by introducing non-fungible tokens (NFTs), which create scarcity. While virtual events and product launches generate revenue, cross-platform integration guarantees accessibility across multiple devices. Cryptocurrency integration powers digital currency transactions, offering safe and flexible payment choices. Data analytics improves the shopping experience, and virtual assistants that work in real-time provide better customer service. A worldwide audience can be reached through accessibility and diversity, while gamification components provide motivation and enjoyment. Ensuring privacy and security while integrating with physical shopping delivers a smooth omnichannel experience that fosters confidence. Taken as a whole, these characteristics herald a new era of metaverse retail by offering consumers a linked, personalized, and dynamic buying experience.

DISCUSSION

The emergence of the metaverse has sparked a paradigm shift in the retail industry that has significantly altered and changed the customer experience. This connected, virtual place is more than simply an online shopping extension; it's a dynamic setting that uses cutting-edge technology to completely change the way consumers engage with items and brands. The development of 3D settings that are immersive within the metaverse is one of the major effects. Virtual stores provide clients an immersive and interactive buying experience that emulates the real world, surpassing the constraints of conventional e-commerce platforms. In the metaverse, social trade assumes new dimensions. A sense of community and social connection are fostered by the ability for customers to explore virtual areas together, share insights, and make decisions in real time. Non-fungible tokens (NFTs) and blockchain technology combine to create the idea of digital ownership, giving virtual goods more value and individuality in the retail industry.

Cross-platform compatibility guarantees accessibility, enabling users to move between devices with ease and yet have a unified, engaging experience. Launches and virtual events in the metaverse provide a sense of exclusivity and excitement that is similar to those of worldwide real events. In order to appeal to a consumer base that is tech-savvy, digital currency transactions backed by cryptocurrency integration offer secure and alternative payment methods. The omnichannel experience is completed by integration with physical retail, which enables customers to move between virtual and real-world shopping venues with ease. In conclusion, the metaverse is having a revolutionary effect on retail by providing a personalized, dynamic, and connected shopping experience that goes beyond the constraints of conventional online and offline retail settings. It's a change that not only satisfies but also foresees the changing demands of today's tech-savvy customers.

CONCLUSION

This study adds to the continuing discussion regarding the metaverse's revolutionary impact on customer experience in the retail industry. This study provides helpful guidance for retailers, industry practitioners, and researchers navigating the metaverse-driven paradigm change in retail by exploring the convergence of immersive technology, customization methods, social commerce dynamics, and emerging business models. Customers are introduced to immersive retail settings in the metaverse that converge the real and virtual worlds. The fundamental nature of how consumers view, interact with, and buy items is being redefined by virtual shops, interactive displays, and augmented experiences.

In the retail story generated by the metaverse, personalization takes center stage. Retailers use the metaverse to design custom experiences and customize their offerings based on customer preferences and behavior. The outcome is a highly customized retail experience that transcends the generic and resonates strongly with each customer. The transactional aspects of retail transform into a world of experiences. Virtual try-ons and interactive product displays allow customers to connect with, investigate, and experiment with products in addition to making purchases, making shopping an exciting and engaging experience.

The metaverse develops into a vibrant center for social commerce that promotes connections between people, the sharing of experiences, and group decision-making. Consumers form connections not only with brands but also with one another, strengthening the social fabric that fosters brand loyalty. While promising, the integration of the metaverse into retail is not without difficulties. In order to guarantee a seamless and secure client experience, strategic investments and a forward-thinking strategy are required. These factors are highlighted by technological challenges, security concerns, and infrastructure requirements.

Retailers must embrace innovation as a pillar of their success and survival in the metaverse. New business models and revenue streams usher in an era where adaptability, innovation, and technological know-how characterize industry leaders. These models and revenue streams are fuelled by the dynamic of the metaverse. This study highlights how important it is for stakeholders to not just adapt but also lead in the metaverse. A dynamic voyage through virtual worlds where innovation, personalization, and community come together to form the retail environment of tomorrow, the consumer experience is no longer a linear trip. Each customer is a collaborator in the production of this ground-breaking masterpiece because the metaverse is more than just a technological marvel; it is the canvas on which the future of retail is being painted. The metaverse beckons as we stand on the cusp of this paradigm shift because it represents more than simply a technology frontier; it represents a place where the very nature of retailing is reinvented and where the consumer experience takes center stage in this enthralling digital narrative.

REFERENCES

Bulearca, M., & Tamarjan, D. (2010). Augmented reality: A sustainable marketing tool. Global business and management research. *International Journal (Toronto, Ont.)*, *2*(2), 237–252.

Fiore, A. M., Lee, S.-E., & Kunz, G. (2004). Individual Differences, Motivation, and Participation in Designing Apparel on the Internet. *Clothing & Textiles Research Journal*, *22*(1), 32–47.

Golf-Papez, M., Heller, J., Hilken, T., Chylinski, M., de Ruyter, K., Keeling, D. I., & Mahr, D. (2022). Embracing falsity through the metaverse: Te case of synthetic customer experiences. *Business Horizons*, *65*(6), 739–749. doi:10.1016/j.bushor.2022.07.007

Johnson, A., Smith, B., & Lee, C. (2021). Exploring the Metaverse: Implications for Retail Engagement. *Journal of Virtual Commerce*, *15*(3), 112–129.

Lee, Y., & Wang, L. (2018). Metaverse Retail: Customization and Customer Experience. *International Journal of Retail & Distribution Management*, *46*(6), 618–635.

Lik-Hang, L. E. E., Braud, T., Zhou, P., Wang, L., Xu, D., Lin, Z., & Hui, P. (2021). *All one needs to know about metaverse: a complete survey on technological singularity, virtual ecosystem, and research agenda*. IEEE.

Smith, R., & Brown, A. (2021). Metaverse Adoption in Retail: Understanding Customer Acceptance. *Journal of Retail Technology*, *17*(4), 321–335.

Tussyadiah, I., & Park, S. (2018). Consumer Evaluation of Hotel Service Robots' Attributes: The Role of Perceived Risk and Emotional Responses. *International Journal of Hospitality Management*, *72*, 47–58.

Williams, M., & Chen, L. (2022). Navigating Virtual Retail: A Study of Consumer Behavior in the Metaverse. *International Journal of Consumer Studies*, *46*(2), 210–225.

Chapter 8
Creator's Economy in the Metaverse:
How Stakeholders in the Retail Industry Will Benefit

Krishna Khanal
https://orcid.org/0009-0003-1369-0952
Westcliff University, USA

Pushkar Khanal
King's College, Nepal

Manju Bala
https://orcid.org/0009-0005-4496-9395
Panipat Institute of Engineering and Technology, India

ABSTRACT

The creator's economy in the metaverse is poised to revolutionize the retail industry by offering an array of benefits to its stakeholders. In this emerging landscape, creators, brands, and retailers alike stand to gain substantially. Creators can leverage the metaverse's limitless creative potential to craft unique and immersive shopping experiences, fostering deeper connections with consumers. Brands can tap into the metaverse's vast and diverse user base to reach new audiences, drive engagement, and experiment with innovative marketing strategies. It is essential to bring various stakeholders together and to integrate the physical and virtual world together to leverage potential synergies and cross-channel benefits. Retailers should adopt a comprehensive and all-encompassing retailing strategy keeping customers and creators in the center and enabling customers to select their preferred shopping channel throughout their entire customer journey.

DOI: 10.4018/979-8-3693-1866-9.ch008

INTRODUCTION

The Metaverse, a concept once confined to the realms of science fiction, is now rapidly becoming a tangible reality. In this digital universe, individuals are transformed into creators crafting immersive experiences and content that blur the boundaries between the physical and virtual worlds (Florida, 2022). This transformative shift has given rise to what is known as the "Creator's Economy," a dynamic ecosystem where creative individuals and businesses leverage technology to generate, distribute, and monetize content (Rieder, 2023). While the impact of the Creator's Economy extends across various sectors, this chapter delves into its profound implications for the retail industry. As stakeholders within the retail landscape increasingly explore the potential of the Metaverse, they are poised to unlock innovative opportunities that could redefine the future of commerce.

In the era of the Metaverse, retail is no longer confined to brick-and-mortar stores or even e-commerce websites. Instead, it transcends physical constraints, immersing consumers in a multifaceted digital realm where creativity knows no bounds. This chapter embarks on a journey to explore how the Creator's Economy, a driving force behind this paradigm shift, intertwines with the retail industry. As the lines between consumers and creators blur, retailers are presented with unprecedented avenues for engagement, personalization, and brand storytelling. From virtual storefronts to augmented reality shopping experiences, the Metaverse offers retailers a transformative canvas to redefine their strategies, forge deeper connections with customers, and ultimately thrive in an evolving landscape where innovation reigns supreme.

Metaverse: The term "Metaverse" refers to a virtual, interconnected, and immersive digital universe or space that transcends the boundaries of the physical world (Mystakidis, 2022). It is a collective virtual shared space where users can interact with each other, digital objects and environments in real time, often through the use of Virtual reality (VR), augmented reality (AR), or other advanced digital technologies (Kamenov, 2021).

Three decades ago, author Neal Stephenson introduced the idea of the metaverse in his novel "Snow Crash" (Stephenson, 1992). Within his literary work, Stephenson envisions a parallel virtual realm in which individuals have the opportunity to both inhabit and engage in work-related activities. These virtual interactions, which transcend the conventional constraints of time and space, are often regarded as the epitome of the internet's capabilities. In the metaverse, users can create, explore, socialize, work, play and conduct various activities, similar to the way the people engage in the physical world (Ball, 2021). It encompasses a wide range of experiences, from virtual world and online games to social media platforms, virtual economies, and immersive simulations. The metaverse is characterized by its vastness, interactivity, and the sense of presence it provides to users, making it significant concepts in the fields of technology, entertainment and digital culture (McKinsey & Company, 2022). It can be described as an expansive system of interconnected virtual realms, as opposed to single virtual world. This system is intended to enhance reality with virtual elements, providing an immersive three-dimensional experience that holds the potential for generating significant profits (Zhao et al., 2022).

Creator's Economy: The combination of advances in technology like artificial intelligence, animation tools, photo editing software, and virtual music production studios along with changes in the job market such as remote and flexible work, has created opportunities for a wide range of creative individuals like bloggers, writers, influencers, artists, and more (Peres et al.,2023). They can now be part of the creator economy by producing, sharing, and making money from their content (Bhargava, 2022). Anyone has the opportunity to become a content creator on social media, where they can connect with potential customers, build a dedicated following, and establish a viable business, all without the need for financial backing or support from an established company. Progress in the field of computing as a whole, and particularly in platform mediation, has resulted in reduced expenses associated with production, distribution and transactions (Poell et al., 2022). Social media has leveled the playing field for talented individuals, offering them a means to generate income based on their abilities. The metaverse holds the promise of further democratizing talent, content and media production, and the growth of creators' businesses. The metaverse provides a more accessible point of entry, requiring creators to have nothing more than a smart device and internet access to begin. Through game engines and digital platforms, creators can concentrate on their content without the need to code. Geographical locations become inconsequential; creators are not obligated to reside in major cities or possess the resources to travel for investors meetings, as they can create, design, and share their work from any location.

Content creators are of growing significance as they function as entrepreneurs and contributors to job creation in various economies (Johnson et al., 2022). The creator's economy is a burgeoning economic paradigm that places creators, artists, influencers and content producers at the forefront of value creation in the digital age (Tafesse & Dayan, 2023). It is characterized by individuals leveraging their skills, talents, and creativity to generate income and build businesses in the digital realm. The rise of social media, online content platforms, and digital marketplaces has empowered creators to reach global audience and monetize their work directly, often bypassing traditional intermediaries. Creators can generate revenue through various means, such as sponsored content, merchandise sales, subscription models, and the sale of non-fungible tokens (NFTs) that represent unique digital assets. The shift towards the creator's economy highlights the growing importance of personal branding, authenticity, and community engagement in the digital landscape, enabling individuals to turn their passions into sustainable careers while reshaping industries like entertainment, art and media.

The Creator's Economy in the Metaverse represents a profound departure from traditional retail paradigms. In this digital frontier, creators, be they individuals or brands, have the power to construct entire virtual worlds, populate them with unique products and experiences, and foster communities that transcend geographical boundaries. This paradigm shift is not merely a technological evolution but a fundamental reimagining of how retail operates. As we embark on this exploration, we will delve into the technologies underpinning this transformation—such as AI-driven image generators, virtual showrooms, and blockchain-based authentication—highlighting their role in reshaping the retail landscape. Moreover, we will shed light on the strategies employed by forward-thinking retail stakeholders as they navigate the opportunities and challenges presented by the Metaverse. By understanding how the Creator's Economy is poised to reshape the retail industry, we can chart a course for a future where innovation, creativity, and customer-centricity reign supreme.

Within the Metaverse, traditional notions of commerce are being redefined. Retailers no longer compete solely on the basis of physical locations or online storefronts; they compete for consumer attention, engagement, and loyalty within immersive, digital realms (Habil, 2023). As we traverse the virtual landscapes of the Creator's Economy, we will uncover how stakeholders in the retail sector can harness this dynamic environment to their advantage. From leveraging virtual influencers to curating interactive shopping experiences, the possibilities are boundless. In this chapter, we will navigate this exciting frontier, exploring the ways in which the retail industry can embrace the Metaverse, adapt to its evolving dynamics, and unlock a new era of innovation and profitability.

Metaverse Creators: Metaverse creators are individuals or entities who design, build, and contribute to the virtual worlds, environments, experiences, and content within the metaverse. They play a pivotal role in shaping the digital universe of the metaverse, often using a combination of artistic, technical, and creative skills. User generated content is a significant factor that enhances the platform's appeal to the user (Yang et al., 2022). Metaverse creators can encompass a wide range of roles and activities, including world builders who design and construct virtual landscapes, content creators producing 3D models and interactive experiences, game developers creating virtual games and simulations, and architects designing virtual building structures. Additionally, social experiences designers focus on promoting community engagement, while avatar and character creators specialize in designing digital persons. Virtual fashion designers create digital clothing, and scripters and developers write code to enable interactive elements within virtual environments. Entrepreneurs in the metaverse may even build and manage virtual economies, including virtual currencies and blockchain-based assets like NFTs.

In addition to their technical and creative contributions, metaverse creators are instrumental in fostering user engagement and enabling personalization within the metaverse. They provide users with the tools and content necessary to customize their digital presence, express their individuality, and engage in a wide range of activities, from social interactions to business ventures. The diversity and innovation brought forth by metaverse creators help shape the metaverse into a dynamic and immersive digital space that continues to evolve, offering unique experiences and opportunities for users across a spectrum of interests and industries.

The Power of Virtual Influencers: Virtual influencers are increasingly gaining recognition as internet celebrities who are reshaping the very essence, significance, and principles of the influencer marketing field, which, in turn, is attracting significant investments (Sands et al., 2022). They are artificial characters or avatars meticulously created and overseen by experts and digital agencies. They function as a strategic tool for brands to effectively engage and connect with their preferred target demographics by leveraging the distinctive digital personas these entities represent. Metaverse influencers are individuals or entities who design, build, and contribute to the virtual worlds, environments, experiences, and content within the metaverse. They play a pivotal role in shaping the digital universe of the metaverse, often using a combination of artistic, technical, and creative skills. Metaverse creators can encompass a wide range of roles and activities, including world builders who design and construct virtual landscapes, content creators producing 3D models and interactive experiences, game developers crafting virtual games and simulations, and architects designing virtual buildings and structures. Additionally, social experience designers focus on promoting community engagement, while avatar and character creators specialize in designing digital personas. Virtual fashion designers create digital clothing, and scripters and developers write code to enable interactive elements within virtual environments. Entrepreneurs in the metaverse may even build and manage virtual economics, including virtual currencies and blockchain based assets like NFTs.

In addition to their technical and creative contributions, metaverse creators are instrumental in fostering user engagement and enabling personalization within the metaverse. They provide users with the tools and content necessary to customize their digital presence, express their individuality, and engage in a wide range of activities, from social interactions to business ventures. Incorporating influencer marketing into your strategy is an effective branding and promotional technique for enhancing brand visibility and engaging with social media user particularly from the Gen Y and Gen Z demographics (Jhawar et al., 2023). The diversity and innovation brought forth by metaverse creators help shape the metaverse into a dynamic and immersive digital space that continues to evolve, offering unique experiences, and opportunities for users across a spectrum of interests and industries.

How Creators Engage With Audiences in the Metaverse: Creators engage with audiences in the metaverse through a variety of immersive methods, harnessing the unique capabilities of virtual environment. They frequently host live streams, virtual events, and concerts, enabling real-time interactions and Q&A sessions. Social platforms within the metaverse serve as hubs for creators to share updates, engage in conversations, and nurture online communities (Rijmenam, 2022). Creators also organize virtual meetups and gatherings, fostering direct connections between fans and fellow enthusiasts. Interactive experiences like immersive storytelling and collaborative projects allow audience to actively participate in the creator's content. User-generated content initiatives, such as fan art and challenges, further enhance community engagement. Additionally, creators may offer customization options for avatars or digital personas, enabling users to express their individuality. Virtual economies and NFT sales provide exclusive incentives for supporters, while collaborations with other influencers and brands expand reach and offer unique cross-promotional opportunities. In essence, creators in the metaverse employ technology and immersive nature of virtual spaces to cultivate deeper, more interactive relationships with their audiences, elevating the sense of community and engagement beyond what is available in the physical world.

The Metaverse as a New Retail Frontier: The metaverse is emerging as a groundbreaking frontier for the retail industry, presenting a transformative opportunity to revolutionize the way consumers shop and interact with brands. In this digital universe, retail is no longer confined to physical stores or even traditional e-commerce websites. Instead, retailers can establish a virtual presence in immersive, interconnected virtual environments where consumers can explore, interact with products, and make purchases in innovative ways. Virtual storefronts and experiences within the metaverse offer retailers the ability to create highly personalized and immersive shopping experiences using augmented reality (AR) and virtual reality (VR) technologies. Customers can try on virtual clothing, see how furniture fits into their homes, or interact with products before making informed purchasing decisions, mimicking the in-store experience. The level of engagement not only enhances customer satisfaction but also enables data collection and analysis that can be used to tailor offerings and marketing strategies effectively.

Moreover, the metaverse provides retailers with the opportunity to experiment with novel business models and revenue streams. The concept of "NFT fashion," where virtual clothing items are sold as non-fungible tokens (NFTs), has gained traction, allowing retailers to tap into the digital fashion market. (Sahay et al., 2022) Virtual economies and blockchain technology enable the creation of unique digital assets and collectibles that can be traded with the metaverse, creating new opportunities for branding and monetization. As the metaverse evolves, retailers must adapt to this new retail frontier to stay competitive and continue providing engaging and personalized shopping experiences for their customers. The metaverse represents not only a digital evolution of retail but also a reimagining of the entire shopping journey, promising to reshape the industry in profound and exciting ways.

Opportunities for Retail Stakeholders in the Metaverse: The metaverse presents a wealth of exciting opportunities of retail stakeholders. Retailers have the chance to establish a novel virtual presence within this digital universe, expanding their reach and engaging customers in immersive and personalized ways. Virtual storefronts, augmented reality (AR) and virtual reality (VR) experiences, and interactive product showcases offers retailers the opportunity to create innovative and engaging shopping environments (Allam et. Al., 2022). The integration of blockchain technology and non-fungible tokens (NFTs) allows for the creation of unique digital assets and collectibles, opening up new revenue streams and branding possibilities. Additionally, collaborations with metaverse creators and influencers can help retailers tap into niche markets and foster brand loyalty. By embracing the metaverse, retail stakeholders can not only stay ahead of the curve but also create entirely new avenues for customer engagement and sales in this exciting digital frontier.

How Creators and Retailers Collaborate: Collaborations between creators and retailers in the metaverse are fostering innovative and mutually beneficial partnerships. Creators bring their expertise in designing immersive virtual experiences and engaging content to the table, while retailers contribute their established brand presence and product offerings. Together, they craft unique metaverse experiences that resonate with audiences. Creators often design virtual storefronts and interactive showcases, enabling retailers to extend their digital reach and connect with consumers in novel ways. These collaborations can result in engaging marketing campaigns, limited edition virtual products, and interactive events that not only drive brand awareness but also enhance the overall shopping experience.

Furthermore, these partnerships enable retailers to tap into the creative talents of metaverse creators to develop brand virtual content (Chen & Cheng, 2022), from digital fashion collections to exclusive in-game items. In return, creators gain access to established customer bases and marketing resources, helping them expand their reach and monetize their metaverse creations. This symbiotic relationship is emblematic of the metaverse's potential to reshape how retail operates, fostering innovation and customer engagement through collaborative efforts between creators and retailers (Vidal-Tomás, 2023). As the metaverse continues to evolve, we can expect even more dynamic and boundary-pushing collaborations that redefine the shopping experience for consumers in this digital frontier.

Leveraging Influencer Marketing in the Metaverse: Leveraging influencer marketing in the metaverse presents a compelling opportunity for brands and creators alike. Influencer, whether human or virtual, hold a significant sway over their dedicated audiences, and their endorsements can drive brand awareness and product engagement. Involving social media influencers with a substantial following to endorse products or services is referred to as influencer marketing (More & Lingam, 2017). In the metaverse, these influencers can amplify their impact by immersing themselves in virtual environments, creating compelling content, and endorsing virtual products and experiences. Brands can partner with metaverse influencers to tap into their followers and reach a highly engaged and targeted demographic. These collaborations can result in innovative marketing campaigns that combine the authenticity of influencer endorsement with the immersive nature of the metaverse, creating unique and memorable experiences for consumers.

The metaverse also introduces the concept of "meta-influencers"- influential virtual characters or entities that exist today within the digital realm. These meta-influencers can develop their own followings, engage with virtual communities, and endorse products and experiences within the metaverse. For brands, collaborating with meta-influencers presents an opportunity to navigate this new digital landscape and leverage their reach to drive sales and engagement. As the metaverse continues to grow and evolve, influencer marketing within this space is poised to become an integral component of brand strategies, bridging the gap between virtual and real-world consumer experiences.

SUCCESS STORIES AND CASE STUDIES

In May 2019, Nike collaborated with the popular video game Fortnite to release a limited-edition virtual sneaker called the "Nike Air Jordan 1. "Players could purchase these virtual sneakers using the game's currency, V-Bucks and then wear them as part of their in game-avatar's outfit (Bonales-Daimiel, 2022). This partnership not only showcased the potential for virtual fashion and branded merchandise in the metaverse but also generated significant buzz and engagement among Fortnite's massive player base.

Decentraland, a blockchain based virtual world, hosted a virtual fashion week in February 2021. During this event, real world fashion brands like Atari and Pranksy partnered with metaverse creators and designers to showcase digital fashion collections. Users could attend fashion shows, explore virtual showrooms, and purchase limited-edition virtual fashion items as NFTs. This collaboration demonstrated the convergence of fashion and the metaverse, highlighting the potential for creator-retailer partnerships to bring innovative fashion experience to the digital realm.

Understanding NFTs (Non-Fungible Tokens): Non-fungible tokens (NFTs) have emerged as a fascinating and revolutionary concept in the world of digital assets. At their core, NFTs are unique digital tokens that represent ownership or proof of authenticity of a specific digital or physical item, often using blockchain technology (Nadini et al., 2021). What sets NFTs apart from traditional cryptocurrencies like Bitcoin or Ethereum is their individuality and non-interchangeability. Each NFTs is distinct, carrying its own metadata that can include details about the item it represents, such as digital art, music, videos, virtual real estate, collectibles, and even real-world assets. Lately, memes, tweets, GIFs have been sold as NFTs (Gadekallu, et al., 2023). NFTs have gained tremendous popularity for their potential to revolutionize various industries, including art, gaming, entertainment, and even real estate, by providing creators and collectors with a secure and transparent way to buy, sell, and trade digital assets.

NFTs as a Means of Fostering Creator-Retailer Partnerships: NFTs have emerged as a dynamic tool for nurturing collaborative relationships between creators and retailers. These digital assets provide a unique opportunity for creators to tokenize their content or creations, such as digital art, music, or collectibles, and collaborate with retailers to offer exclusive NFT-based merchandise or experiences (Buffaz, 2023). By leveraging blockchain technology, NFTs enable creators to maintain control over their intellectual property rights and ensure that they receive a fair share of the revenue generated from their work. This empowers both established and emerging artists to monetize their art in novel ways and reach a global audience through retail partnerships.

Retailers, on the other hand, benefit from these partnerships by gaining access to a fresh and engaged customer base drawn to the unique allure of NFTs. These collaborations can result in limited-edition NFT releases tied to physical products, immersive virtual shopping experiences in metaverse environments, or even exclusive access to events and merchandise drops (Yuan & Yang, 2022). By embracing NFTs retailers can tap into the authenticity and rarity associated with these tokens, fostering a sense of community and exclusivity around their brand. In essence, NFTs offer a bridge between creators and retailers, enabling them to collaborate in innovative ways that not only enhance brand management but also provide exciting new revenue streams for both parties in the rapidly evolving digital landscape. For example: Art exhibitions serve as a stage for artist from across the globe, offering them the means to advance their creative pursuits through showcasing, presenting their work, and publishing. For visitors, these exhibitions provide an interactive setting for art education and the opportunity to engage with both fellow artists and visitors (Vosinakis & Xenakis, 2011).

Preparing for the Metaverse Retail Revolution: In order to bring the ambitious metaverse vision to life, there is a requirement for a fresh infrastructure that possess revolutionary capabilities, along with a substantial 1000-fold increase in computational power. This upgraded infrastructure should be capable of storing and transmitting data at exceptionally high speeds. At the same time, preparing for a metaverse retail revolution requires a multifaceted approach for businesses. First and foremost, companies should invest in understanding metaverse technologies and their potential applications within their industry. This involves staying informed about emerging trends, partnerships and developments in the metaverse space. Moreover, cultivating a digital-first mindset and infrastructure is crucial, as seamless integration with the metaverse will be essential (George et al., 2021). Brands should consider developing virtual storefronts, creating digital assets, and exploring NFT-based collaborations to establish a metaverse presence.

In addition, fostering digital literacy among employees, customers and other relevant stakeholder is a key, as the metaverse success relies on user engagement and adoption. Brands should also prioritize data privacy and security measures to safeguard user information in this digital realm. Lastly, building a strong online community and social presence can help businesses connect with users in the metaverse, as community engagement and brand loyalty will continue to be significant factors in the evolving retail landscape (Filipova, 2023). By proactively embracing these strategies and staying agile in response to metaverse developments, businesses can position themselves to thrive in the transformative world of metaverse retail.

CONCLUSION

The rise of the Creator's Economy within the Metaverse represents a revolutionary paradigm shift for the retail industry. This transformation offers a multitude of opportunities and benefits for various stakeholders. Creators, brands, and retailers are all poised to reap the rewards of this emerging landscape. Creators can leverage the limitless creative potential of the Metaverse to craft immersive shopping experiences, forging deeper connections with consumers. Brands can tap into the vast and diverse user base of the Metaverse to reach new audiences, drive engagement, and experiment with innovative marketing strategies. For retailers, the Metaverse opens doors to new avenues for immersive customer experiences, innovative marketing strategies, and unique product offerings, potentially revolutionizing how they engage with consumers and drive revenue growth. To fully harness the potential of the Metaverse and unlock its synergies, it is crucial for stakeholders to integrate the physical and virtual worlds, putting creators at the center and allowing customers to choose their preferred shopping channel throughout their entire customer journey.

REFERENCES

Allam, Z., Sharifi, A., Bibri, S. E., Jones, D. S., & Krogstie, J. (2022). The metaverse as a virtual form of smart cities: Opportunities and challenges for environmental, economic, and social sustainability in urban futures. *Smart Cities*, *5*(3), 771–801. doi:10.3390/smartcities5030040

Balaghi, A. A. (2022). *A multichain approach is the future of the blockchain industry*https://cointelegraph.com/news/a-multichain-approach-is-the-future-of-the-blockchain-industry

Buffaz, P., Alkhudary, R., & Guibert, N. (2023). *Harnessing the Power of NFTs in the Retail Industry*. HAL.

Chen, R., Perry, P., Boardman, R., & McCormick, H. (2022). Augmented reality in retail: A systematic review of research foci and future research agenda. *International Journal of Retail & Distribution Management*, *50*(4), 498–518. doi:10.1108/IJRDM-11-2020-0472

Chen, Y., & Cheng, H. (2022). The economics of the metaverse: A comparison with the real economy. *Metaverse*, *3*(1), 19. doi:10.54517/met.v3i1.1802

Daimiel, G. B., Eva, C. M. E., & Ormaechea, S. L. (2022). Análisis del uso del advergaming y metaverso en España y México. *Revista Latina de Comunicación Social*, *80*(80), 155–178. doi:10.4185/RLCS-2022-1802

Dwivedi, Y. K., Hughes, L., Baabdullah, A. M., Ribeiro-Navarrete, S., Giannakis, M., Al Debei, M. M., Dennehy, D., Metri, B., Buhalis, D., Cheung, C. M. K., Conboy, K., Doyle, R., Dubey, R., Dutot, V., Felix, R., Goyal, D. P., Gustafsson, A., Hinsch, C., Jebabli, I., ... Wamba, S. F. (2022). Metaverse beyond the hype: Multidisciplinary perspectives on emerging challenges, opportunities, and agenda for research, practice and policy. *International Journal of Information Management*, *66*(July), 102542. doi:10.1016/j.ijinfomgt.2022.102542

Filipova, I. A. (2023). Creating the Metaverse: Consequences for Economy, Society, and Law. *Journal of Digital Technologies and Law*, *1*(1), 7–32. doi:10.21202/jdtl.2023.1

Florida, R. (2022). *The rise of the creator economy*. Retrieved October 25, 2023, from https://creativeclass.com/reports/The_Rise_of_the_Creator_Economy.pdf

Gadekallu, T. R., Wang, W., Yenduri, G., Ranaweera, P., Pham, Q. V., da Costa, D. B., & Liyanage, M. (2023). Blockchain for the Metaverse: A review. *Future Generation Computer Systems*, *143*, 401–419. doi:10.1016/j.future.2023.02.008

George, A. H., Fernando, M., George, A. S., Baskar, T., & Pandey, D. (2021). Metaverse: The next stage of human culture and the internet. *International Journal of Advanced Research Trends in Engineering and Technology*, *8*(12), 1–10.

Habil, S. G. M., El-Deeb, S., & El-Bassiouny, N. (2023). The metaverse era: leveraging augmented reality in the creation of novel customer experience. Management & Sustainability: An Arab Review. ahead-of-print. doi:10.1108/MSAR-10-2022-0051

Jhawar, A., Kumar, P., & Varshney, S. (2023). *The emergence of virtual influencers: A shift in the influencer marketing paradigm*. Young Consumers Insight and Ideas for Responsible Marketers.

Kshetri, N. (2021). Blockchain-enabled metaverse: Challenges, solutions, and future directions. *Journal of Business Research*, *135*, 492–499.

Mäyrä, F. (2020). The metaverse and imaginary worlds. In T. Arnab, I. Dunwell, & S. Debattista (Eds.), *Serious games and edutainment applications* (pp. 11–30). Springer.

Nadini, M., Alessandretti, L., Di Giacinto, F., Martino, M., Aiello, L. M., & Baronchelli, A. (2021). Mapping the NFT revolution: Market trends, trade networks, and visual features. *Scientific Reports*, *11*(1), 20902. doi:10.1038/s41598-021-00053-8 PMID:34686678

Pamucar, D., Deveci, M., Gokasar, I., Tavana, M., & Köppen, M. (2022). A metaverse assessment model for sustainable transportation using ordinal priority approach and Aczel-Alsina norms. *Technological Forecasting and Social Change*, *182*, 121778. doi:10.1016/j.techfore.2022.121778

Periyasami, S., & Periyasamy, A. P. (2022). Metaverse as Future Promising Platform Business Model: Case Study on Fashion Value Chain. *Businesses*, *2*(4), 527–545. doi:10.3390/businesses2040033

Rieder, B., Borra, E., Coromina, Ò., & Matamoros-Fernández, A. (2023). Making a Living in the Creator Economy: A Large-Scale Study of Linking on YouTube. *Social Media + Society*, *9*(2). Advance online publication. doi:10.1177/20563051231180628

Sahay, S., Mahajan, N., Malik, S., & Kaur, J. (2022, August). Metaverse: Research based analysis and impact on economy and business. In *2022 2nd Asian Conference on Innovation in Technology (ASIANCON)* (pp. 1-8). IEEE.

Sands, S., Campbell, C. L., Plangger, K., & Ferraro, C. (2022). Unreal influence: Leveraging AI in influencer marketing. *European Journal of Marketing*, *56*(6), 1721–1747. doi:10.1108/EJM-12-2019-0949

Van Rijmenam, M. (2022). *Step into the metaverse: How the immersive internet will unlock a trillion-dollar social economy*. John Wiley & Sons.

Vidal-Tomás, D. (2023). The illusion of the metaverse and meta-economy. *International Review of Financial Analysis*, *86*, 102560. doi:10.1016/j.irfa.2023.102560

Vosinakis, S., & Xenakis, I. (2011). *A Virtual World Installation in an Art Exhibition: Providing a Shared Interaction Space for Local and Remote Visitors*. Academic Press.

Yuan, Y., & Yang, Y. (2022). Embracing the Metaverse: Mechanism and logic of a new digital economy. *Metaverse*, *3*(2), 15. doi:10.54517/m.v3i2.1814

Zhao, Y., Jiang, J., Chen, Y., Liu, R., Yang, Y., Xue, X., & Chen, S. (2022). Metaverse: Perspectives from graphics, interactions and visualization. *Visual Informatics*, *6*(1), 56–67. Advance online publication. doi:10.1016/j.visinf.2022.03.002

Chapter 9
Metaverse's Significance for Smart Cities and the Retail Sector:
Facilitating Technologies and Upcoming Approaches

Hemlata Parmar
Manipal University Jaipur, India

Utsav Krishan Murari
Sharda University, India

ABSTRACT

The past few decades have observed a worldwide metaverse development. User-interactive, digitally produced settings make up the metaverse. The metaverse could revolutionize, reshape, and redefine smart cities through enhancing infrastructure, modernizing services provided by governments, enhancing convenience, speeding up the growth of the economy, and encouraging long-term viability. In this study, the authors explain how using the metaverse towards smart cities might spur development and enhance its implementation. They cover essential metaverse innovations, their top advantages, and smart city implementations. They demonstrate metaverse technology's applicability throughout sectors with active initiatives and cases. They also highlight and address major research hurdles that are preventing the metaverse from reaching its maximum capacity. They conclude with additional investigation objectives for developing the metaverse and smart city interconnectivity.

DOI: 10.4018/979-8-3693-1866-9.ch009

INTRODUCTION

The Metaverse, a concept once confined to the realms of science fiction, is now rapidly becoming a tangible reality. In this digital universe, individuals are transformed into creators crafting immersive experiences and content that blur the boundaries between the physical and virtual worlds (Florida, 2022). This transformative shift has given rise to what is known as the "Creator's Economy," a dynamic ecosystem where creative individuals and businesses leverage technology to generate, distribute, and monetize content (Rieder, 2023). While the impact of the Creator's Economy extends across various sectors, this chapter delves into its profound implications for the retail industry. As stakeholders within the retail landscape increasingly explore the potential of the Metaverse, they are poised to unlock innovative opportunities that could redefine the future of commerce.

In the era of the Metaverse, retail is no longer confined to brick-and-mortar stores or even e-commerce websites. Instead, it transcends physical constraints, immersing consumers in a multifaceted digital realm where creativity knows no bounds. This chapter embarks on a journey to explore how the Creator's Economy, a driving force behind this paradigm shift, intertwines with the retail industry. As the lines between consumers and creators blur, retailers are presented with unprecedented avenues for engagement, personalization, and brand storytelling. From virtual storefronts to augmented reality shopping experiences, the Metaverse offers retailers a transformative canvas to redefine their strategies, forge deeper connections with customers, and ultimately thrive in an evolving landscape where innovation reigns supreme.

METAVERSE

The term "Metaverse" refers to a virtual, interconnected, and immersive digital universe or space that transcends the boundaries of the physical world (Mystakidis, 2022). It is a collective virtual shared space where users can interact with each other, digital objects and environments in real time, often through the use of Virtual reality (VR), augmented reality (AR), or other advanced digital technologies (Kamenov, 2021).

Three decades ago, author Neal Stephenson introduced the idea of the metaverse in his novel "Snow Crash" published in 1992 (Stephenson, 2003). Within his literary work, Stephenson envisions a parallel virtual realm in which individuals have the opportunity to both inhabit and engage in work-related activities. These virtual interactions, which transcend the conventional constraints of time and space, are often regarded as the epitome of the internet's capabilities. In the metaverse, users can create, explore, socialize, work, play and conduct various activities, similar to the way the people engage in the physical world (Ball, 2021). It encompasses a wide range of experiences, from virtual world and online games to social media platforms, virtual economies, and immersive simulations. The metaverse is characterized by its vastness, interactivity, and the sense of presence it provides to users, making it significant concepts in the fields of technology, entertainment and digital culture (McKinsey & Company, 2022). It can be described as an expansive system of interconnected virtual realms, as opposed to single virtual world. This system is intended to enhance reality with virtual elements, providing an immersive three-dimensional experience that holds the potential for generating significant profits (Zhao et al., 2022).

CREATOR'S ECONOMY

The combination of advances in technology like artificial intelligence, animation tools, photo editing software, and virtual music production studios along with changes in the job market such as remote and flexible work, has created opportunities for a wide range of creative individuals like bloggers, writers, influencers, artists, and more (Peres et al., 2023). They can now be part of the creator economy by producing, sharing, and making money from their content (Bhargava, 2022). Anyone has the opportunity to become a content creator on social media, where they can connect with potential customers, build a dedicated following, and establish a viable business, all without the need for financial backing or support from an established company. Progress in the field of computing as a whole, and particularly in platform mediation, has resulted in reduced expenses associated with production, distribution and transactions (Poell et al., 2022). Social media has leveled the playing field for talented individuals, offering them a means to generate income based on their abilities. The metaverse holds the promise of further democratizing talent, content and media production, and the growth of creators' businesses. The metaverse provides a more accessible point of entry, requiring creators to have nothing more than a smart device and internet access to begin. Through game engines and digital platforms, creators can concentrate on their content without the need to code. Geographical locations become inconsequential; creators are not obligated to reside in major cities or possess the resources to travel for investors meetings, as they can create, design, and share their work from any location.

Content creators are of growing significance as they function as entrepreneurs and contributors to job creation in various economies (Johnson et al., 2022). The creator's economy is a burgeoning economic paradigm that places creators, artists, influencers and content producers at the forefront of value creation in the digital age (Tafesse & Dayan, 2023). It is characterized by individuals leveraging their skills, talents, and creativity to generate income and build businesses in the digital realm. The rise of social media, online content platforms, and digital marketplaces has empowered creators to reach global audience and monetize their work directly, often bypassing traditional intermediaries. Creators can generate revenue through various means, such as sponsored content, merchandise sales, subscription models, and the sale of non-fungible tokens (NFTs) that represent unique digital assets. The shift towards the creator's economy highlights the growing importance of personal branding, authenticity, and community engagement in the digital landscape, enabling individuals to turn their passions into sustainable careers while reshaping industries like entertainment, art and media.

The Creator's Economy in the Metaverse represents a profound departure from traditional retail paradigms. In this digital frontier, creators, be they individuals or brands, have the power to construct entire virtual worlds, populate them with unique products and experiences, and foster communities that transcend geographical boundaries. This paradigm shift is not merely a technological evolution but a fundamental reimagining of how retail operates. As we embark on this exploration, we will delve into the technologies underpinning this transformation—such as AI-driven image generators, virtual showrooms, and blockchain-based authentication—highlighting their role in reshaping the retail landscape. Moreover, we will shed light on the strategies employed by forward-thinking retail stakeholders as they navigate the opportunities and challenges presented by the Metaverse. By understanding how the Creator's Economy is poised to reshape the retail industry, we can chart a course for a future where innovation, creativity, and customer-centricity reign supreme.

Within the Metaverse, traditional notions of commerce are being redefined. Retailers no longer compete solely on the basis of physical locations or online storefronts; they compete for consumer attention, engagement, and loyalty within immersive, digital realms (Metry Habil et al., 2023). As we traverse the virtual landscapes of the Creator's Economy, we will uncover how stakeholders in the retail sector can harness this dynamic environment to their advantage. From leveraging virtual influencers to curating interactive shopping experiences, the possibilities are boundless. In this chapter, we will navigate this exciting frontier, exploring the ways in which the retail industry can embrace the Metaverse, adapt to its evolving dynamics, and unlock a new era of innovation and profitability.

METAVERSE CREATORS

Metaverse creators are individuals or entities who design, build, and contribute to the virtual worlds, environments, experiences, and content within the metaverse. They play a pivotal role in shaping the digital universe of the metaverse, often using a combination of artistic, technical, and creative skills. User generated content is a significant factor that enhances the platform's appeal to the user (Yang et al., 2022). Metaverse creators can encompass a wide range of roles and activities, including world builders who design and construct virtual landscapes, content creators producing 3D models and interactive experiences, game developers creating virtual games and simulations, and architects designing virtual building structures. Additionally, social experiences designers focus on promoting community engagement, while avatar and character creators specialize in designing digital persons. Virtual fashion designers create digital clothing, and scripters and developers write code to enable interactive elements within virtual environments. Entrepreneurs in the metaverse may even build and manage virtual economies, including virtual currencies and blockchain-based assets like NFTs.

In addition to their technical and creative contributions, metaverse creators are instrumental in fostering user engagement and enabling personalization within the metaverse. They provide users with the tools and content necessary to customize their digital presence, express their individuality, and engage in a wide range of activities, from social interactions to business ventures. The diversity and innovation brought forth by metaverse creators help shape the metaverse into a dynamic and immersive digital space that continues to evolve, offering unique experiences and opportunities for users across a spectrum of interests and industries.

THE POWER OF VIRTUAL INFLUENCERS

Virtual influencers are increasingly gaining recognition as internet celebrities who are reshaping the very essence, significance, and principles of the influencer marketing field, which, in turn, is attracting significant investments (Sands et al., 2022). They are artificial characters or avatars meticulously created and overseen by experts and digital agencies. They function as a strategic tool for brands to effectively engage and connect with their preferred target demographics by leveraging the distinctive digital personas these entities represent. Metaverse influencers are individuals or entities who design, build, and contribute to the virtual worlds, environments, experiences, and content within the metaverse. They play a pivotal role in shaping the digital universe of the metaverse, often using a combination of artistic, technical, and creative skills. Metaverse creators can encompass a wide range of roles and activities, including world builders who design and construct virtual landscapes, content creators producing 3D models and interactive experiences, game developers crafting virtual games and simulations, and architects designing virtual buildings and structures. Additionally, social experience designers focus on promoting community engagement, while avatar and character creators specialize in designing digital personas. Virtual fashion designers create digital clothing, and scripters and developers write code to enable interactive elements within virtual environments. Entrepreneurs in the metaverse may even build and manage virtual economics, including virtual currencies and blockchain based assets like NFTs.

In addition to their technical and creative contributions, metaverse creators are instrumental in fostering user engagement and enabling personalization within the metaverse. They provide users with the tools and content necessary to customize their digital presence, express their individuality, and engage in a wide range of activities, from social interactions to business ventures. Incorporating influencer marketing into your strategy is an effective branding and promotional technique for enhancing brand visibility and engaging with social media user particularly from the Gen Y and Gen Z demographics (Jhawar et al., 2023). The diversity and innovation brought forth by metaverse creators help shape the metaverse into a dynamic and immersive digital space that continues to evolve, offering unique experiences, and opportunities for users across a spectrum of interests and industries.

HOW CREATORS ENGAGE WITH AUDIENCES IN THE METAVERSE

Creators engage with audiences in the metaverse through a variety of immersive methods, harnessing the unique capabilities of virtual environment. They frequently host live streams, virtual events, and concerts, enabling real-time interactions and Q&A sessions. Social platforms within the metaverse serve as hubs for creators to share updates, engage in conversations, and nurture online communities (Rijmenam, 2022). Creators also organize virtual meetups and gatherings, fostering direct connections between fans and fellow enthusiasts. Interactive experiences like immersive storytelling and collaborative projects allow audience to actively participate in the creator's content. User-generated content initiatives, such as fan art and challenges, further enhance community engagement. Additionally, creators may offer customization options for avatars or digital personas, enabling users to express their individuality. Virtual economies and NFT sales provide exclusive incentives for supporters, while collaborations with other influencers and brands expand reach and offer unique cross-promotional opportunities. In essence, creators in the metaverse employ technology and immersive nature of virtual spaces to cultivate deeper, more interactive relationships with their audiences, elevating the sense of community and engagement beyond what is available in the physical world.

THE METAVERSE AS A NEW RETAIL FRONTIER

The metaverse is emerging as a groundbreaking frontier for the retail industry, presenting a transformative opportunity to revolutionize the way consumers shop and interact with brands. In this digital universe, retail is no longer confined to physical stores or even traditional e-commerce websites. Instead, retailers can establish a virtual presence in immersive, interconnected virtual environments where consumers can explore, interact with products, and make purchases in innovative ways. Virtual storefronts and experiences within the metaverse offer retailers the ability to create highly personalized and immersive shopping experiences using augmented reality (AR) and virtual reality (VR) technologies. Customers can try on virtual clothing, see how furniture fits into their homes, or interact with products before making informed purchasing decisions, mimicking the in-store experience. The level of engagement not only enhances customer satisfaction but also enables data collection and analysis that can be used to tailor offerings and marketing strategies effectively.

Moreover, the metaverse provides retailers with the opportunity to experiment with novel business models and revenue streams. The concept of "NFT fashion," where virtual clothing items are sold as non-fungible tokens (NFTs), has gained traction, allowing retailers to tap into the digital fashion market (Sahay et al., 2022). Virtual economies and blockchain technology enable the creation of unique digital assets and collectibles that can be traded with the metaverse, creating new opportunities for branding and monetization. As the metaverse evolves, retailers must adapt to this new retail frontier to stay competitive and continue providing engaging and personalized shopping experiences for their customers. The metaverse represents not only a digital evolution of retail but also a reimagining of the entire shopping journey, promising to reshape the industry in profound and exciting ways.

OPPORTUNITIES FOR RETAIL STAKEHOLDERS IN THE METAVERSE

The metaverse presents a wealth of exciting opportunities of retail stakeholders. Retailers have the chance to establish a novel virtual presence within this digital universe, expanding their reach and engaging customers in immersive and personalized ways. Virtual storefronts, augmented reality (AR) and virtual reality (VR) experiences, and interactive product showcases offers retailers the opportunity to create innovative and engaging shopping environments (Allam et. Al., 2022). The integration of blockchain technology and non-fungible tokens (NFTs) allows for the creation of unique digital assets and collectibles, opening up new revenue streams and branding possibilities. Additionally, collaborations with metaverse creators and influencers can help retailers tap into niche markets and foster brand loyalty. By embracing the metaverse, retail stakeholders can not only stay ahead of the curve but also create entirely new avenues for customer engagement and sales in this exciting digital frontier.

HOW CREATORS AND RETAILERS COLLABORATE

Collaborations between creators and retailers in the metaverse are fostering innovative and mutually beneficial partnerships. Creators bring their expertise in designing immersive virtual experiences and engaging content to the table, while retailers contribute their established brand presence and product offerings. Together, they craft unique metaverse experiences that resonate with audiences. Creators often design virtual storefronts and interactive showcases, enabling retailers to extend their digital reach and connect with consumers in novel ways. These collaborations can result in engaging marketing campaigns, limited edition virtual products, and interactive events that not only drive brand awareness but also enhance the overall shopping experience.

Furthermore, these partnerships enable retailers to tap into the creative talents of metaverse creators to develop brand virtual content (Chen & Cheng, 2022), from digital fashion collections to exclusive in-game items. In return, creators gain access to established customer bases and marketing resources, helping them expand their reach and monetize their metaverse creations. This symbiotic relationship is emblematic of the metaverse's potential to reshape how retail operates, fostering innovation and customer engagement through collaborative efforts between creators and retailers (Vidal-Tomás, 2023). As the metaverse continues to evolve, we can expect even more dynamic and boundary-pushing collaborations that redefine the shopping experience for consumers in this digital frontier.

LEVERAGING INFLUENCER MARKETING IN THE METAVERSE

Leveraging influencer marketing in the metaverse presents a compelling opportunity for brands and creators alike. Influencer, whether human or virtual, hold a significant sway over their dedicated audiences, and their endorsements can drive brand awareness and product engagement. Involving social media influencers with a substantial following to endorse products or services is referred to as influencer marketing (More & Lingam, 2017). In the metaverse, these influencers can amplify their impact by immersing themselves in virtual environments, creating compelling content, and endorsing virtual products and experiences. Brands can partner with metaverse influencers to tap into their followers and reach a highly engaged and targeted demographic. These collaborations can result in innovative marketing campaigns that combine the authenticity of influencer endorsement with the immersive nature of the metaverse, creating unique and memorable experiences for consumers.

The metaverse also introduces the concept of "meta-influencers"- influential virtual characters or entities that exist today within the digital realm. These meta-influencers can develop their own followings, engage with virtual communities, and endorse products and experiences within the metaverse. For brands, collaborating with meta-influencers presents an opportunity to navigate this new digital landscape and leverage their reach to drive sales and engagement. As the metaverse continues to grow and evolve, influencer marketing within this space is poised to become an integral component of brand strategies, bridging the gap between virtual and real-world consumer experiences.

SUCCESS STORIES AND CASE STUDIES

In May 2019, Nike collaborated with the popular video game Fortnite to release a limited-edition virtual sneaker called the "Nike Air Jordan 1. "Players could purchase these virtual sneakers using the game's currency, V-Bucks and then wear them as part of their in game-avatar's outfit (Daimiel et al., 2022). This partnership not only showcased the potential for virtual fashion and branded merchandise in the metaverse but also generated significant buzz and engagement among Fortnite's massive player base.

Decentraland, a blockchain based virtual world, hosted a virtual fashion week in February 2021. During this event, real world fashion brands like Atari and Pranksy partnered with metaverse creators and designers to showcase digital fashion collections. Users could attend fashion shows, explore virtual showrooms, and purchase limited-edition virtual fashion items as NFTs. This collaboration demonstrated the convergence of fashion and the metaverse, highlighting the potential for creator-retailer partnerships to bring innovative fashion experience to the digital realm.

UNDERSTANDING NFTS (NON-FUNGIBLE TOKENS)

Non-fungible tokens (NFTs) have emerged as a fascinating and revolutionary concept in the world of digital assets. At their core, NFTs are unique digital tokens that represent ownership or proof of authenticity of a specific digital or physical item, often using blockchain technology (Nadini et al., 2021). What sets NFTs apart from traditional cryptocurrencies like Bitcoin or Ethereum is their individuality and non-interchangeability. Each NFTs is distinct, carrying its own metadata that can include details about the item it represents, such as digital art, music, videos, virtual real estate, collectibles, and even real-world assets. Lately, memes, tweets, GIFs have been sold as NFTs (Gadekallu, et al., 2023). NFTs have gained tremendous popularity for their potential to revolutionize various industries, including art, gaming, entertainment, and even real estate, by providing creators and collectors with a secure and transparent way to buy, sell, and trade digital assets.

NFTS AS A MEANS OF FOSTERING CREATOR-RETAILER PARTNERSHIPS

NFTs have emerged as a dynamic tool for nurturing collaborative relationships between creators and retailers. These digital assets provide a unique opportunity for creators to tokenize their content or creations, such as digital art, music, or collectibles, and collaborate with retailers to offer exclusive NFT-based merchandise or experiences (Buffaz, 2023). By leveraging blockchain technology, NFTs enable creators to maintain control over their intellectual property rights and ensure that they receive a fair share of the revenue generated from their work. This empowers both established and emerging artists to monetize their art in novel ways and reach a global audience through retail partnerships.

Retailers, on the other hand, benefit from these partnerships by gaining access to a fresh and engaged customer base drawn to the unique allure of NFTs. These collaborations can result in limited-edition NFT releases tied to physical products, immersive virtual shopping experiences in metaverse environments, or even exclusive access to events and merchandise drops (Yuan & Yang, 2022). By embracing NFTs retailers can tap into the authenticity and rarity associated with these tokens, fostering a sense of community and exclusivity around their brand. In essence, NFTs offer a bridge between creators and retailers, enabling them to collaborate in innovative ways that not only enhance brand management but also provide exciting new revenue streams for both parties in the rapidly evolving digital landscape. For example: Art exhibitions serve as a stage for artist from across the globe, offering them the means to advance their creative pursuits through showcasing, presenting their work, and publishing. For visitors, these exhibitions provide an interactive setting for art education and the opportunity to engage with both fellow artists and visitors (Vosinakis & Xenakis, 2011).

PREPARING FOR THE METAVERSE RETAIL REVOLUTION

In order to bring the ambitious metaverse vision to life, there is a requirement for a fresh infrastructure that possess revolutionary capabilities, along with a substantial 1000-fold increase in computational power. This upgraded infrastructure should be capable of storing and transmitting data at exceptionally high speeds. At the same time, preparing for a metaverse retail revolution requires a multifaceted approach for businesses. First and foremost, companies should invest in understanding metaverse technologies and their potential applications within their industry. This involves staying informed about emerging trends, partnerships and developments in the metaverse space. Moreover, cultivating a digital-first mindset and infrastructure is crucial, as seamless integration with the metaverse will be essential (George et al., 2021). Brands should consider developing virtual storefronts, creating digital assets, and exploring NFT-based collaborations to establish a metaverse presence.

In addition, fostering digital literacy among employees, customers and other relevant stakeholder is a key, as the metaverse success relies on user engagement and adoption. Brands should also prioritize data privacy and security measures to safeguard user information in this digital realm. Lastly, building a strong online community and social presence can help businesses connect with users in the metaverse, as community engagement and brand loyalty will continue to be significant factors in the evolving retail landscape (Filipova, 2023). By proactively embracing these strategies and staying agile in response to metaverse developments, businesses can position themselves to thrive in the transformative world of metaverse retail.

CONCLUSION

The rise of the Creator's Economy within the Metaverse represents a revolutionary paradigm shift for the retail industry. This transformation offers a multitude of opportunities and benefits for various stakeholders. Creators, brands, and retailers are all poised to reap the rewards of this emerging landscape. Creators can leverage the limitless creative potential of the Metaverse to craft immersive shopping experiences, forging deeper connections with consumers. Brands can tap into the vast and diverse user base of the Metaverse to reach new audiences, drive engagement, and experiment with innovative marketing strategies. For retailers, the Metaverse opens doors to new avenues for immersive customer experiences, innovative marketing strategies, and unique product offerings, potentially revolutionizing how they engage with consumers and drive revenue growth. To fully harness the potential of the Metaverse and unlock its synergies, it is crucial for stakeholders to integrate the physical and virtual worlds, putting creators at the center and allowing customers to choose their preferred shopping channel throughout their entire customer journey.

REFERENCES

Allam, Z., Sharifi, A., Bibri, S. E., Jones, D. S., & Krogstie, J. (2022). The metaverse as a virtual form of smart cities: Opportunities and challenges for environmental, economic, and social sustainability in urban futures. *Smart Cities*, *5*(3), 771–801.

Ball, M. (2021). *Framework for The Metaverse*. Retrieved from https://www.matthewball.vc/all/forwardtothemetabveseprimer

Bhargava, H. K. (2022). The Creator Economy: Managing Ecosystem Supply, Revenue-Sharing, and Platform Design. *Management Science*. Advance online publication.

Buffaz, P., Alkhudary, R., & Guibert, N. (2023). *Harnessing the Power of NFTs in the Retail Industry. Post-Print hal-04164085*. HAL.

Chen, Y., & Cheng, H. (2022). The economics of the metaverse: A comparison with the real economy. *Metaverse*, *3*(1), 19.

Daimiel, G., Bonales, G., Martínez Estrella, E. C., & Liberal Ormaechea, S. (2022). Análisis del uso del advergaming y metaverso en España y México. *Revista Latina de Comunicación Social*, *80*, 155–178.

Filipova, I. A. (2023). Creating the Metaverse: Consequences for Economy, Society, and Law. *Journal of Digital Technologies and Law*, *1*(1), 7–32.

Florida, R. (2022). *The rise of the creator economy*. Retrieved October 25, 2023, from https://creativeclass.com/reports/The_Rise_of_the_Creator_Economy.pdf

Gadekallu, T. R., Wang, W., Yenduri, G., Ranaweera, P., Pham, Q. V., da Costa, D. B., & Liyanage, M. (2023). Blockchain for the Metaverse: A review. *Future Generation Computer Systems*, *143*, 401–419.

George, A. H., Fernando, M., George, A. S., Baskar, T., & Pandey, D. (2021). Metaverse: The next stage of human culture and the internet. *International Journal of Advanced Research Trends in Engineering and Technology*, *8*(12), 1–10.

Jhawar, A., Kumar, P., & Varshney, S. (2023). *The emergence of virtual influencers: A shift in the influencer marketing paradigm*. Young Consumers Insight and Ideas for Responsible Marketers.

Johnson, N. E., Short, J. C., Chandler, J., & Jordan, S. M. (2022). Introducing the contentpreneur: Making the case for research on content creation-based online platforms. *Journal of Business Venturing Insights*, *18*(6), e00328. doi:10.1016/j.jbvi.2022.e00328

Kamenov, K. (2021). *Immersive Experience—The 4th Wave in Tech: Learning the Ropes*. Retrieved from https://www.accenture.com/gb-en/blogs/blogs-immersive-experience-wave-learning-ropes

McKinsey & Company. (2022). *Value creation in the metaverse*. https:// www.mckinsey.com/business-functions/growth-marketing-and-sales/ our-insights/ value-creation-in-the-metaverse

Metry Habil, S. G., El-Deeb, S., & El-Bassiouny, N. (2023). The Metaverse Era: Leveraging Augmented Reality in the Creation of Novel Customer Experience. *Management & Sustainability: An Arab Review.*

More, J. S., & Lingam, C. (2017). A SI model for social media influencer maximization. *Applied Computing and Informatics,* 1-7. https://doi.org/ doi:10.1016/j.aci.2017.11.001

Mystakidis, S. (2022). *Metaverse. Encyclopedia*. Academic Press.

Nadini, M., Alessandretti, L., Di Giacinto, F., Martino, M., Aiello, L. M., & Baronchelli, A. (2021). Mapping the NFT revolution: Market trends, trade networks, and visual features. *Scientific Reports*, *11*(1), 20902.

Peres, R., Schreier, M., Schweidel, D., & Sorescu, A. (2023). On ChatGPT and beyond: How generative artificial intelligence may affect research, teaching, and practice. *International Journal of Research in Marketing*, *40*(2), 269–275.

Poell, T., Nieborg, D. B., & Duffy, B. E. (2022). Spaces of negotiation: Analyzing platform power in the news industry. *Digital Journalism (Abingdon, England)*, *0*(0), 1–19. doi:10.1080/21670811.2022.2103011

Rieder, B., Borra, E., Coromina, Ò., & Matamoros-Fernández, A. (2023). Making a Living in the Creator Economy: A Large-Scale Study of Linking on YouTube. *Social Media + Society*, *9*(2). Advance online publication. doi:10.1177/20563051231180628

Sahay, S., Mahajan, N., Malik, S., & Kaur, J. (2022, August). Metaverse: Research based analysis and impact on economy and business. In *2022 2nd Asian Conference on Innovation in Technology (ASIANCON)* (pp. 1-8). IEEE.

Sands, S., Campbell, C. L., Plangger, K., & Ferraro, C. (2022). Unreal influence: Leveraging AI in influencer marketing. *European Journal of Marketing*, *56*(6), 1721–1747.

Stephenson, N. (2003). *Snow Crash: A Novel*. Random House Publishing Group.

Tafesse, W., & Dayan, M. (2023). Content creators' participation in the creator economy: Examining the effect of creators' content sharing frequency on user engagement behavior on digital platforms. *Journal of Retailing and Consumer Services*, *73*(C).

Vidal-Tomás, D. (2023). The illusion of the metaverse and meta-economy. *International Review of Financial Analysis*, *86*, 102560.

Vosinakis, S., & Xenakis, I. (2011). *A Virtual World Installation in an Art Exhibition: Providing a Shared Interaction Space for Local and Remote Visitors. In Step into the metaverse: How the immersive internet will unlock a trillion-dollar social economy*. John Wiley & Sons.

Yang, B., Yang, S., Lv, Z., Wang, F., & Olofsson, T. (2022). Application of Digital Twins and Meta- verse in the Field of Fluid Machinery Pumps and Fans: A Review. *Sensors (Basel)*, *22*(23), 9294.

Yuan, Y., & Yang, Y. (2022). Embracing the Metaverse: Mechanism and logic of a new digital economy. *Metaverse*, *3*(2), 15.

Zhao, Y., Jiang, J., Chen, Y., Liu, R., Yang, Y., Xue, X., & Chen, S. (2022). Metaverse: Perspectives from graphics, interactions and visualization. *Visual Informatics*. Advance online publication. doi:10.1016/j.visinf.2022.03.002

Chapter 10
Retail Supply Chain Management:
Ensuring Product Availability and Reducing Out-of-Stock Incidents in India

Manoj Govindaraj
https://orcid.org/0000-0003-2830-7875
VelTech Rangarajan Dr. Sagunthala R&D Institute of Science and Technology, India

Chandramowleeswaran Gnanasekaran
VelTech Rangarajan Dr. Sagunthala R&D Institute of Science and Technology, India

Ravishankar Krishnan
VelTech Rangarajan Dr. Sagunthala R&D Institute of Science and Technology, India

Parvez Khan
Atria University, India

Sinh Duc Hoang
Ho Chi Minh City University of Foreign Languages – Information Technology, Vietnam

ABSTRACT

In the dynamic landscape of the Indian retail industry, the seamless functioning of the supply chain is paramount to ensuring product availability and minimizing out-of-stock incidents. The flexibility of the supply chain is essential to effectively address challenges within the food supply chain. This research delves into the complexities and challenges faced by retailers in

DOI: 10.4018/979-8-3693-1866-9.ch010

India as they strive to manage their supply chains effectively and ensure a consistent flow of products to meet consumer demands. The objective of this study is to comprehensively analyze the practices, strategies, and technologies employed by retailers in India to enhance supply chain management, ultimately reducing out-of-stock incidents. With the rapid growth of e-commerce and changing consumer expectations, retailers face mounting pressure to optimize their supply chains to remain competitive and maintain customer satisfaction. The study contributes to the ongoing dialogue on the role of supply chain management in ensuring the success and sustainability of retail businesses in India's rapidly evolving market.

INTRODUCTION

The retail industry in India has witnessed significant growth and transformation in recent years, driven by a burgeoning consumer market, increasing disposable incomes, and a shift towards organized retail. As a result, retailers are faced with the challenge of meeting consumer demand while ensuring that products are consistently available on the shelves. The problem of out-of-stock incidents has become a critical issue that retailers must address to maintain customer satisfaction and stay competitive in the market (Schleper, et al (2021). Retail supply chain management plays a pivotal role in ensuring product availability, optimizing inventory levels, and reducing out-of-stock incidents. A well-functioning supply chain is the backbone of the retail sector, linking manufacturers, distributors, and retailers in a complex web of activities that ultimately deliver products to consumers. In this context, it is essential for retailers to have a holistic understanding of their supply chain and implement strategies that minimize out-of-stock incidents, which can lead to lost sales, dissatisfied customers, and brand erosion (Frederico, G. F. (2021). This paper aims to delve into the challenges and opportunities within the Indian retail supply chain, specifically focusing on strategies and best practices to ensure product availability and reduce out-of-stock incidents. It will explore various aspects of supply chain management, including demand forecasting, inventory optimization, distribution network design, and the integration of technology to streamline operations. By addressing these key areas, retailers can enhance their operational efficiency, improve customer satisfaction, and drive sustainable growth in the dynamic Indian retail market (Walker, J., et al (2022). Furthermore, this research will examine the unique characteristics and constraints of the Indian retail environment, such as diverse consumer preferences, varying regional demand patterns, infrastructure limitations, and regulatory considerations. These factors make it crucial for retailers to adapt their supply chain strategies to meet the specific needs of the Indian market (Kumar, S., et al (2021). In the subsequent sections, we will discuss the current state of the retail industry in India, the challenges associated with out-of-stock incidents, and the potential consequences for retailers. We will also explore the key elements of an effective retail supply chain, including demand forecasting, inventory management, and distribution network optimization. Additionally, we will highlight the role of technology and data analytics in enhancing supply chain performance (Taylor, D et al (2020). By understanding these components and implementing best practices, retailers can work towards a future where out-of-stock incidents are minimized, product availability is optimized, and customer satisfaction is maximized (Ziady, H. (2020). The content analysis conducted in these studies involved the synthesis of existing information regarding various aspects of supply chain disruptions. This encompassed categorizing the types of disruptions, assessing their impact on supply chains, scrutinizing resilience methods integrated into supply chain design, and evaluating recovery strategies proposed within the studies, often supported by cost-benefit analyses. Furthermore, our review delved into prevalent modeling approaches associated with this subject matter, providing indicative examples, and also explored the information technology tools that play a pivotal role in bolstering resilience and mitigating disruption risks (Katsaliaki, et al (2022).

REVIEW OF THE STUDY

Alok Raj et al (2020), in their paper entitled "Supply chain management during and post-COVID-19 pandemic: Mitigation strategies and practical lessons learned" It is evident that the most prominent challenges within the supply chain are inconsistency in supply and suboptimal manufacturing, closely followed by the scarcity of labor and issues related to vehicle unavailability and delays. In-depth discussions with experts have enabled us to identify appropriate mitigation strategies, both in the short-term and long-term. With a focus on addressing these challenges and drawing upon the dynamic capability theory as a framework to enhance supply chain resilience, we have devised strategies that are effective not only in mitigating the current crises but also in preparing for future adversities of a similar nature and magnitude. Short-term strategies encompass actions such as diversifying the vendor base by selecting multiple suppliers in proximity to the primary manufacturing facility, reevaluating safety and reserve stock levels, and implementing employee welfare programs to incentivize skilled migrant workers. Conversely, long-term strategies involve embracing end-to-end digital technologies, leveraging advanced artificial intelligence and machine learning techniques, establishing real-time visibility control towers that harness big data, formulating comprehensive Business Continuity Plans, and exploring the use of autonomous vehicles and drones for line haul transport and last-mile deliveries, respectively. These strategies are designed to enhance supply chain resilience and adaptability, making them essential not only in the present crisis but also in preparation for future challenges of a similar scale and nature.

Berdymyrat Ovezmyradov (2022), in his paper entitled "Product availability and stockpiling in times of pandemic: causes of supply chain disruptions and preventive measures in retailing" The assumptions outlined in this research are practical in the context of retailing, particularly when faced with the challenges associated with profit maximization techniques rooted in the news vendor model. Nonetheless, broadening the scope of the study to encompass alternative business objectives and inventory strategies could offer valuable insights with wider applicability. The exploration of diverse business objectives and inventory policies would be instrumental in generating insights that extend beyond the specific focus of the current study. Such an approach would provide practitioners with a broader range of solutions and strategies, especially when it comes to determining optimal purchasing limits. This broader perspective could be immensely beneficial for decision-makers in the retail industry, allowing them to tailor their inventory management practices to their specific business goals and operational contexts.

Nikolicic, et al (2021), in their article entitled "Reducing Food Waste in the Retail Supply Chains by Improving Efficiency of Logistics Operations" concluded that the advancement of sustainable supply chains is primarily centered on enhancing economic, environmental, and social outcomes. Within this context, the paramount objective is to minimize waste, with particular significance in the food industry. Numerous initiatives have been initiated to combat food waste in supply chains, including food recovery and donation, food waste valorization, and repurposing for animal feed. However, this research primarily focuses on waste prevention. This paper investigates the impact of alterations in inventory management, supported by the implementation of Radio-Frequency Identification (RFID) and contemporary information and communication technologies, in relation to waste reduction in food supply chains. Given RFID technology's potential for logistics and supply chain management, including rapid reading, simultaneous reading of multiple objects, even when not in the line of sight, substantial data storage capacity, direct product communication, and traceability, it was deemed valuable to explore this technology as an initial step towards full process digitization. In retail supply chains, where a substantial volume of perishable food products undergo handling, any reduction in waste, time, and expenses represents a significant business advantage. The established inventory performance positively impacts the economic aspects of supermarket and producer operations. The quantification of these effects for standard goods flows constitutes the primary contribution of this research and lays the groundwork for further investigations in the realm of sustainability.

Serpil Aday, Mehmet Seckin Aday (2020), in their paper entitled "Impact of COVID-19 on the food supply chain Food Quality and Safety" Amid a pandemic, ensuring the uninterrupted flow of the agricultural and food supply chain, a critical sector alongside healthcare, becomes imperative in averting a food crisis and mitigating adverse effects on the global economy. While significant disruptions have not yet been evident in food supply chains, the future remains uncertain. Consequently, each nation must recognize the gravity of the situation and be prepared to adjust measures as needed in response to the pandemic's evolution. Flexibility within the supply chain is crucial to effectively address challenges in food supply.

Shahab Derhamia, et al (2020), in their paper entitled "Assessing product availability in omnichannel retail networks in the presence of on-demand inventory transshipment and product substitution?" It has been established that the proposed model is adaptable for integration into an optimization framework aimed at addressing inventory planning challenges. The primary goal of this optimization model is to maximize product availability across a network of retail outlets. Within the context of assortment planning for an interconnected network of retailers, two distinct cases can be contemplated: Centralized Ordering System: In this scenario, a unified replenishment strategy is employed, and the replenishment orders for neighboring retail centers are collectively determined. The objective is to optimize product availability throughout the entire network. Decentralized Ordering Method: In this case, each individual retail center independently formulates its assortment plan while taking into account the product availability within other retail centers. The aim is to optimize product availability while allowing each retail center to make its assortment decisions autonomously. These two approaches represent different strategies for achieving the overarching goal of maximizing product availability in a network of interconnected retail outlets. The choice between centralized and decentralized ordering methods will depend on the specific operational context and the desired level of coordination among retail centers within the network.

Shikha Puri, et al (2023), in their paper entitled "Analyzing the Retail Supply Chain Attributes for Improving Product Availability to Satisfy Customer Needs & Reducing Expenses, In conclusion, the shift toward a customer-centric approach in retail supply chain management represents a strategic response to the dynamic retail landscape's challenges and opportunities. By giving precedence to customer needs, retailers can attain operational efficiency, elevate customer satisfaction, and secure a competitive advantage in the continually evolving marketplace. This approach not only fulfills the immediate goal of enhancing supply chain performance but also positions retailers for sustained success in the long term.

OBJECTIVES OF THE RESEARCH

1. To understand the current state of the retail industry in India, including its growth, challenges, and opportunities.
2. To identify the key factors and challenges specific to the Indian retail supply chain that contribute to out-of-stock incidents.
3. To examine best practices and strategies for demand forecasting in the Indian retail context, considering diverse consumer preferences and regional variations.
4. To investigate inventory management techniques that can help retailers optimize stock levels while minimizing out-of-stock occurrences.

METHODOLOGY

We will gather secondary data from a variety of sources, which encompass existing literature, reports, government publications, books, journals, magazines, online resources, and other pertinent materials. In the course of this study, we have obtained data from sources that include journals, magazines, websites, and similar outlets.

The Current State of the Retail Industry in India, Including Its Growth, Challenges, and Opportunities

The retail industry in India was experiencing significant growth and undergoing several notable changes. However, please note that the situation may have evolved since then, and it is advisable to consult the latest sources and statistics for the most up-to-date information. Here's an overview of the state of the retail industry in India at that time:

Growth:

- **Economic Growth:** India's retail sector was closely tied to the country's economic growth. With a steadily growing economy, a burgeoning middle class, and increasing disposable incomes, the retail industry had been expanding.
- **E-commerce Boom:** The e-commerce sector had witnessed explosive growth. Several homegrown e-commerce companies had emerged as major players, offering a wide range of products and services. This digital transformation was changing the way consumers shopped.
- **Organized Retail:** The organized retail segment, including large supermarket chains and organized brick-and-mortar stores, was expanding. Consumers were increasingly turning to organized retail for a more organized and convenient shopping experience.

Challenges:

- **Infrastructure Challenges:** India faced infrastructure limitations, including inadequate storage and transportation facilities, which could affect the supply chain and product availability.
- **Regulatory Complexities:** The Indian retail industry had complex and varied regulations that differed from state to state. Understanding and navigating these regulations could be challenging for retailers.
- **Intense Competition:** The retail sector in India was highly competitive, with both traditional and e-commerce players vying for market share. This competition placed pressure on pricing and profit margins.
- **Consumer Diversity:** India's diverse consumer base had varying preferences, regional variations, and price sensitivity. Retailers needed to tailor their strategies to cater to this diversity effectively.

Opportunities:

- **Rural Market Expansion:** With increasing urbanization and improving infrastructure in rural areas, retailers were exploring opportunities to expand their reach into these markets.

- **Technology Adoption:** Technology adoption, including mobile commerce, data analytics, and supply chain optimization, offered retailers a chance to enhance efficiency and customer experiences.
- **Private Labels:** Retailers were increasingly introducing private label products, which provided higher profit margins and differentiated them from competitors.
- **Omni-channel Retailing:** Many retailers were adopting omni-channel strategies, combining their online and offline presence to provide a seamless shopping experience.
- **Consumer Experience:** Retailers were focusing on enhancing the overall shopping experience, including personalized marketing, loyalty programs, and improved customer service.
- **Sustainability:** There was a growing emphasis on sustainability and responsible retail practices, reflecting the evolving consumer values and preferences.

To Identify the Key Factors and Challenges Specific to the Indian Retail Supply Chain That Contribute to Out-of-Stock Incidents

Identifying the key factors and challenges specific to the Indian retail supply chain that contribute to out-of-stock incidents is crucial for developing effective strategies to reduce such incidents. While the specific challenges may evolve over time, here are some of the common factors that have historically contributed to out-of-stock incidents in the Indian retail supply chain:

Demand Variability and Forecasting:

- **Diverse Consumer Preferences:** India's diverse population with varying preferences across regions, cultures, and income levels can make accurate demand forecasting challenging. Retailers must adapt to localized demand patterns.
- **Seasonal Fluctuations:** India experiences significant seasonal variations in demand, such as festivals, monsoons, and holiday seasons, which can strain the supply chain if not adequately anticipated.

Inventory Management:

- **Inadequate Inventory Visibility:** Limited visibility into stock levels, especially in fragmented supply chains, can lead to stockouts.

- **Working Capital Constraints:** Many retailers face working capital limitations that may prevent them from maintaining ideal inventory levels.

Distribution Challenges:

- **Poor Infrastructure:** Inadequate transportation and warehousing infrastructure in some regions can lead to supply chain bottlenecks and delays.
- **Last-Mile Delivery Difficulties:** The challenge of reaching customers in remote or congested areas can result in delivery delays and, subsequently, out-of-stock incidents.

Regulatory Complexities:

- **Complex Taxation:** India's complex tax system (e.g., Goods and Services Tax or GST) may impact supply chain efficiency and inventory management.
- **State-Specific Regulations:** Varied state regulations related to permits, licenses, and movement of goods can create operational challenges.

Supplier Reliability:

- **Supplier Issues:** Reliance on suppliers, especially for perishable goods, can be risky if suppliers face disruptions or quality issues.

Supply Chain Fragmentation:

- **Multiple Intermediaries:** A fragmented supply chain with many intermediaries can lead to information loss and inefficiencies, making it difficult to manage inventory effectively.

Data and Technology:

- **Limited Data Integration:** Inadequate integration of data from various points in the supply chain can hinder real-time visibility and decision-making.
- **Technology Adoption:** Uneven technology adoption and digitalization across the supply chain can lead to inefficiencies.

Seasonal Labor:

- **Labor Availability:** The availability of seasonal labor for tasks like stocking, packing, and transportation can be inconsistent and challenging to manage during peak demand periods.

Product Shelf Life:

- **Perishable Goods:** The retail supply chain for perishable goods, such as fresh produce and dairy, requires stringent management to prevent waste and out-of-stock incidents.

Consumer Behavior:

- **Impulse Buying:** Indian consumers often engage in impulsive buying, which can lead to unexpected spikes in demand.
- **Price Sensitivity:** Price-driven shopping behavior may make it difficult for retailers to hold excess inventory without impacting profit margins.

To mitigate out-of-stock incidents, retailers need to tailor their supply chain strategies, including inventory management, distribution, and demand forecasting, to address these specific challenges. Technology, data analytics, and a customer-centric approach can help improve supply chain visibility and responsiveness, reducing the risk of stockouts and improving customer satisfaction. Additionally, understanding regional and seasonal variations in demand and optimizing inventory levels accordingly is essential for success in the Indian retail market.

Best Practices and Strategies for Demand Forecasting in the Indian Retail Context, Considering Diverse Consumer Preferences and Regional Variations

Demand forecasting in the Indian retail context can be particularly challenging due to the diverse consumer preferences and regional variations present in the country. To address these complexities, retailers can implement the following best practices and strategies for demand forecasting:

1. Data Analytics and Big Data:

Utilize advanced data analytics and big data technologies to process and analyze large volumes of data. This can include sales data, historical demand patterns, customer feedback, and even external data sources like weather and social trends.

2. Machine Learning and AI:

Implement machine learning and artificial intelligence algorithms to identify hidden patterns and correlations within data. These technologies can adapt to changing consumer preferences and regional trends.

3. Localized Forecasting:

Recognize that demand patterns can vary significantly from one region to another. Implement region-specific forecasting models that consider local factors such as cultural events, festivals, and economic conditions.

4. Customer Segmentation:

Segment customers based on their preferences and behaviors. This allows for more accurate forecasts by tailoring inventory and marketing strategies to specific customer groups.

5. Collaborative Forecasting:

Collaborate with suppliers and distributors to share data and insights, ensuring that the entire supply chain is aligned with demand forecasts. This minimizes the risk of stockouts caused by upstream disruptions.

6. Real-Time Data:

Leverage real-time data streams to adjust forecasts dynamically. For instance, monitor social media trends and feedback to respond quickly to changing customer sentiment.

7. Predictive Analytics for Seasonality:

Use predictive analytics to anticipate and prepare for seasonal spikes in demand. This can include adjusting inventory levels and marketing strategies well in advance.

8. Forecast Review and Adjustment:

Regularly review and adjust forecasts based on actual sales and market feedback. Be flexible and adaptive in fine-tuning demand predictions.

9. Promotion and Pricing Analysis:

Consider the impact of promotions and pricing changes on demand. Analyze historical data to understand how sales promotions affect consumer behavior.

10. Cross-Functional Collaboration:

Facilitate collaboration between different departments, such as marketing, sales, and supply chain, to incorporate diverse perspectives into forecasting processes.

11. Inventory Optimization:

Implement inventory management systems that optimize stock levels based on demand forecasts. Avoid overstocking, which ties up capital, and under stocking, which results in out-of-stock incidents.

12. Demand Sensing:

Implement demand sensing techniques that use real-time data to react quickly to demand fluctuations. This allows for agile adjustments in supply chain operations.

13. Customer Feedback Loops:

Establish feedback mechanisms to gather insights from customers directly. Use surveys, feedback forms, and online reviews to understand their preferences and concerns.

14. Scenario Planning:

Develop scenarios for various demand situations, including optimistic and pessimistic scenarios. These scenarios can guide decision-making and risk mitigation strategies.

15. Continuous Learning and Improvement:

Continuously evaluate the accuracy of forecasts and incorporate lessons learned into future forecasting models. Be open to experimentation and innovation in your forecasting methods.

Demand forecasting in the Indian retail context requires a dynamic and data-driven approach that accounts for the diverse and evolving nature of consumer preferences and regional variations. By combining advanced technologies with localized insights, retailers can better align their supply chains with customer demand, reduce out-of-stock incidents, and enhance overall customer satisfaction.

Inventory Management Techniques That Can Help Retailers Optimize Stock Levels While Minimizing Out-of-Stock Occurrences

Effective inventory management is crucial for retailers to optimize stock levels and minimize out-of-stock occurrences. Retailers must strike a balance between ensuring products are available to meet customer demand while avoiding excessive inventory holding costs. Here are some inventory management techniques that can help achieve this balance:

- **ABC Analysis:**

Categorize your products into "A," "B," and "C" groups based on their importance and sales frequency. Allocate more resources to managing "A" items, as they are high-value and high-demand, while being more lenient with "C" items.

- **Just-In-Time (JIT) Inventory:**

Implement JIT inventory practices to receive goods from suppliers as they are needed, reducing excess stock and warehousing costs.

- **Safety Stock:**

Maintain a safety stock level for high-demand items to act as a buffer against unexpected spikes in demand, supplier delays, or other disruptions.

- **Reorder Point (ROP):**

Set reorder points for each product based on its lead time and demand variability. Reorder when the inventory level reaches the ROP to prevent stock outs.

- **Economic Order Quantity (EOQ):**

Calculate the EOQ for each product, finding the optimal order quantity that minimizes total inventory costs. This ensures you're not over ordering or under ordering.

- **Batch Ordering:**

Group similar items into batches for ordering. This can help reduce ordering costs and optimize the utilization of storage space.

- **Demand Forecasting:**

Employ accurate demand forecasting techniques to anticipate consumer demand. This can help you align inventory levels with expected sales, reducing stock outs and overstocking.

- **Inventory Turnover Ratio:**

Regularly calculate the inventory turnover ratio to measure how quickly products are sold. Higher turnover indicates efficient inventory management.

- **Supplier Collaboration:**

Collaborate with suppliers to improve lead times and order accuracy, reducing the need for excessive safety stock.

- **Drop Shipping:**

Consider drop shipping for certain products. This entails having suppliers ship products directly to customers, eliminating the need for warehousing and reducing inventory carrying costs.

- **Cross-Docking:**

Implement cross-docking for fast-moving products. This involves transferring products directly from inbound shipments to outbound shipments, reducing storage time.

- **Technology and Inventory Management Software:**

Utilize inventory management software that provides real-time visibility into stock levels and automates reordering processes. This technology can enhance accuracy and efficiency.

- **Rapid Replenishment Programs:**

Collaborate with suppliers on rapid replenishment programs for frequently sold items, enabling quick restocking.

- **Dead Stock Management:**

Identify slow-moving or obsolete inventory and implement strategies to clear or liquidate these items.

- **Multi-Echelon Inventory Optimization:**

Optimize inventory levels throughout the supply chain, not just at the retailer level, to minimize overall supply chain costs and improve availability.

- **Continuous Monitoring and Analysis:**

Continuously monitor and analyze inventory performance, adjusting your inventory management strategies as needed to adapt to changing market conditions and customer demand.

Effective inventory management is an ongoing process that requires a combination of these techniques, tailored to the specific needs and characteristics of your retail business. By optimizing stock levels and reducing out-of-stock occurrences, retailers can improve customer satisfaction, reduce carrying costs, and enhance overall operational efficiency.

Suggestions

Localization Strategies: Retailers operating in India should prioritize the implementation of localization strategies. These strategies should encompass offering products tailored to specific regions, adjusting inventory levels to align with local demand patterns, and crafting marketing campaigns that are region-specific (Dolgui, A., & Ivanov, D., 2021).

Collaboration with Suppliers: Retailers should foster stronger collaboration with their suppliers to enhance supply chain efficiency. This can be achieved by encouraging suppliers to adopt contemporary inventory management practices and provide precise demand forecasts, ultimately reducing lead times and minimizing the risk of out-of-stock incidents (Ghadge, A., Er, M., Ivanov, D., & Chaudhuri, A., 2021).

Technology Adoption: Embracing state-of-the-art technology and data analytics is pivotal for improving supply chain visibility, enhancing demand forecasting accuracy, and optimizing inventory levels. This modernization enables real-time decision-making and more effective stock management (Hecht, A. A., Biehl, E., Barnett, D. J., & Neff, R. A., 2019).

Data-Driven Decision-Making: Retailers should place a strong emphasis on continuous data collection and analysis to refine demand forecasting accuracy. This entails utilizing various data sources, including customer feedback, sales data, and external information, to fine-tune inventory management strategies.

Omni-channel Retailing: The development of a seamless omni-channel retailing strategy is crucial. This approach integrates online and offline channels, allowing customers to shop and receive products through multiple avenues, thereby reducing the risk of out-of-stock incidents (Ovezmyradov, B., & Kurata, H., 2019).

Regulatory Compliance: Staying well-informed about regulatory changes and ensuring compliance with tax and trade regulations is of utmost importance. Such compliance can have a substantial impact on the operations of the supply chain (Yang, H., & Schrage, L., 2009).

By implementing these strategies, retailers can not only address the challenges of the Indian retail landscape but also optimize their supply chains, leading to improved product availability and reduced out-of-stock incidents.

CONCLUSION

The retail sector in India is currently undergoing rapid growth and transformation, primarily driven by a burgeoning consumer market and the shift towards organized retail. However, one of the critical challenges that retailers face is the occurrence of out-of-stock incidents, which they must address to uphold customer satisfaction and remain competitive. A well-optimized supply chain is the cornerstone for ensuring product availability while minimizing these out-of-stock occurrences (Yang, J. et al, 2021). To excel in the Indian retail market, retailers must adapt to the unique challenges and opportunities stemming from diverse consumer preferences and regional variations. The implementation of effective demand forecasting, inventory management techniques and the optimization of distribution networks hold the key to significantly reducing these out-of-stock incidents (Queiroz, M. et al, 2022). Furthermore, embracing technology, data analytics, and fostering collaboration with suppliers can markedly enhance supply chain performance. This enables retailers to respond swiftly to the ever-evolving dynamics of the market. By concentrating on these strategies and accounting for the specific nuances of the Indian retail landscape, retailers can not only mitigate out-of-stock incidents but also elevate customer satisfaction levels and bolster their long-term growth prospects. In conclusion, the journey towards ensuring product availability and minimizing out-of-stock incidents in the Indian retail sector requires a multifaceted approach that takes into account the challenges and opportunities inherent in this dynamic market. Retailers that adapt to these conditions and invest in effective supply chain management practices are better positioned to thrive and prosper within the Indian retail landscape.

REFERENCES

Aday, S., & Aday, M. S. (2020, December). Impact of COVID-19 on the food supply chain. *Food Quality and Safety*, *4*(4), 167–180. doi:10.1093/fqsafe/fyaa024

Delasay, M., Jain, A., & Kumar, S. (2021). Impacts of the COVID-19 Pandemic on Grocery Retail Operations: An Analytical Model. *Production and Operations Management, 31*(5), 2237–2255. doi:10.1111/poms.13717 PMID:35601843

Derhamia, Montreuila, & Bau. (2020). *Assessing product availability in omnichannel retail networks in the presence of on-demand inventory transshipment and product substitution?* Academic Press.

Dohmen, A. E., Merrick, J. R., Saunders, L. W., Stank, T. T. P., & Goldsby, T. J. (2022). When preemptive risk mitigation is insufficient: The effectiveness of continuity and resilience techniques during COVID-19. *Production and Operations Management*. Advance online publication. doi:10.1111/poms.13677

Dolgui, A., & Ivanov, D. (2021). Ripple effect and supply chain disruption management: New trends and research directions. *International Journal of Production Research, 59*(1), 102–109. doi:10.1080/00207543.2021.1840148

Eppen, G. D. (1979). Effects of centralization on expected costs in a multi-location newsboy problem. *Management Science, 25*(5), 498–501. doi:10.1287/mnsc.25.5.498

Frederico, G. F. (2021). Towards a supply chain 4.0 on the post-COVID-19 pandemic: a conceptual and strategic discussion for more resilient supply chains. *Rajagiri Management Journal*.

Gerchak, Y., & Mossman, D. (1992). On the effect of demand randomness on inventories and costs. *Operations Research, 40*(4), 804–807. doi:10.1287/opre.40.4.804

Ghadge, A., Er, M., Ivanov, D., & Chaudhuri, A. (2021). Visualisation of ripple effect in supply chains under long-term, simultaneous disruptions: A system dynamics approach. *International Journal of Production Research*. Advance online publication. doi:10.1080/00207543.2021.1987547

Golubeva, O. (2021). Firms' performance during the COVID-19 outbreak: international evidence from 13 countries. *Corporate Governance: The International Journal of Business in Society*.

Guan, D., Wang, D., Hallegatte, S., Davis, S. J., Huo, J., Li, S., & Gong, P. (2020). Global supply-chain effects of COVID-19 control measures. *Nature Human Behaviour, 4*(6), 577–587. doi:10.1038/s41562-020-0896-8 PMID:32493967

Hecht, A. A., Biehl, E., Barnett, D. J., & Neff, R. A. (2019). Urban food supply chain resilience for crises threatening food security: A qualitative study. *Journal of the Academy of Nutrition and Dietetics*, *119*(2), 211–224. doi:10.1016/j.jand.2018.09.001 PMID:30527912

Hendalianpour, A., Hamzehlou, M., Feylizadeh, M. R., Xie, N., & Shakerizadeh, M. H. (2020). Coordination and competition in two-echelon supply chain using grey revenue-sharing contracts. *Grey Systems: Theory and Application*.

Herold, D. M., Nowicka, K., Pluta-Zaremba, A., & Kummer, S. (2021). COVID-19 and the pursuit of supply chain resilience: Reactions and "lessons learned" from logistics service providers (LSPs). *Supply Chain Management*, *26*(6), 702–714. doi:10.1108/SCM-09-2020-0439

Hillier, F. S., & Lieberman, G. J. (2004). *Introduction to Operations Research*. McGrawHill.

Ho, T. H., Tang, C. S., & Bell, D. R. (1998). Rational shopping behavior and the option value of variable pricing. *Management Science, 44*(12-part-2), S145–S160.

Ivanov, D. (2020). Predicting the impacts of epidemic outbreaks on global supply chains: A simulation-based analysis on the coronavirus outbreak (COVID-19/SARS-CoV-2) case. *Transportation Research Part E, Logistics and Transportation Review*, *136*, 101922. doi:10.1016/j.tre.2020.101922 PMID:32288597

Ivanov, D. (2021). Supply chain viability and the COVID-19 pandemic: A conceptual and formal generalisation of four major adaptation strategies. *International Journal of Production Research*, *59*(12), 3535–3552. doi:10.1080/00207543.2021.1890852

Ivanov, D., & Dolgui, A. (2020). Viability of intertwined supply networks: Extending the supply chain resilience angles towards survivability. A position paper motivated by COVID-19 outbreak. *International Journal of Production Research*, *58*(10), 2904–2915. doi:10.1080/00207543.2020.1750727

Ivanov, D., & Dolgui, A. (2021). OR-methods for coping with the ripple effect in supply chains during COVID-19 pandemic: Managerial insights and research implications. *International Journal of Production Economics*, *232*, 107921. doi:10.1016/j.ijpe.2020.107921 PMID:32952301

Johnson, M. (2020). Who Hoards? The Personality of Stockpiling Behavior. *Psychology Today*.

Jumrisko, M. (2020). *Singapore Grocery Chain Starts Limiting How Much People Can Buy*. Bloomberg.

Kaplan, E. H. (2020). OM Forum—COVID-19 scratch models to support local decisions. *Manufacturing & Service Operations Management*, *22*(4), 645–655. doi:10.1287/msom.2020.0891

Kapser, S., Abdelrahman, M., & Bernecker, T. (2021). Autonomous delivery vehicles to fight the spread of Covid-19–How do men and women differ in their acceptance? *Transportation Research Part A, Policy and Practice*, *148*, 183–198. doi:10.1016/j.tra.2021.02.020 PMID:33776251

Katsaliaki, P. G., & Kumar, S. (2022). Supply chain disruptions and resilience: A major review and future research agenda. *Annals of Operations Research*, *319*(1), pages965–1002. doi:10.1007/s10479-020-03912-1 PMID:33437110

Koerber, T., & Schiele, H. (2021). Is COVID-19 a turning point in stopping global sourcing? Differentiating between declining continental and increasing transcontinental sourcing. *Journal of Global Operations and Strategic Sourcing*. doi:10.1108/JGOSS-02-2021-0018

Kronblad, C., & Pregmark, J. E. (2021). Responding to the COVID-19 crisis: the rapid turn toward digital business models. *Journal of Science and Technology Policy Management*. doi:10.1108/JSTPM-10-2020-0155

Kumar, S., Xu, C., Ghildayal, N., Chandra, C., & Yang, M. (2021). Social media effectiveness as a humanitarian response to mitigate influenza epidemic and COVID-19 pandemic. *Annals of Operations Research*. Advance online publication. doi:10.1007/s10479-021-03955-y PMID:33531729

Lee, H. L., Padmanabhan, V., & Whang, S. (1997). Information distortion in a supply chain: The bullwhip effect. *Management Science*, *43*(4), 546–558. doi:10.1287/mnsc.43.4.546

Li, D., & Dong, C. (2021). Government regulations to mitigate the shortage of life-saving goods in the face of a pandemic. *European Journal of Operational Research*, *301*(3), 942–955. doi:10.1016/j.ejor.2021.11.042

Li, Y., Wang, X., Gong, T., & Wang, H. (2022). Breaking out of the pandemic: How can firms match internal competence with external resources to shape operational resilience? *Journal of Operations Management*. Advance online publication. doi:10.1002/joom.1176

Liu, K., Liu, C., Xiang, X., & Tian, Z. (2021). Testing facility location and dynamic capacity planning for pandemics with demand uncertainty. *European Journal of Operational Research*, *304*(1), 150–168. doi:10.1016/j.ejor.2021.11.028 PMID:34848916

Liu, Y., Wang, D. D., & Xu, Q. (2020). A supply chain coordination mechanism with suppliers' effort performance level and fairness concern. *Journal of Retailing and Consumer Services*, *53*, 101950. doi:10.1016/j.jretconser.2019.101950

Lorentz, H., Laari, S., Meehan, J., Eßig, M., & Henke, M. (2021). An attention-based view of supply disruption risk management: Balancing biased attention processing for improved resilience in the COVID-19 context. *International Journal of Operations & Production Management*, *41*(13), 152–177. doi:10.1108/IJOPM-06-2021-0381

Manuj, I., & Mentzer, J. T. (2008). Global supply chain risk management strategies. *International Journal of Physical Distribution & Logistics Management*, *38*(3), 192–223. doi:10.1108/09600030810866986

Matarazzo, M., & Diamantopoulos, A. (2022). Applying reactance theory to study consumer responses to COVID restrictions: A note on model specification. *International Marketing Review*. Advance online publication. doi:10.1108/IMR-12-2021-0370

Metters, R. (1997). Quantifying the bullwhip effect in supply chains. *Journal of Operations Management*, *15*(2), 89–100. doi:10.1016/S0272-6963(96)00098-8

Mouratidis, K., & Peters, S. (2022). COVID-19 impact on tele activities: Role of built environment and implications for mobility. *Transportation Research Part A, Policy and Practice*, *158*, 251–270. doi:10.1016/j.tra.2022.03.007 PMID:35291720

Mower, J. M., & Pedersen, E. L. (2018). Manufacturer, retailer and consumer misbehavior in the United States during the Second World War. Fashion. *Fashion, Style & Popular Culture*, *5*(1), 41–57. doi:10.1386/fspc.5.1.41_1

Nagurney, A. (2021a). Optimization of supply chain networks with inclusion of labor: Applications to COVID-19 pandemic disruptions. *International Journal of Production Economics, 235*, 108080. doi:10.1016/j.ijpe.2021.108080 PMID:36570047

Nagurney, A. (2021b). Supply chain game theory network modeling under labor constraints: Applications to the Covid-19 pandemic. *European Journal of Operational Research, 293*(3), 880–891. doi:10.1016/j.ejor.2020.12.054 PMID:33519049

Nikolicic, S., Kilibarda, M., Maslaric, M., Mircetic, D., & Bojic, S. (2021). Reducing Food Waste in the Retail Supply Chains by Improving Efficiency of Logistics Operations. *Sustainability (Basel), 13*(12), 6511. doi:10.3390/su13126511

Ovezmyradov. (2022). *Product availability and stockpiling in times of pandemic: causes of supply chain disruptions and preventive measures in retailing*. doi:10.1007/s10479-022-05091-7

Ovezmyradov, B., & Kurata, H. (2019). Effects of customer response to fashion product stockout on holding costs, order sizes, and profitability in omnichannel retailing. *International Transactions in Operational Research, 26*(1), 200–222. doi:10.1111/itor.12511

Palau-Saumell, R., Matute, J., Derqui, B., & Meyer, J. H. (2021). The impact of the perceived risk of COVID-19 on consumers' attitude and behavior toward locally produced food. *British Food Journal, 123*(13), 281–301. doi:10.1108/BFJ-04-2021-0380

Passetti, E. E., Battaglia, M., Bianchi, L., & Annesi, N. (2021). Coping with the COVID-19 pandemic: The technical, moral and facilitating role of management control. *Accounting, Auditing & Accountability Journal, 34*(6), 1430–1444. doi:10.1108/AAAJ-08-2020-4839

Penco, L., Ciacci, A., Benevolo, C., & Torre, T. (2021). Open social innovation for surplus food recovery and aid during COVID-19 crisis: The case of Fondazione Banco Alimentare Onlus. *British Food Journal*. Advance online publication. doi:10.1108/BFJ-02-2021-0116

Pournader, M., Kach, A., & Talluri, S. (2020). A review of the existing and emerging topics in the supply chain risk management literature. *Decision Sciences, 51*(4), 867–919. doi:10.1111/deci.12470 PMID:34234385

Puri, Agarwal, Kumar, Thandayuthapani, & Baja. (2023). *Analyzing the Retail Supply Chain Attributes for Improving Product Availability to Satisfy Customer Needs & Reducing Expenses*. Academic Press.

Queiroz, M. M., Wamba, S. F., Jabbour, C. J. C., & Machado, M. C. (2022). Supply chain resilience in the UK during the coronavirus pandemic: A resource orchestration perspective. *International Journal of Production Economics, 245*, 108405. doi:10.1016/j.ijpe.2021.108405 PMID:35002082

Raassens, N., Haans, H., & Mullick, S. (2021). Surviving the hectic early phase of the COVID-19 pandemic: A qualitative study to the supply chain strategies of food service firms in times of a crisis. *International Journal of Logistics Management*. Advance online publication. doi:10.1108/IJLM-01-2021-0013

Raj, A., Mukherjee, A. A., de Sousa Jabbour, A. B. L., & Srivastava, S. K. (2022, March). Supply chain management during and post-COVID-19 pandemic: Mitigation strategies and practical lessons learned. *Journal of Business Research, 142*, 1125–1139. doi:10.1016/j.jbusres.2022.01.037 PMID:35079190

Remko, V. H. (2020). Research opportunities for a more resilient post-COVID-19 supply chain–closing the gap between research findings and industry practice. *International Journal of Operations & Production Management, 40*(4), 341–355. doi:10.1108/IJOPM-03-2020-0165

Repko, M. (2021). *Costco brings back purchase limits on toilet paper, cleaning supplies and More*. CNBC.

Rey, J. (2020). *Amazon is banning the sale of N95 and surgical masks to the general public*. Vox.

Rodrigue, J. P. (2016). *The Geography of Transport Systems*. Taylor & Francis. doi:10.4324/9781315618159

Rozhkov, M., Ivanov, D., Blackhurst, J., & Nair, A. (2022). Adapting supply chain operations in anticipation of and during the COVID-19 pandemic. *Omega, 110*, 102635. doi:10.1016/j.omega.2022.102635 PMID:35291412

Salaverria, L. (2020). Manufacturers, retailers seek lifting of purchase limits. *Philippine Daily Inquirer*.

Salvietti, G., Ziliani, C., Teller, C., Ieva, M., & Ranfagni, S. (2022). Omnichannel retailing and post-pandemic recovery: Building a research agenda. *International Journal of Retail & Distribution Management, 50*(8/9), 1156–1181. doi:10.1108/IJRDM-10-2021-0485

Sanci, E., Daskin, M. S., Hong, Y. C., Roesch, S., & Zhang, D. (2021). Mitigation strategies against supply disruption risk: A case study at the Ford Motor Company. *International Journal of Production Research.* Advance online publication. doi:10.1080/00207543.2021.1975058

Satish, K., Venkatesh, A., & Manivannan, A. S. R. (2021). Covid-19 is driving fear and greed in consumer behaviour and purchase pattern. *South Asian Journal of Marketing, 2*(2), 113–129. doi:10.1108/SAJM-03-2021-0028

Schlegelmilch, B. B., Sharma, K., & Garg, S. (2022). Employing machine learning for capturing COVID-19 consumer sentiments from six countries: A methodological illustration. *International Marketing Review.* Advance online publication. doi:10.1108/IMR-06-2021-0194

Schleper, M. C., Gold, S., Trautrims, A., & Baldock, D. (2021). Pandemic-induced knowledge gaps in operations and supply chain management: COVID-19's impacts on retailing. *International Journal of Operations & Production Management, 41*(3), 193–205. doi:10.1108/IJOPM-12-2020-0837

Schmitt, A. J., Sun, S. A., Snyder, L. V., & Shen, Z. J. M. (2015). Centralization versus decentralization: Risk pooling, risk diversification, and supply chain disruptions. *Omega, 52*, 201–212. doi:10.1016/j.omega.2014.06.002

Shen, Z. M., & Sun, Y. (2021). Strengthening supply chain resilience during COVID-19: A case study of JD. com. *Journal of Operations Management.* Advance online publication. doi:10.1002/joom.1161

Shih, W. (2022). From Just-In-Time to Just-In-Case: Is Excess and Obsolete Next? *Forbes.*

Shou, B., Xiong, H., & Shen, X. M. (2013). *Consumer panic buying and quota policy under supply disruptions.* Working paper. Hong Kong: City University of Hong Kong.

Siebert, B. (2020). *Coronavirus hoarder tries to return $10,000 worth of goods to Adelaide supermarket.* ABC Radio.

Singh, J. P., Dwivedi, Y. K., Rana, N. P., Kumar, A., & Kapoor, K. K. (2019). Event classification and location prediction from tweets during disasters. *Annals of Operations Research, 283*(1), 737–757. doi:10.1007/s10479-017-2522-3

Singh, S., Kumar, R., Panchal, R., & Tiwari, M. K. (2021). Impact of COVID-19 on logistics systems and disruptions in food supply chain. *International Journal of Production Research, 59*(7), 1993–2008. doi:10.1080/00207543.2020.1792000

Stiff, R., Johnson, K., & Tourk, K. A. (1975). *Scarcity and hoarding: economic and social explanations and marketing implications.* ACR North American Advances.

Su, X., & Zhang, F. (2008). Strategic customer behavior, commitment, and supply chain performance. *Management Science, 54*(10), 1759–1773. doi:10.1287/mnsc.1080.0886

Sucky, E. (2009). The bullwhip effect in supply chains—An overestimated problem? *International Journal of Production Economics, 118*(1), 311–322. doi:10.1016/j.ijpe.2008.08.035

Swinney, R. (2011). Selling to strategic consumers when product value is uncertain: The value of matching supply and demand. *Management Science, 57*(10), 1737–1751. doi:10.1287/mnsc.1110.1360

Taylor, D., Pritchard, A., Duhan, D., & Mishra, S. (2020). What's behind the empty grocery shelves? *Supply Chain Management Review*, 1–4.

Terazono, E., & Evans, J. (2020). How coronavirus is affecting pasta's complex supply chain. *Financial Times.*

Thomas, L. (2020). *Coronavirus wreaks havoc on retail supply chains globally, even as China's factories come back online*. CNBC.

Tolk, A., Harper, A., & Mustafee, N. (2021). Hybrid models as transdisciplinary research enablers. *European Journal of Operational Research, 291*(3), 1075–1090. doi:10.1016/j.ejor.2020.10.010 PMID:33078041

Tsao, Y. C., Raj, P., & Raj, P. V. (2019). Product substitution with customer segmentation under panic buying behavior. *Scientia Iranica*. Advance online publication. doi:10.24200/sci.2019.5099.1093

Tsiligianni, C., Tsiligiannis, A., & Tsiliyannis, C. (2022). A stochastic inventory model of COVID-19 and robust, real-time identification of carriers at large and infection rate via asymptotic laws. *European Journal of Operational Research, 304*(1), 42–56. doi:10.1016/j.ejor.2021.12.037 PMID:35035055

Tyko, K. (2022). Grocery stores still have empty shelves amid supply chain disruptions,omicron and winter storms. *USA Today*.

Van Oorschot, K. E., Van Wassenhove, L. N., & Jahre, M. (2022). Collaboration–competition dilemma in flattening the COVID-19 curve. *Production and Operations Management*. Advance online publication. doi:10.1111/poms.13709 PMID:35601840

Walker, J., Brewster, C., Fontinha, R., Haak-Saheem, W., Benigni, S., Lamperti, F., & Ribaudo, D. (2022). The unintended consequences of the pandemic on non-pandemic research activities. *Research Policy, 51*(1), 104369. doi:10.1016/j.respol.2021.104369 PMID:34565926

Yang, H., & Schrage, L. (2009). Conditions that cause risk pooling to increase inventory. *European Journal of Operational Research, 192*(3), 837–851. doi:10.1016/j.ejor.2007.10.064

Yang, J., Xie, H., Yu, G., & Liu, M. (2021). Antecedents and consequences of supply chain risk management capabilities: An investigation in the post-coronavirus crisis. *International Journal of Production Research, 59*(5), 1573–1585. doi:10.1080/00207543.2020.1856958

Ye, F., Liu, K., Li, L., Lai, K. H., Zhan, Y., & Kumar, A. (2022). Digital supply chain management in the COVID-19 crisis: An asset orchestration perspective. *International Journal of Production Economics, 245*, 108396. doi:10.1016/j.ijpe.2021.108396 PMID:34931109

Ziady, H. (2020). *Panic buying is forcing supermarkets to ration food and other supplies*. CNN Business.

Chapter 11
Role of the Digital India Movement to Incorporate the Digital Technologies in the Indian System:
Adoption of Artificial Intelligence

Jaskirat Singh Rai
https://orcid.org/0000-0001-5453-0267
Chitkara Business School, Chitkara University, India

Megha Goyal
Chitkara Business School, Chitkara University, India

ABSTRACT

The objective of this study was to investigate the substantial influence of artificial intelligence (AI) on the adoption of digital technologies in India, with a specific focus on the post-Digital India Movement era. This study examines the various manners in which artificial intelligence (AI) technology has facilitated advancements in multiple programmatic domains. The utilization of artificial intelligence (AI) has facilitated financial inclusion, enhanced accessibility to healthcare and education, and contributed to the broader socioeconomic progress of India by ways of decentralization and international cooperation. This study also examines the challenges and ethical concerns associated with the utilization of artificial intelligence within the framework of digital technology adoption in India. The findings of this study illustrate the capacity of artificial intelligence (AI) to expedite the realization of Digital India's goals.

DOI: 10.4018/979-8-3693-1866-9.ch011

INTRODUCTION

The adoption of artificial intelligence (AI) is quickly increasing in our modern environment. Artificial intelligence (AI) can enhance and magnify human intelligence, hence enhancing individuals' interaction with the environment and their efficiency. This is accomplished by enabling sophisticated cognitive processes, including logical thinking, sensory interpretation, knowledge assimilation, problem-solving, and the capacity to make well-informed decisions (Tai, M.C., 2020). Artificial intelligence (AI) has the ability to carry out sophisticated data gathering and consolidation, analysis, and computational operations. The potential of artificial intelligence (AI) technology extends to different fields, including transportation, logistics, education, healthcare, military, and banking systems. Its purpose is to tackle ongoing difficulties inside our society. Artificial intelligence (AI) has the capacity to offer significant assistance in addressing key issues encountered in our nation, namely in the areas of agriculture, healthcare, and finance in rural regions of India.

The Indian government is actively striving to improve the human capital on a national scale and attract foreign investment to India. The primary focus of these endeavors is primarily on the younger demographic and includes initiatives such as Skill India, Make in India, and Digital India. In 2016, India ranked third among the G20 nations as a prominent center for start-ups specializing in artificial intelligence (AI). India has had a significant increase in the number of start-ups that are employing artificial intelligence within the country (Shankar, 2020).

DIGITAL INDIA MOVEMENT AND ADOPTION OF DIGITAL TECHNOLOGIES

The Digital India campaign was launched on July 1, 2015, with the aim of providing electronic infrastructure to citizens and promoting the use of digital technologies in the Indian financial system. The main aim is to decentralize the Indian system and streamline the delivery of government services to Indian citizens through the use of digital technology, thereby reducing their dependence on traditional paperwork (Mohanata, 2017). The Department of Electronics and Information Technology (Deity) is accountable for its guidance and direction. The government's effectiveness is augmented by the "digital India" initiative, which also fosters the expansion of electronic services, products, gadgets, manufacturing, and employment prospects. The

Indian government implemented the Digital India program with the objective of expanding high-speed internet connectivity to rural areas (Gaur, 2017).

The aim of the concept is to create a system that is distinguished by active involvement, clarity, and promptness in addressing issues. Technology acts as a channel, successfully combining the extensive capabilities of the internet and the accessibility of global knowledge, with the goal of promoting education and awareness inside the villages of India. The "Digital India" program is not only a promotional endeavor, but rather a necessity for our country, considering the substantial section of our people that still lacks access to the government of India's new services. The establishment of Digital India aims to foster inclusive growth in several sectors such as banking and finance, electronic services, commodities, manufacturing, and employment possibilities (SKIREC, 2017).

The Indian government implemented the Digital India program with the objective of enabling convenient online access to government services for the population. This objective is achieved by enhancing online infrastructure, consistently raising awareness among Indian citizens, and improving internet connectivity. India has attained self-sufficiency in the field of digital technology. Within the Indian setting, a significant segment of the younger demographic has received training in information technology (IT) and embraced sophisticated digital technologies. However, the present condition of technical infrastructure and digital facilities has yet to completely harness their potential in terms of use.

AI IN E-GOVERNANCE

Artificial intelligence (AI) is commonly used in electronic governance (e-governance) to automate routine activities and processes. Government websites and portals are progressively including chatbots and virtual assistants powered by artificial intelligence (AI). These AI-powered applications are designed to help individuals with various chores and provide prompt solutions to their requests. This guarantees that individuals obtain precise and consistent information, thereby maximizing efficiency for both citizens and government officials. The utilization of artificial intelligence (AI) is essential in the realm of data analytics since it enables governments to make well-informed decisions grounded in facts. Artificial Intelligence has the capacity to detect patterns, deviations, and areas of potential issues by analyzing large datasets. This skill is particularly beneficial in the Indian financial system as it allows for the use of predictive policing to improve the effective distribution of resources and the deterrence of criminal actions.

Artificial intelligence (AI) is rapidly utilized in the Indian banking and e-governance industry primarily to analyze financial data and predict potential issues, allowing for proactive identification of banking system failures. Artificial intelligence (AI) is an influential instrument that is transforming the realm of electronic governance (e-governance). The improvement of effectiveness and productivity in the provision of public services is accompanied by a rise in accessibility and responsiveness to the requirements of the general people. The application of Artificial Intelligence (AI) in the field of e-government involves multiple aspects, including automation, data analytics, security, and decision-making. Nevertheless, it also engenders apprehensions over security, privacy, and the adaptability of workers. To maximize the effective use of artificial intelligence (AI) in e-government, governments must find a careful balance between protecting individuals' rights and interests, while also encouraging innovation. The attainment of a more effective and citizen-focused administration relies heavily on maintaining this harmonious equilibrium (Chopra, 2020).

AI IN FINANCIAL EDUCATION

Artificial intelligence (AI) is widely acknowledged as a disruptive influence in the realm of financial education. The integration of artificial intelligence (AI) technology is causing a revolution in the approaches to education and sharing of information inside financial organizations. The incorporation of artificial intelligence (AI) into financial settings is transforming the Indian financial system by improving the accessibility, efficiency, and customization of teaching approaches. Financial institutions utilize AI algorithms to evaluate the strengths and weaknesses of a banking system, and subsequently rectify any irregularities according to their preferred speed and learning modality. According to Verma (2018), this approach ensures that people engage in the financial institutions acquire comprehensive understanding of the innovative fintech content and maintains their engagement in the learning process.

AI-powered chatbots, in conjunction with financial educators, offer immediate and tailored support to individuals who are quick to embrace fintech services. Individuals have the chance to acquire answers to their questions at any given moment, thereby promoting a deeper comprehension of financial matters. Furthermore, these technologies reduce the workload for financial institutions, enabling them to dedicate their time and resources to more demanding duties. The widespread use of artificial intelligence has facilitated the expansion and development of financial services, as well as the widespread adoption of digital services by the general public. Financial institutions powered by artificial intelligence can efficiently serve a broad customer base at the same time, allowing consumers from different areas to access high-quality financial services.

DIGITAL TECHNOLOGIES IN AGRICULTURE

The agriculture sector is undergoing a major transformation in which the use of digital technology, such as artificial intelligence (AI), is becoming increasingly important. Farmers and other participants in the agricultural industry are utilizing artificial intelligence (AI) to improve crop yield, optimize resource allocation, and tackle issues related to food security, financial sustainability, and environmental preservation. The use of artificial intelligence (AI) solutions is enabling the conversion of agriculture into a data-driven, accurate, and environmentally aware industry. Precision farming use artificial intelligence (AI) tools, including satellite imaging, drones, and remote sensing, to gather data on crop health, weather patterns, and soil conditions. The aforementioned data is subjected to processing using machine learning techniques to furnish farmers with vital insights. This technology improves agricultural output and maximizes resource usage by equipping farmers with essential information to make well-informed decisions regarding the timing and placement of planting, irrigation, fertilizing, and harvesting activities. Drones, outfitted with cameras, sensors, and artificial intelligence (AI) capabilities, have the capacity to effectively and precisely monitor large agricultural areas. The observers possess the capacity to detect agricultural concerns, such as insect infestations, disease outbreaks, or nutritional deficits, related to crops. The alert highlights the importance of early detection in enabling timely actions by farmers, hence avoiding crop damage and decreasing reliance on fertilizers and herbicides (Shah, 2020).

Artificial intelligence has also affected the agriculture supply chain. The efficient application of artificial intelligence algorithms and predictive analytics in logistics guarantees the punctual transportation of agricultural products to marketplaces. Moreover, this approach not only helps to reduce waste but also assists in preventing food spoiling. AI-powered solutions are employed to address the difficulties presented by limited resources and climate change. Artificial Intelligence can assist farmers in efficiently adapting to changing climate conditions and improving water management practices by employing sophisticated methods like monitoring meteorological trends and evaluating soil conditions. In addition, the utilization of artificial intelligence (AI) in the identification of genetic characteristics that contribute to enhanced plant resilience against diseases and drought conditions has proven to be beneficial in the field of agricultural breeding (Shah, 2020).

DIGITAL TECHNOLOGIES IN HEALTHCARE

Healthcare professionals are advancing in the field of therapeutic innovations, improving the accuracy of diagnoses, and raising the quality of patient care by utilizing digital technology like artificial intelligence (AI). The healthcare industry is making significant progress in terms of precision, effectiveness, and patient-focused treatment by incorporating artificial intelligence (AI) in tasks such as data analysis, picture recognition, and predictive modeling. The application of artificial intelligence in healthcare provides substantial benefits, with diagnostic precision being particularly remarkable. Machine learning algorithms can be utilized to examine large datasets consisting of clinical research, patient data, and medical records to detect trends and irregularities. According to Hotjar (2023), this technology assists medical professionals in achieving a higher level of precision when identifying patients, particularly in scenarios when human judgment may be limited.

Radiology is progressively utilizing artificial intelligence (AI) algorithms to analyze and interpret diagnostic imaging modalities such as computed tomography (CT), magnetic resonance imaging (MRI), and X-rays. The algorithms demonstrate a significantly high accuracy rate in recognizing early indicators of anomalies or diseases, such as cancer. This method decreases the probability of an inaccurate diagnosis while simultaneously improving the effectiveness of the diagnostic process. Artificial intelligence (AI) is making significant progress in the field of pathology, particularly in its capacity to examine tissue samples and precisely identify cancer cells. This technological advancement grants pathologists extra time and improves the accuracy of their diagnostic operations. Artificial intelligence (AI) can aid in the early detection of heart conditions by assisting in the monitoring and analysis of electrocardiograms (ECGs). AI-powered chatbots and virtual assistants can efficiently handle duties like booking appointments, sending medication reminders, and providing patients with health-related information. These features contribute to improving patient involvement and guaranteeing reliable administration of medicine. Artificial intelligence (AI) is essential in enabling the customization of treatments. AI systems have the ability to customize treatment plans, forecast probable adverse effects, and optimize medicine doses by analyzing a patient's genetic and medical data. Tai (2020) suggests that the adoption of personalized medicine has the capacity to reduce healthcare costs and minimize negative reactions, while also improving patient outcomes.

CHALLENGES AND CONCERNS IN ADOPTING AI AND SOLUTIONS

1. Ethical Concerns and Bias in AI

The deployment of artificial intelligence (AI) raises numerous consequential ethical issues that require meticulous examination and resolution. Artificial intelligence (AI) systems rely extensively on data for training and decision-making, especially in the realm of machine learning algorithms. If artificial intelligence relies on skewed or unrepresentative data, it has the potential to perpetuate existing prejudices. Prejudice can appear in diverse manifestations, including biases pertaining to socioeconomic class, ethnicity, or gender. AI systems may unintentionally demonstrate bias in favor of certain demographic groups throughout the hiring process, resulting in the generation of unfair outcomes.

Solution: To tackle these problems, AI developers and organizations must prioritize carefulness while choosing and examining training data, with the goal of reducing bias. It is necessary to create algorithms that demonstrate accountability, transparency, and comprehensibility. To guarantee ethical implementation, it is crucial to develop legislation and ethical norms that regulate the responsible adoption of artificial intelligence (AI).

DATA PRIVACY AND SECURITY

The growing adoption of artificial intelligence (AI) has raised substantial concerns over the protection of data security and privacy, resulting in increased scrutiny and careful consideration. AI systems frequently utilize significant volumes of data, including data that is confidential and delicate in nature. This situation increases the probability of data misuse and breaches. It is crucial to guarantee the security of sensitive data against unauthorized access and to ensure its ethical management.

Solution: Organizations utilizing artificial intelligence (AI) must adhere to data protection laws, such as the Health Insurance Portability and Accountability Act (HIPAA) in the United States and the General Data Protection Regulation (GDPR) in Europe. Utilizing data encryption and anonymization strategies can bolster data security and privacy within artificial intelligence (AI) systems.

WORKFORCE DISRUPTION

The emergence of artificial intelligence (AI) and its capacity for automating work and optimizing processes has led to investigations into the possibility of job displacement. The application of artificial intelligence (AI) holds potential in automating mundane and repetitive activities in several industries, while also offering possibilities for the discovery of new career paths. The potential ramifications of this circumstance may impact multiple areas of the economy, including manufacturing, customer service, and data input, in relation to employment.

Solution: To tackle this problem, companies must give high importance to workforce planning and the execution of re-skilling and up-skilling programs. An effective approach to address concerns about job displacement entails offering individuals training chances to acquire the skills required for engaging in new occupations that involve collaborating with AI systems and effectively utilizing human-AI interaction.

2. Cost and Resource Constraints

The implementation of artificial intelligence (AI) solutions can incur significant costs, particularly for smaller firms and organizations. The creation, installation, and maintenance of AI systems need substantial financial and technological resources. The potential impediment to the widespread adoption of artificial intelligence (AI) lies in the financial burden associated with acquiring the necessary hardware, software, and expertise.

Solution: To address this matter, it is recommended to collaborate with artificial intelligence (AI) vendors, do thorough research on cost-effective alternatives, and leverage cloud-based solutions. AI-as-a-Service (AIaaS) offerings have the potential to benefit smaller organizations by providing them with access to AI capabilities, hence eliminating the need for extensive infrastructure or specialized expertise (Karim.S, 2021).

Government Initiatives and Policies to Boost AI and Digitalization in India:

India has emerged as a significant contributor in the domains of artificial intelligence (AI) and digitalization, driven by its focus on transforming into a knowledge-based economy and fostering a digitally empowered society. The government acknowledges the significant potential of these technologies in enhancing economic development, bolstering national security, and enhancing the overall quality of life for inhabitants. Several initiatives and policies have been implemented with the aim of achieving these aims (Gaur, 2017).

1. **Digital India**

Broadband for All: Broadband for all initiative aims to facilitate widespread availability of cost-effective and high-speed internet connectivity to individuals throughout the country, thereby enabling equitable access to digital services, including in geographically isolated regions.

Digital Infrastructure: The primary objective of the program is to establish the essential digital infrastructure, including data centers and networks, in order to facilitate the provision of digital services by the government.

Digital Literacy: The objective of a digital literacy program is to enhance the digital literacy skills of individuals, with a special focus on those residing in rural regions, enabling them to effectively utilize digital technology (Yadav, 2021).

2. National Policy on Electronics (NPE): Driving Electronics Manufacturing

The National Policy on Electronics was implemented in 2019 with the objective of positioning India as a global hub for the development and manufacturing of electronic systems. The primary goals of the strategy are to enhance employment opportunities, promote innovation in the field of electronics, and stimulate investment in the electronics manufacturing industry. The inclusion of these factors is crucial in facilitating the nation's transition towards digitalization. Furthermore, the NPE prioritizes research and development in advanced domains like as artificial intelligence (AI), recognizing its crucial role in the production of electronic goods and services (MieTY, 2020),

3. National Policy on Software Products (NPSP): Promoting Software Product Ecosystem

The National Policy on Software Products was implemented in the year 2019 with the objective of promoting the growth and development of the software product industry in India. This statement underscores the importance of software products in facilitating the process of digital transformation and recognizes the imperative of fostering an environment that fosters entrepreneurial endeavors and promotes innovation. The NPSP additionally facilitates research and development in these domains, highlighting the significance of artificial intelligence (AI) and emerging technologies in the development of software products.

4. AI and Emerging Technologies

The National AI Strategy was implemented in 2020, wherein the government established the National Artificial Intelligence Portal. This portal was designed to function as a central repository of information and resources pertaining to advancements in artificial intelligence within India. The document encompasses an AI strategy that delineates the overarching vision and objective for the integration and utilization of artificial intelligence inside the nation. The National Mission on Quantum Technologies, initiated in the year 2020, seeks to expedite the advancement of research and development in the field of quantum technologies. These technologies have the capacity to bring about transformative changes in multiple domains, such as cryptography and data security (Srivastava, S. K., 2018).

5. International Collaboration and Agreements

India acknowledges the significance of engaging in international cooperation pertaining to artificial intelligence (AI) and digitalization. The government has entered into agreements and established collaborations with multiple nations, such as the United States and Japan, with the aim of promoting research, fostering innovation, and facilitating the interchange of technology. International collaborations play a pivotal role in facilitating India's access to global experience, investments, and technology, hence bolstering its ongoing digitization endeavors.

6. Skill Development and Education

The successful implementation of digitalization and AI necessitates a workforce that possesses the necessary skills and expertise. The government has implemented a variety of skill development programs and initiatives aimed at equipping the Indian workforce with the necessary competencies to thrive in the digital era. Notable initiatives encompass the Skill India program as well as endeavor to integrate artificial intelligence (AI) and digital literacy into educational courses.

Artificial Intelligence (AI) possesses the potential to enhance public services, revolutionize industries, and enhance the overall well-being of individuals. This analysis examines the potential of artificial intelligence (AI) in India's digital future and its capacity to stimulate the nation's growth and development.

1. Industry Transformation and Innovation:

Artificial intelligence (AI) is expected to play a pivotal role in expediting the sector's transition. India is endeavouring to enhance its manufacturing skills through initiatives such as the "Make in India" program. Artificial Intelligence (AI) has the potential to contribute to various aspects of business operations, including supply chain management, quality assurance, and manufacturing efficiency. In addition, the utilization of artificial intelligence (AI) will facilitate the development of novel products and solutions labeled as "Designed in India," with the intention of targeting global markets (Srivastava, S. K., 2018).

2. Agriculture and Food Security:

Artificial intelligence (AI) possesses the capacity to revolutionize the agricultural sector through enhancements in production forecasting, optimization of crop management practices, and rectification of inefficiencies within the supply chain. Farmers will be able to acquire data-driven insights through the utilization of smart farming practices that are enabled by artificial intelligence (AI) and the Internet of Things (IoT). According to Shah (2020), the enhancement of food security holds significant importance for India's socioeconomic progress, alongside the augmentation of agricultural productivity.

3. Education skilling and Job creation

Artificial intelligence (AI) possesses the capacity to tailor instructional methods in order to cater to the unique requirements of each student. This transition possesses the capacity to address the disparity in educational outcomes and cultivate a citizenry that is proficient in digital literacy. The cultivation of a knowledge-driven society will be significantly facilitated by the utilization of adaptive learning platforms, intelligent tutoring systems, and online education. The implementation of artificial intelligence (AI) is anticipated to bring about transformations in various occupations, rather than completely eradicating them. As automation assumes responsibility for dull and repetitive tasks, labor can shift its focus towards creative and strategic activities. According to Srivastava (2018), India stands to benefit from embracing skill development initiatives that focus on equipping its workers for AI-related employment and fostering economic expansion.

4. Smart Cities and Governance

The utilization of artificial intelligence (AI) applications plays a crucial role in the advancement of smart cities. AI-driven urban planning has the potential to enhance various aspects of urban development, including traffic control, energy efficiency, and infrastructure management. According to Srivastava (2018), artificial intelligence (AI) has the potential to enhance government services through the optimization of processes, resulting in improved efficiency, accessibility, and a stronger focus on citizen needs. This utilization of AI can contribute to India's pursuit of its social development goals.

5. Inclusivity and Accessibility

Artificial intelligence has the potential to contribute to the reduction of the digital gap by ensuring its beneficial integration throughout all sectors of society. This inclusivity can be advantageous for rural areas, vulnerable populations, and individuals with disabilities. The utilization of artificial intelligence (AI) driven accessibility features possesses the capacity to facilitate the participation of all individuals in social development initiatives and the digital economy. According to Shanker (2020),

CONCLUSION

The influence of artificial intelligence (AI) on the Digital India initiative is significant, encompassing various sectors and holding the potential to redefine both economic growth and social advancement. Artificial intelligence (AI) is a remarkable technological advancement that holds significant importance in India's Digital India plan. The nation is being steered towards technological advancement, societal advancement, and economic prosperity. In conjunction with its digital initiatives, the strategic approach of the Indian government towards artificial intelligence (AI) establishes a comprehensive framework for progress. The impact of artificial intelligence (AI) on the Digital India initiative extends beyond technological advancements, encompassing transformative effects on individuals' lives and the potential to foster a more promising future for all. The progress of India in achieving digital empowerment, facilitated by the integration of artificial intelligence, serves as a testament to its commitment to progress and inclusive growth.

REFERENCES

Gaur, A. (2016). *A Study Impact of Digital India in Make in India Program in IT and BPM Sector.* Presented in the AIMS International Conference at MICA, Ahmadabad.

Hotjar. (2023). *The impact of Artificial intelligence on 5 industries*. Retrieved from https://www.hotjar.com/blog/ai-impact-industries-1/

Jain, P. (2017). Role of Digital India Movement in a Country. *A Journal of Advances in Management IT & Social Sciences*, *7*(7), 13–17.

Karim, S., Sandu, N., & Kayastha, M. (2021). The challenges and opportunities of adopting artificial intelligence (AI) in Jordan's healthcare transformation. *Global Journal of Information Technology*, *11*(2), 35–46. doi:10.18844/gjit.v11i2.6546

Mohanta, G., Debasish, S. S., & Nanda, S. K. (2017). A Study on Growth and Prospect of Digital India Campaign. *Saudi Journal of Business and Management Studies*, *2*(7), 727–731.

Shanker, S. (2020). Digital India empowered by artificial intelligence. *An International Bilingual Peer Reviewed Refereed Research Journal*, *7*(26), 149–154.

Sharma, G. D., Yadav, A., & Chopra, R. (2020). Artificial intelligence and effective governance: A review, critique and research agenda. *Sustainable Futures : An Applied Journal of Technology, Environment and Society*, *2*(2), 100–104. doi:10.1016/j.sftr.2019.100004

Srivastava, S. K. (2018). Artificial Intelligence: Way forward for India. *Journal of Information Systems and Technology Management*, *15*, 1–23. doi:10.4301/S1807-1775201815004

Swalehin, M. (2021). Digital Divide and digital Inclusive policies in India: A sociological study. *International Journal of Trend in Scientific Research and Development*, *2*(1), 232–238.

Tai, M. C. (2020). The Impact of Artificial Intelligence on Human Society and Bioethics. *Tzu-Chi Medical Journal*, *32*(4), 339. doi:10.4103/tcmj.tcmj_71_20 PMID:33163378

Talaviya, T., Shah, D. N., Patel, N., Yagnik, H., & Shah, M. (2020). Implementation of artificial intelligence in agriculture for optimisation of irrigation and application of pesticides and herbicides. *Artificial Intelligence in Agriculture*, *4*, 58–73. doi:10.1016/j.aiia.2020.04.002

Verma, M. (2018). Artificial intelligence and its scope in different areas with special reference to the field of education. *International Journal of Advanced Educational Research*, *3*(1), 5–10.

Yadav, S. (2021). Digital India Programme: An Overview. *International Journal of Creative Research Thoughts*, *9*(2), 15–20.

Compilation of References

Aaker, D. (1991). *Managing brand equity: Capitalizing on the value of a brand name*. The Free Press.

Abadie, A., Diamond, A., & Hainmueller, J. (2011). Synth: An r package for synthetic control methods in comparative case studies. *Journal of Statistical Software*, *42*(13). Advance online publication. doi:10.18637/jss.v042.i13

Aday, S., & Aday, M. S. (2020, December). Impact of COVID-19 on the food supply chain. *Food Quality and Safety*, *4*(4), 167–180. doi:10.1093/fqsafe/fyaa024

Addis, M., & Holbrook, M. B. (2001). On the conceptual link between mass customisation and experiential consumption: An explosion of subjectivity. *Journal of Consumer Behaviour*, *1*(1), 50–66. doi:10.1002/cb.53

Aguaded, J. I., & Tirado, R. (2010). Ordenadores en los pupitres: Informática y telemática en el proceso de enseñanza-aprendizaje en los centros TIC de Andalucía. *Pixel-Bit. Revista de Medios y Educación*, *36*, 5–28.

Aleksandar, A. (2022). *Alibaba Cloud accused of violating China's cybersecurity law*. Academic Press.

Allah Pitchay, A., Ganesan, Y., Zulkifli, N. S., & Khaliq, A. (2022). Determinants of customers' intention to use online food delivery application through smartphone in Malaysia. *British Food Journal*, *124*(3), 732–753. doi:10.1108/BFJ-01-2021-0075

Allam, Z., Sharifi, A., Bibri, S. E., Jones, D. S., & Krogstie, J. (2022). The metaverse as a virtual form of smart cities: Opportunities and challenges for environmental, economic, and social sustainability in urban futures. *Smart Cities*, *5*(3), 771–801. doi:10.3390/smartcities5030040

Anderman, E., & Dawson, H. S. (2011). Learning with motivation. In R. E. Mayer & P. A. Alexander (Eds.), *Handbook of research on learning and instruction* (pp. 219–241). Routledge.

Angrist, J. D., & Pischke, J. S. (2008). Mostly Harmless Econometrics: An Empiricist's Companion. Princeton University Press.

Apptuts, E. (2022). *Microsoft Mesh: Microsoft's gambit into the metaverse, AppTuts.net -Aplicativos Android, iPhone, iPad, Mac OSX e Windows.* Available at: https://www.apptuts.net/en/tutorial/android/microsoft-mesh-gambit-metaverse/

Área, M., Cepeda, O., González, D. and Sanabria, A. (2010). Un análisis de las actividades didácticas con TIC en aulas de educación secundaria. *Un análisis de las actividades didácticas con TIC en aulas de educación secundaria*, *38*, 187-199.

Atkinson, J. W. (1976). *An introduction to motivation.* Van Nostrand.

Ausubel, D. P. (1968). *Educational psychology: A cognitive view.* Holt, Rinehart and Winston.

Ausubel, D. P., Novak, J. D., & Hanesian, H. (1991). *Psicologia educativa: Un punto de vista cognoscitivo.* Trillas.

Avery, J., Steenburgh, T. J., Deighton, J., & Caravella, M. (2012). Adding bricks to clicks: Predicting the patterns of cross-channel elasticities over time. *Journal of Marketing*, *76*(3), 96–111. doi:10.1509/jm.09.0081

Bakos, J. Y. (1997). Reducing buyer search costs: Implications for electronic marketplaces. *Management Science*, *43*(12), 1676–1692. doi:10.1287/mnsc.43.12.1676

Balaghi, A. A. (2022). *A multichain approach is the future of the blockchain industry*https://cointelegraph.com/news/a-multichain-approach-is-the-future-of-the-blockchain-industry

Ball, M. (2021). *Framework for The Metaverse.* Retrieved from https://www.matthewball.vc/all/forwardtothemetabveseprimer

Ball, M. (n.d.-a). *Framework for the Metaverse.* Available online: https://www.matthewball.vc/all/forwardtothemetaverseprimer

Ball, M. (n.d.-b). *The Metaverse: What It Is, Where to Find It, Who Will Build It, and Fortnite.* Available online: https://www.matthewball.vc/all/themetaverse

Bandura, A. (1986). From thought to action: Mechanisms of personal agency. *The Journal of Psychology*, *15*, 1–17.

Bang, H., & Robins, J. M. (2005). Doubly robust estimation in missing data and causal inference models. *Biometrics, 61*(4), 962–972.

Barré, R., & David, B. (2004, May). Participative and coherent scenario building: An input/output balance model: The case of the French national futuris operation. In *Proceedings of the EUUS Scientific Seminar: New Technology Foresight, Forecasting & Assessment Methods in Seville, Spain* (pp. 3-14). Academic Press.

BBC. (2016). *France Data Authority criticises Windows 10 over privacy.* BBC News. Available at: https://www.bbc.com/news/technology-36854909

Bella, S. (2019, November 4). *Book Review: The Age of Surveillance Capitalism: The Fight for a Human Future at the New Frontier of Power by Shoshana Zuboff | LSE Review of Books.* LSE Review of Books. Available at: https://blogs.lse.ac.uk/lsereviewofbooks/2019/11/04/book-review-the-age-of-surveillancecapitalism-the-fight-for-the-future-at-the-new-frontier-of-power-by-shoshana-zuboff/

Berkhout, F., & Hertin, J. (2002). Foresight futures scenarios: Developing and applying a participative strategic planning tool. *Greener Management International*, *2002*(37), 37–52. doi:10.9774/GLEAF.3062.2002.sp.00005

Bhargava, H. K. (2022). The Creator Economy: Managing Ecosystem Supply, Revenue-Sharing, and Platform Design. *Management Science*. Advance online publication.

Blackburn, J. D., Guide, V. D. R. Jr, Souza, G. C., & Van Wassenhove, L. N. (2004). Reverse supply chains for commercial returns. *California Management Review*, *46*(2), 6–22. doi:10.2307/41166207

Bodoni, S. (2021). *Amazon gets record $888 million EU Fine Over Data violations.* ACEDS. Available at: https://aceds.org/stephanie-bodoni-amazon-gets-record-888-million-eu-fineover-data-violations

Bosworth, A., & Clegg, N. (2021). *Building the Metaverse Responsibly.* Available online: https://about.fb.com/news/2021/09/building-the-metaverse-responsibly/

Brakus, J. J., Schmitt, B. H., & Zarantonello, L. (2009). Brand experience: What is it? How is it measured? Does it affect loyalty? *Journal of Marketing*, *73*(3), 52–68. doi:10.1509/jmkg.73.3.052

Brennan, M., & Macnutt, L. (2006). *Learning Styles and Learning to Program: An Experiment in Adapting Online Resources to Match a Student's Learning Style*. Institute Of Technology Blanchardstown.

Brynjolfsson, E., Hu, Y. J., & Rahman, M. S. (2009). Battle of the retail channels: How product selection and geography drive cross-channel competition. *Management Science*, *55*(11), 1755–1765. doi:10.1287/mnsc.1090.1062

Buffaz, P., Alkhudary, R., & Guibert, N. (2023). *Harnessing the Power of NFTs in the Retail Industry*. HAL.

Buffaz, P., Alkhudary, R., & Guibert, N. (2023). *Harnessing the Power of NFTs in the Retail Industry. Post-Print hal-04164085*. HAL.

Bulearca, M., & Tamarjan, D. (2010). Augmented reality: A sustainable marketing tool. Global business and management research. *International Journal (Toronto, Ont.)*, *2*(2), 237–252.

Burgos, J. (2022). *Alibaba shares jump as Chinese e-commerce giant posts record transactions, Forbes*. Forbes Magazine.

Cachon, G., Gallino, S., & Olivares, M. (2013). *Does adding inventory increase sales? Evidence of a scarcity effect in us automobile dealerships*. Working Paper.

Caro, E. O., & Monroy, M. N. (2008). *Relación de los ambientes hipertextuales de aprendizaje gráfico y sonoro, con los estilos de aprendizaje verbal y visual*. Avances en Sistemas e Informática.

Carpenter, D. (2021). *Digital Marketing, the metaverse, and web 3.0, Digital Marketing Agency based in Seattle, Connection Model*. Available at:https://www.connectionmodel.com/blog/digital-marketing-the-metaverse-and-web-3.0

Carrascal, S., Magro, M., Anguita, J., & Espada, M. (2019). Acquisition of Competences for Sustainable Development through Visual Thinking. A Study in Rural Schools in Mixco, Guatemala. *Sustainability (Basel)*, *11*(8), 1–18. doi:10.3390/su11082317

Chalmers, D. (2003). *The matrix as metaphysics*. Available at:https://www.consc.net/papers/matrix.pdf

Chalmers, D. J. (2022). Reality+: Virtual worlds and the problems of philosophy. Penguin UK.

Chekola, M. G. (1974). *The concept of happiness*. University of Michigan.

Chen, H. S., Liang, C. H., Liao, S. Y., & Kuo, H. Y. (2020). Consumer attitudes and purchase intentions toward food delivery platform services. *Sustainability (Basel)*, *12*(23), 1–18. doi:10.3390/su122310177

Chen, R., Perry, P., Boardman, R., & McCormick, H. (2022). Augmented reality in retail: A systematic review of research foci and future research agenda. *International Journal of Retail & Distribution Management*, *50*(4), 498–518. doi:10.1108/IJRDM-11-2020-0472

Chen, Y., & Cheng, H. (2022). The economics of the metaverse: A comparison with the real economy. *Metaverse*, *3*(1), 19. doi:10.54517/met.v3i1.1802

Ciaravino, C. (2022). *Fashion Brands arrive in the metaverse*. The Cryptonomist. Available at: https://cryptonomist.ch/2022/07/20/fashion-brands-arrive-in-the-metaverse/?amp=1

CNN. (2022). *Meta fast facts*. CNN. Cable News Network. Available at: https://edition.cnn.com/2014/02/11/world/facebook-fast-facts/index.html

Coffield, F. J., Moseley, D. V., Hall, E., & Ecclestone, K. (2004a). *Learning styles and pedagogy in post-16 learning: A systematic and critical review*. Learning and Skills Research Centre.

Coffield, F. J., Moseley, D. V., Hall, E., & Ecclestone, K. (2004b). *Learning styles: What research has to say to practice*. Learning and Skills Research Centre.

Conklin, W. A., & McLeod, A. (2009). Introducing the information technology security essential body of knowledge framework. *Journal of Information Privacy and Security*, *5*(2), 27–41. doi:10.1080/15536548.2009.10855862

Coughlan, A. T., Anderson, E., Stern, L. W., & Ansary, A. I. (2006). *Marketing channels*. Pearson/Prentice Hall.

Cowley, D. (1991). *Understanding brands by ten people who do*. Kogan Page.

Cryptostars. (2022). *The metaverse is coming*. Available at: https://blog.cryptostars.is/themetaverse-is-coming-c0c8de3b5a99

Daimiel, G. B., Eva, C. M. E., & Ormaechea, S. L. (2022). Análisis del uso del advergaming y metaverso en España y México. *Revista Latina de Comunicación Social*, *80*(80), 155–178. doi:10.4185/RLCS-2022-1802

Dave, A. (2020). *Meta partners with Balenciaga, Prada, and Thom Browne and launches Digital Fashion Marketplace, The Block*. The Block.

Davis, K., Christodoulou, J., Seider, S., & Gardner, H. (2011). The theory of multiple intelligences. In R. J. Sternberg & S. B. Kaufman (Eds.), *Cambridge Handbook of Intelligence* (pp. 485–503). Cambridge University Press. doi:10.1017/CBO9780511977244.025

Davis, S., Gerstner, E., & Hagerty, M. (1995). Money back guarantees in retailing: Matching products to consumer tastes. *Journal of Retailing*, *71*(1), 7–22. doi:10.1016/0022-4359(95)90010-1

Deci, E. L., & Ryan, R. M. (1985). *Intrinsic motivation and self-determination in human behavior*. Plenum. doi:10.1007/978-1-4899-2271-7

Decker, K. (2022) *Into the metaverse: How digital twins can change the Business Landscape*. Entrepreneur. Entrepreneur. Available at: https://www.entrepreneur.com/article/425444

Delasay, M., Jain, A., & Kumar, S. (2021). Impacts of the COVID-19 Pandemic on Grocery Retail Operations: An Analytical Model. *Production and Operations Management*, *31*(5), 2237–2255. doi:10.1111/poms.13717 PMID:35601843

Derhamia, Montreuila, & Bau. (2020). *Assessing product availability in omnichannel retail networks in the presence of on-demand inventory transshipment and product substitution?* Academic Press.

Di Pietro, R., & Cresci, S. (2021, December). Metaverse: Security and Privacy Issues. In *2021 Third IEEE International Conference on Trust, Privacy and Security in Intelligent Systems and Applications (TPS-ISA)* (pp. 281-288). IEEE.

Digital Watch Observatory. (n.d.). Available at: https://dig.watch/updates/alibaba-cloud-accusedviolating-chinas-cybersecurity-law

Dohmen, A. E., Merrick, J. R., Saunders, L. W., Stank, T. T. P., & Goldsby, T. J. (2022). When preemptive risk mitigation is insufficient: The effectiveness of continuity and resilience techniques during COVID-19. *Production and Operations Management*. Advance online publication. doi:10.1111/poms.13677

Dolgui, A., & Ivanov, D. (2021). Ripple effect and supply chain disruption management: New trends and research directions. *International Journal of Production Research*, *59*(1), 102–109. doi:10.1080/00207543.2021.1840148

Donath, J. (2007). Signals in social supernets. *Journal of Computer-Mediated Communication*, *13*(1), 231–251. doi:10.1111/j.1083-6101.2007.00394.x

Duan, H., Li, J., Fan, S., Lin, Z., Wu, X., & Cai, W. (2021, October). Metaverse for social good: A university campus prototype. In *Proceedings of the 29th ACM International Conference on Multimedia* (pp. 153-161). 10.1145/3474085.3479238

Dunn, R. (1984). Learning style: State of the science. *Theory into Practice*, *23*(1), 10–19. doi:10.1080/00405848409543084

Dweck, C. S., & Leggett, E. L. (1988). A social cognitive approach to motivation and personality. *Psychological Review*, *95*(2), 256–273. doi:10.1037/0033-295X.95.2.256

Dwivedi, Y. K., Hughes, L., Baabdullah, A. M., Ribeiro-Navarrete, S., Giannakis, M., Al Debei, M. M., Dennehy, D., Metri, B., Buhalis, D., Cheung, C. M. K., Conboy, K., Doyle, R., Dubey, R., Dutot, V., Felix, R., Goyal, D. P., Gustafsson, A., Hinsch, C., Jebabli, I., ... Wamba, S. F. (2022). Metaverse beyond the hype: Multidisciplinary perspectives on emerging challenges, opportunities, and agenda for research, practice and policy. *International Journal of Information Management*, *66*(July), 102542. doi:10.1016/j.ijinfomgt.2022.102542

Elliott, E. S., & Dweck, C. S. (1988). Goals: An approach to motivation and achievement. *Journal of Personality and Social Psychology*, *54*(1), 5–12. doi:10.1037/0022-3514.54.1.5 PMID:3346808

Eppen, G. D. (1979). Noteeffects of centralization on expected costs in a multi-location newsboy problem. *Management Science*, *25*(5), 498–501. doi:10.1287/mnsc.25.5.498

Fahey, L., & Randall, R. M. (Eds.). (1997). *Learning from the future: Competitive foresight scenarios*. John Wiley & Sons.

Felder, R. M., & Silverman, L. K. (1988). Learning and Teaching Styles in Engineering Education. *Engineering Education*, *78*(7), 674–681.

Filipova, I. A. (2023). Creating the Metaverse: Consequences for Economy, Society, and Law. *Journal of Digital Technologies and Law*, *1*(1), 7–32. doi:10.21202/jdtl.2023.1

Fink, C. (2021). Facebook releases Blockbuster app for remote work, Forbes. *Forbes Magazine*. Available at: https://www.forbes.com/sites/charliefink/2021/08/19/facebook-releasesblockbuster-app-for-remote-work/?sh=4346462652fd

Fiore, A. M., Lee, S.-E., & Kunz, G. (2004). Individual Differences, Motivation, and Participation in Designing Apparel on the Internet. *Clothing & Textiles Research Journal*, *22*(1), 32–47.

Florida, R. (2022). *The rise of the creator economy*. Retrieved October 25, 2023, from https://creativeclass.com/reports/The_Rise_of_the_Creator_Economy.pdf

Forman, C., Ghose, A., & Goldfarb, A. (2009). Competition between local and electronic markets: How the benefit of buying online depends on where you live. *Management Science*, *55*(1), 47–57. doi:10.1287/mnsc.1080.0932

Frankenfield, J. (2022). Digital currency types, characteristics, Pros & Cons, future uses. *Investopedia*. Available at: https://www.investopedia.com/terms/d/digitalcurrency.asp

Franzoni, A. L., Assar, S., Defude, B., & Rojas, J. (2008). Student Learning Styles Adaptation Method Based on Teaching Strategies and Electronic Media. *2008 Eighth IEEE International Conference on Advanced Learning Technologies*, 778-782. https://doi.org/10.1109/ICALT.2008.149

Frederico, G. F. (2021). Towards a supply chain 4.0 on the post-COVID-19 pandemic: a conceptual and strategic discussion for more resilient supply chains. *Rajagiri Management Journal*.

Fu, Z. (2022). *Alibaba takes a step further into the metaverse by launching a new shopping venue*. PingWest. Available at: https://en.pingwest.com/a/10257

Gadekallu, T. R., Wang, W., Yenduri, G., Ranaweera, P., Pham, Q. V., da Costa, D. B., & Liyanage, M. (2023). Blockchain for the Metaverse: A review. *Future Generation Computer Systems*, *143*, 401–419. doi:10.1016/j.future.2023.02.008

Gallino, S., & Moreno, A. (2014). Integration of online and offline channels in retail: The impact of sharing reliable inventory availability information. *Management Science*, *60*(6), 1434–1451. doi:10.1287/mnsc.2014.1951

García, F. J., & Doménech, F. (1997). Motivación, aprendizaje y rendimiento escolar. *Revista Electrónica de Motivación y Emoción*, *1*, 1-8. http://reme.uji.es/articulos/pa0001/texto.html

Gardner, H. (2006). *Multiple intelligences: New horizons*. Basic Books.

Gaur, A. (2016). *A Study Impact of Digital India in Make in India Program in IT and BPM Sector.* Presented in the AIMS International Conference at MICA, Ahmadabad.

Gensler, S., Leeflang, P., & Skiera, B. (2012). Impact of online channel use on customer revenues and costs to serve: Considering product portfolios and self-selection. *International Journal of Research in Marketing*, *29*(2), 192–201. doi:10.1016/j.ijresmar.2011.09.004

George, A. H., Fernando, M., George, A. S., Baskar, T., & Pandey, D. (2021). Metaverse: The next stage of human culture and the internet. *International Journal of Advanced Research Trends in Engineering and Technology*, *8*(12), 1–10.

Gerchak, Y., & Mossman, D. (1992). On the effect of demand randomness on inventories and costs. *Operations Research*, *40*(4), 804–807. doi:10.1287/opre.40.4.804

Ghadge, A., Er, M., Ivanov, D., & Chaudhuri, A. (2021). Visualisation of ripple effect in supply chains under long-term, simultaneous disruptions: A system dynamics approach. *International Journal of Production Research*. Advance online publication. doi:10.1080/00207543.2021.1987547

Ghose, A., Smith, M. D., & Telang, R. (2006). Internet exchanges for used books: An empirical analysis of product cannibalization and welfare impact. *Information Systems Research*, *17*(1), 3–19. doi:10.1287/isre.1050.0072

Golf-Papez, M., Heller, J., Hilken, T., Chylinski, M., de Ruyter, K., Keeling, D. I., & Mahr, D. (2022). Embracing falsity through the metaverse: Te case of synthetic customer experiences. *Business Horizons*, *65*(6), 739–749. doi:10.1016/j.bushor.2022.07.007

Golubeva, O. (2021). Firms' performance during the COVID-19 outbreak: international evidence from 13 countries. *Corporate Governance: The International Journal of Business in Society*.

González, Á. L., Navarro, Ó., Sánchez-Verdejo, F. J., & Muelas, Á. (2020). Psychological Well-Being and Intrinsic Motivation: Relationship in Students Who Begin University Studies at the School of Education in Ciudad Real. *Frontiers in Psychology*, *11*(2054), 1–10. doi:10.3389/fpsyg.2020.02054 PMID:33013520

Gross, R., & Acquisti, A. (2005, November). Information revelation and privacy in online social networks. In *Proceedings of the 2005 ACM workshop on Privacy in the electronic society* (pp. 71-80). 10.1145/1102199.1102214

Guan, D., Wang, D., Hallegatte, S., Davis, S. J., Huo, J., Li, S., & Gong, P. (2020). Global supply-chain effects of COVID-19 control measures. *Nature Human Behaviour*, *4*(6), 577–587. doi:10.1038/s41562-020-0896-8 PMID:32493967

Guide, V. D. R. Jr, Souza, G. C., Van Wassenhove, L. N., & Blackburn, J. D. (2006). Time value of commercial product returns. *Management Science*, *52*(8), 1200–1214. doi:10.1287/mnsc.1060.0522

Gursoy, D., Malodia, S., & Dhir, A. (2022). The metaverse in the hospitality and tourism industry: An overview of current trends and future research directions. *Journal of Hospitality Marketing & Management*, *31*(5), 527–534. doi:10.1080/19368623.2022.2072504

Habil, S. G. M., El-Deeb, S., & El-Bassiouny, N. (2023). The metaverse era: leveraging augmented reality in the creation of novel customer experience. Management & Sustainability: An Arab Review. ahead-of-print. doi:10.1108/MSAR-10-2022-0051

Haeckel, S. H., Carbone, L. P., & Berry, L. L. (2003). How to lead the customer experience. *Marketing Management*, *12*(1), 18–18.

Han, D. I. D., Bergs, Y., & Moorhouse, N. (2022). Virtual reality consumer experience escapes: Preparing for the metaverse. *Virtual Reality (Waltham Cross)*, *26*(4), 1443–1458. doi:10.1007/s10055-022-00641-7

Harari, Y. N. (2018). *Why Technology Favors Tyranny, The Atlantic*. Atlantic Media Company. Available at: https://www.theatlantic.com/magazine/archive/2018/10/yuval-noah-hararitechnology-tyranny/568330/

Hawk, T. F., & Shah, A. J. (2007). Using Learning Style Instruments to Enhance Student Learning. *Decision Sciences Journal of Innovative Education*, *5*(1), 1–19. doi:10.1111/j.1540-4609.2007.00125.x

Heath, A. (2021). *Mark Zuckerberg on why Facebook is rebranding to Meta, The Verge*. The Verge. Available at: https://www.theverge.com/22749919/mark-zuckerberg-facebookmeta-company-rebrand

Hecht, A. A., Biehl, E., Barnett, D. J., & Neff, R. A. (2019). Urban food supply chain resilience for crises threatening food security: A qualitative study. *Journal of the Academy of Nutrition and Dietetics*, *119*(2), 211–224. doi:10.1016/j.jand.2018.09.001 PMID:30527912

Hendalianpour, A., Hamzehlou, M., Feylizadeh, M. R., Xie, N., & Shakerizadeh, M. H. (2020). Coordination and competition in two-echelon supply chain using grey revenue-sharing contracts. *Grey Systems: Theory and Application*.

Henning, B., & Vorderer, P. (2001). Psychological escapism: Predicting the amount of television viewing by need for cognition. *Journal of Communication*, *51*(1), 100–120. doi:10.1111/j.1460-2466.2001.tb02874.x

Heo, M., & Toomey, N. (2020). Learning with multimedia: The effects of gender, type of multimedia learning resources, and spatial ability. *Computers & Education*, *146*, 1–12. doi:10.1016/j.compedu.2019.103747

Hernández, A. (2017). Enseñar E/LE a la primera generación de nativos digitales. *Foro de profesores de E/LE*, *13*, 165-176.

Hernandez, O. (2022). W*eb3 watch: Disney and Walmart Target Young Audiences in the metaverse*. Blockworks. Available at: https://blockworks.co/web3-watch-disney-andwalmart-target-young-audiences-in-the-metaverse

Herold, D. M., Nowicka, K., Pluta-Zaremba, A., & Kummer, S. (2021). COVID-19 and the pursuit of supply chain resilience: Reactions and "lessons learned" from logistics service providers (LSPs). *Supply Chain Management*, *26*(6), 702–714. doi:10.1108/SCM-09-2020-0439

Herrman, J., & Browning, K. (2021, Oct. 29). Are we in the metaverse yet? *The New York Times*.

Hillier, F. S., & Lieberman, G. J. (2004). *Introduction to Operations Research*. McGrawHill.

Hirschberg, Rajko, Schumacher, & M. W. (2016). *The changing market for food delivery*. doi:10.1109/FIE.1994.580625

Ho, T. H., Tang, C. S., & Bell, D. R. (1998). Rational shopping behavior and the option value of variable pricing. *Management Science, 44*(12-part-2), S145–S160.

Hoeffler, S., & Keller, K. L. (2002). Building brand equity through corporate societal marketing. *Journal of Public Policy & Marketing*, *21*(1), 78–89. doi:10.1509/jppm.21.1.78.17600

Holbrook, M. B., & Hirschman, E. C. (1982). The experiential aspects of consumption: Consumer fantasies, feelings, and fun. *The Journal of Consumer Research*, *9*(2), 132–140. doi:10.1086/208906

Hollensen, S., Kotler, P., & Opresnik, M. O. (2022). Metaverse—The new marketing universe. *The Journal of Business Strategy*.

Hootsuite Inc. (2020). *More than half of the people on Earth now use social media*. Available at: https://www.hootsuite.com/newsroom/press-releases/more-than-half-of-the-people-onearth-now-use-social-media

Horta, P. M., Matos, J. D. P., & Mendes, L. L. (2022). Food promoted on an online food delivery platform in a Brazilian metropolis during the coronavirus disease (COVID-19) pandemic: A longitudinal analysis. *Public Health Nutrition*, *25*(5), 1336–1345. doi:10.1017/S1368980022000489 PMID:35232512

Hotjar. (2023). *The impact of Artificial intelligence on 5 industries*. Retrieved from https://www.hotjar.com/blog/ai-impact-industries-1/

IBEF. (2018). *E-commerce industry in India*. Retrieved from https://www.ibef.org/industry/ecommerce.aspx

Ivanov, D. (2020). Predicting the impacts of epidemic outbreaks on global supply chains: A simulation-based analysis on the coronavirus outbreak (COVID-19/SARS-CoV-2) case. *Transportation Research Part E, Logistics and Transportation Review*, *136*, 101922. doi:10.1016/j.tre.2020.101922 PMID:32288597

Ivanov, D. (2021). Supply chain viability and the COVID-19 pandemic: A conceptual and formal generalisation of four major adaptation strategies. *International Journal of Production Research*, *59*(12), 3535–3552. doi:10.1080/00207543.2021.1890852

Ivanov, D., & Dolgui, A. (2020). Viability of intertwined supply networks: Extending the supply chain resilience angles towards survivability. A position paper motivated by COVID-19 outbreak. *International Journal of Production Research*, *58*(10), 2904–2915. doi:10.1080/00207543.2020.1750727

Ivanov, D., & Dolgui, A. (2021). OR-methods for coping with the ripple effect in supply chains during COVID-19 pandemic: Managerial insights and research implications. *International Journal of Production Economics*, *232*, 107921. doi:10.1016/j.ijpe.2020.107921 PMID:32952301

Jain, P. (2017). Role of Digital India Movement in a Country. *A Journal of Advances in Management IT & Social Sciences*, *7*(7), 13–17.

Jaloza, L. B. (2022). *Connect 2021: Our vision for the metaverse.* Tech at Meta. Available at:https://tech.fb.com/ar-vr/2021/10/connect-2021-our-vision-for-the-metaverse/

Jhawar, A., Kumar, P., & Varshney, S. (2023). *The emergence of virtual influencers: A shift in the influencer marketing paradigm.* Young Consumers Insight and Ideas for Responsible Marketers.

Johnson, B. (2010). Privacy no longer a social norm, says Facebook founder. *The Guardian.* https://www.theguardian.com/technology/2010/jan/11/facebook-privacy

Johnson, A., Smith, B., & Lee, C. (2021). Exploring the Metaverse: Implications for Retail Engagement. *Journal of Virtual Commerce*, *15*(3), 112–129.

Johnson, M. (2020). Who Hoards? The Personality of Stockpiling Behavior. *Psychology Today.*

Johnson, N. E., Short, J. C., Chandler, J., & Jordan, S. M. (2022). Introducing the contentpreneur: Making the case for research on content creation-based online platforms. *Journal of Business Venturing Insights*, *18*(6), e00328. doi:10.1016/j.jbvi.2022.e00328

Jordannovet. (2022). *Mark Zuckerberg envisions a billion people in the metaverse spending hundreds of dollars each, CNBC.* CNBC. Available at: https://www.cnbc.com/2022/06/22/mark-zuckerberg-envisions-1-billion-people-in-themetaverse.html

Jumrisko, M. (2020). *Singapore Grocery Chain Starts Limiting How Much People Can Buy.* Bloomberg.

Kamenov, K. (2021). *Immersive Experience—The 4th Wave in Tech: Learning the Ropes*. Retrieved from https://www.accenture.com/gb-en/blogs/blogs-immersive-experience-wave-learning-ropes

Kaplan, E. H. (2020). OM Forum—COVID-19 scratch models to support local decisions. *Manufacturing & Service Operations Management*, *22*(4), 645–655. doi:10.1287/msom.2020.0891

Kapser, S., Abdelrahman, M., & Bernecker, T. (2021). Autonomous delivery vehicles to fight the spread of Covid-19–How do men and women differ in their acceptance? *Transportation Research Part A, Policy and Practice*, *148*, 183–198. doi:10.1016/j.tra.2021.02.020 PMID:33776251

Karim, S., Sandu, N., & Kayastha, M. (2021). The challenges and opportunities of adopting artificial intelligence (AI) in Jordan's healthcare transformation. *Global Journal of Information Technology*, *11*(2), 35–46. doi:10.18844/gjit.v11i2.6546

Kastrenakes, J., & Heath, A. (2021). *Facebook is spending at least $10 billion this year on its metaverse division, The Verge*. The Verge. Available at: https://www.theverge.com/2021/10/25/22745381/facebook-reality-labs-10-billionmetaverse

Katsaliaki, P. G., & Kumar, S. (2022). Supply chain disruptions and resilience: A major review and future research agenda. *Annals of Operations Research*, *319*(1), pages965–1002. doi:10.1007/s10479-020-03912-1 PMID:33437110

Keeble, M., Adams, J., & Burgoine, T. (2022). Investigating experiences of frequent online food delivery service use: A qualitative study in UK adults. *BMC Public Health*, *22*(1), 1–14. doi:10.1186/s12889-022-13721-9 PMID:35842625

Keeble, M., Adams, J., Sacks, G., Vanderlee, L., White, C. M., Hammond, D., & Burgoine, T. (2020). Use of online food delivery services to order food prepared away-from-home and associated sociodemographic characteristics: A cross-sectional, multi-country analysis. *International Journal of Environmental Research and Public Health*, *17*(14), 1–17. doi:10.3390/ijerph17145190 PMID:32709148

Keller, K. L. (1993). Conceptualizing, measuring and managing customer-based brand equity. *Journal of Marketing*, *57*(1), 1–22. doi:10.1177/002224299305700101

Keller, K. L. (1998). *Strategic brand management building, measuring, and managing brand equity*. Prentice Hall.

Keller, K. L. (2003). *Strategic brand management: Building, measuring and managing brand equity* (4th ed.). Prentice-Hall.

Kelly, N. M. (2018). "Works like Magic": Metaphor, Meaning, and the GUI in Snow Crash. *Science Fiction Studies*, *45*(1), 69–90. doi:10.5621/sciefictstud.45.1.0069

Kelly, S. M. (2021). *Facebook changes its company name to Meta | CNN business*. CNN.

Khan, I., & Rahman, Z. (2015). A review and future directions of brand experience research. *International Strategic Management Review*, *3*(1–2), 1–14. doi:10.1016/j.ism.2015.09.003

Kian, T. S., & Yusoff, W. F. W. (2015). Intrinsic-Extrinsic motivation revisited: Exploring their definitions. *International Journal of Management Sciences*, *6*(3), 136–140.

Koerber, T., & Schiele, H. (2021). Is COVID-19 a turning point in stopping global sourcing? Differentiating between declining continental and increasing transcontinental sourcing. *Journal of Global Operations and Strategic Sourcing*. doi:10.1108/JGOSS-02-2021-0018

Kosow, H., & Gaßner, R. (2008). *Methods of future and scenario analysis: overview, assessment, and selection criteria* (Vol. 39). DEU.

Kosow, H., & Gassner, R. (2008). *Methods of future and scenario analysis: Overview, assessment, and selection criteria*. Deutsches Institut für Entwicklungspolitik.

Kramer, S. (2022). Council post: Metaverse privacy concerns: Are we thinking about our data? *Forbes Magazine*. Available at: https://www.forbes.com/sites/forbestechcouncil/2022/06/01/metaverse-privacy-concerns are- we-thinking-about-our-data/

Kronblad, C., & Pregmark, J. E. (2021). Responding to the COVID-19 crisis: the rapid turn toward digital business models. *Journal of Science and Technology Policy Management*. doi:10.1108/JSTPM-10-2020-0155

Kshetri, N. (2021). Blockchain-enabled metaverse: Challenges, solutions, and future directions. *Journal of Business Research*, *135*, 492–499.

Kumar, S., Xu, C., Ghildayal, N., Chandra, C., & Yang, M. (2021). Social media effectiveness as a humanitarian response to mitigate influenza epidemic and COVID-19 pandemic. *Annals of Operations Research*. Advance online publication. doi:10.1007/s10479-021-03955-y PMID:33531729

Laidler, J. (2019). *Harvard professor says surveillance capitalism is undermining democracy*. Academic Press.

Lee, H. L., Padmanabhan, V., & Whang, S. (1997). Information distortion in a supply chain: The bullwhip effect. *Management Science*, *43*(4), 546–558. doi:10.1287/mnsc.43.4.546

Lee, Y., & Wang, L. (2018). Metaverse Retail: Customization and Customer Experience. *International Journal of Retail & Distribution Management*, *46*(6), 618–635.

Li, C., Mirosa, M., & Bremer, P. (2020). Review of online food delivery platforms and their impacts on sustainability. *Sustainability (Basel)*, *12*(14), 1–17. doi:10.3390/su12145528

Li, D., & Dong, C. (2021). Government regulations to mitigate the shortage of life-saving goods in the face of a pandemic. *European Journal of Operational Research*, *301*(3), 942–955. doi:10.1016/j.ejor.2021.11.042

Lik-Hang, L. E. E., Braud, T., Zhou, P., Wang, L., Xu, D., Lin, Z., & Hui, P. (2021). *All one needs to know about metaverse: a complete survey on technological singularity, virtual ecosystem, and research agenda*. IEEE.

Liu, K., Liu, C., Xiang, X., & Tian, Z. (2021). Testing facility location and dynamic capacity planning for pandemics with demand uncertainty. *European Journal of Operational Research*, *304*(1), 150–168. doi:10.1016/j.ejor.2021.11.028 PMID:34848916

Liu, Y., Wang, D. D., & Xu, Q. (2020). A supply chain coordination mechanism with suppliers' effort performance level and fairness concern. *Journal of Retailing and Consumer Services*, *53*, 101950. doi:10.1016/j.jretconser.2019.101950

Li, Y., Wang, X., Gong, T., & Wang, H. (2022). Breaking out of the pandemic: How can firms match internal competence with external resources to shape operational resilience? *Journal of Operations Management*. Advance online publication. doi:10.1002/joom.1176

Lord, J. (2022). *Franklin Templeton Launches Metaverse ETF in Europe*. Available at: https://www.etfstrategy.com/franklin-templeton-launches-metaverse-etf-in-europe-10339/

Lorentz, H., Laari, S., Meehan, J., Eßig, M., & Henke, M. (2021). An attention-based view of supply disruption risk management: Balancing biased attention processing for improved resilience in the COVID-19 context. *International Journal of Operations & Production Management*, *41*(13), 152–177. doi:10.1108/IJOPM-06-2021-0381

Manuj, I., & Mentzer, J. T. (2008). Global supply chain risk management strategies. *International Journal of Physical Distribution & Logistics Management, 38*(3), 192–223. doi:10.1108/09600030810866986

Maslow, A. H. (1954). *Motivation and personality*. Harper & Row Publishers Inc.

Matarazzo, M., & Diamantopoulos, A. (2022). Applying reactance theory to study consumer responses to COVID restrictions: A note on model specification. *International Marketing Review*. Advance online publication. doi:10.1108/IMR-12-2021-0370

Mäyrä, F. (2020). The metaverse and imaginary worlds. In T. Arnab, I. Dunwell, & S. Debattista (Eds.), *Serious games and edutainment applications* (pp. 11–30). Springer.

McAuley, E., Duncan, T., & Tammen, V. V. (1987). Psychometric properties of the Intrinsic Motivation Inventory in a competitive sport setting: A confirmatory factor analysis. *Research Quarterly for Exercise and Sport, 60*(1), 48–58. doi:10.1080/02701367.1989.10607413 PMID:2489825

McClelland, D. C. (1958). Methods of measuring human motivation. In J. W. Atkinson (Ed.), *Motives in fantasy, action, and society* (pp. 7–42). D. Van Nostrand Company Inc.

McInerney, D. M., Marsh, H. W., & Yeung, A. S. (2003). Toward a hierarchical goal theory model of school motivation. *Journal of Applied Measurement, 4*, 335–357. PMID:14523254

McKinsey & Company. (2022). *Value creation in the metaverse*. https:// www. mckinsey.com/business-functions/growth-marketing-and-sales/ our-insights/ value-creation-in-the-metaverse

McKinsey & Company. (2022). *Value creation in the metaverse.* McKinsey & Company. Available at: https://www.mckinsey.com/capabilities/growth-marketing-and sales/ourinsights/value-creation-in-the-metaverse

Meggsauer. (2022). *Jeff Bezos keeps a 16-year-old framed magazine as a 'reminder' that Amazon's most profitable service was once just a 'risky bet', CNBC*. CNBC. Available at: https://www.cnbc.com/2022/05/20/why-jeff-bezos-keeps-a-reminder-that-aws-was-oncejust-a-risky-bet.html

Mehrolia & Alagarsamy Subburaj. (2020). Customers response to online food delivery services during COVID-19 outbreak. *Int J Consumer Studies.*

Metry Habil, S. G., El-Deeb, S., & El-Bassiouny, N. (2023). The Metaverse Era: Leveraging Augmented Reality in the Creation of Novel Customer Experience. *Management & Sustainability: An Arab Review.*

Metters, R. (1997). Quantifying the bullwhip effect in supply chains. *Journal of Operations Management*, *15*(2), 89–100. doi:10.1016/S0272-6963(96)00098-8

Microsoft Center. (2022). *Microsoft to acquire Activision Blizzard to bring the joy and community of gaming to everyone, across every device, Stories.* Available at: https://news.microsoft.com/2022/01/18/microsoft-to-acquire-activision-blizzard-to-bringthe-joy-and-community-of-gaming-to-everyone-across-every-device

Mietzner, D., & Reger, G. (2005). Advantages and disadvantages of scenario approaches for strategic foresight. *International Journal Technology Intelligence and Planning*, *1*(2), 220–239. doi:10.1504/IJTIP.2005.006516

Mileva, G. (2022). *Understanding the metaverse through real-world examples.* Influencer Marketing Hub. Available at: https://influencermarketinghub.com/metaverse-examples/

Mittal, V., & Kamakura, W. A. (2001). Satisfaction, repurchase intent, and repurchase behavior: Investigating the moderating effect of customer characteristics. *JMR, Journal of Marketing Research*, *38*(1), 131–142. doi:10.1509/jmkr.38.1.131.18832

Mohanta, G., Debasish, S. S., & Nanda, S. K. (2017). A Study on Growth and Prospect of Digital India Campaign. *Saudi Journal of Business and Management Studies*, *2*(7), 727–731.

More, J. S., & Lingam, C. (2017). A SI model for social media influencer maximization. *Applied Computing and Informatics,* 1-7. https://doi.org/doi:10.1016/j.aci.2017.11.001

Morgado, L. (2008). Interconnecting virtual worlds. *Journal of Virtual Worlds Research*, 1.

Moro Visconti, R. (2022) From physical reality to the internet and the metaverse: A Multilayer Network valuation. SSRN *Electronic Journal*, 101–133. doi:10.2139/ssrn.4054674

Mouratidis, K., & Peters, S. (2022). COVID-19 impact on tele activities: Role of built environment and implications for mobility. *Transportation Research Part A, Policy and Practice*, *158*, 251–270. doi:10.1016/j.tra.2022.03.007 PMID:35291720

Mower, J. M., & Pedersen, E. L. (2018). Manufacturer, retailer and consumer misbehavior in the United States during the Second World War. Fashion. *Fashion, Style & Popular Culture*, *5*(1), 41–57. doi:10.1386/fspc.5.1.41_1

MSFT. (2021). *Introducing Microsoft Mesh: Here can be anywhere*. Available at: https://www.microsoft.com/en-us/mesh

Muangmee, C., Kot, S., Meekaewkunchorn, N., Kassakorn, N., & Khalid, B. (2021). Factors determining the behavioral intention of using food delivery apps during covid-19 pandemics. *Journal of Theoretical and Applied Electronic Commerce Research*, *16*(5), 1297–1310. doi:10.3390/jtaer16050073

Murphy, H. (2022). Facebook owner Meta Targets Finance with 'Zuck Bucks' and creator coins, subscribe to read. *Financial Times*. Available at: https://www.ft.com/content/50fbe9ba-32c8-4caf-a34e-234031019371

Mystakidis, S. (2022). *Metaverse. Encyclopedia*. Academic Press.

Nadini, M., Alessandretti, L., Di Giacinto, F., Martino, M., Aiello, L. M., & Baronchelli, A. (2021). Mapping the NFT revolution: Market trends, trade networks, and visual features. *Scientific Reports*, *11*(1), 20902. doi:10.1038/s41598-021-00053-8 PMID:34686678

Nagurney, A. (2021a). Optimization of supply chain networks with inclusion of labor: Applications to COVID-19 pandemic disruptions. *International Journal of Production Economics*, *235*, 108080. doi:10.1016/j.ijpe.2021.108080 PMID:36570047

Nagurney, A. (2021b). Supply chain game theory network modeling under labor constraints: Applications to the Covid-19 pandemic. *European Journal of Operational Research*, *293*(3), 880–891. doi:10.1016/j.ejor.2020.12.054 PMID:33519049

Needle, D. (2022). *The metaverse explained: Everything you need to know, WhatIs.com*. TechTarget. Available at: https://www.techtarget.com/whatis/feature/The-metaverseexplained-Everything-you-need-to-know

Neilson, R. E., & Wagner, C. J. (2000). Strategic scenario planning at CA International. *Knowledge Management Review*, *12*, 4–21.

News Network. (n.d.). Available at: https://www.cnn.com/2021/10/28/tech/facebook-markzuckerberg-keynote-announcements/index.html

Nikolicic, S., Kilibarda, M., Maslaric, M., Mircetic, D., & Bojic, S. (2021). Reducing Food Waste in the Retail Supply Chains by Improving Efficiency of Logistics Operations. *Sustainability (Basel)*, *13*(12), 6511. doi:10.3390/su13126511

Ning, H., Wang, H., Lin, Y., Wang, W., Dhelim, S., Farha, F., & Daneshmand, M. (2021). *A Survey on Metaverse: The State-of-the-art, Technologies, Applications, and Challenges*. arXiv:2111.09673.

Novak, T. (2012). Quality of virtual life. Transformative consumer research for personal and collective well-being. *Revista Fronteiras*, 225–246.

O'Flaherty, K. (2022). *The Data Game: What Amazon knows about you and how to stop it, The Guardian.* Guardian News and Media. Available at: https://www.theguardian.com/technology/2022/feb/27/the-data-game-what-amazonknows-about-you-and-how-to-stop-it

Osemeke, M., & Adegboyega, S. (2017). Critical Review and Comparison between Maslow, Herzberg and McClelland's Theory of Needs. *FUNAI Journal of Accounting*, *1*(1), 161–173.

Ovezmyradov. (2022). *Product availability and stockpiling in times of pandemic: causes of supply chain disruptions and preventive measures in retailing*. doi:10.1007/s10479-022-05091-7

Ovezmyradov, B., & Kurata, H. (2019). Effects of customer response to fashion product stockout on holding costs, order sizes, and profitability in omnichannel retailing. *International Transactions in Operational Research*, *26*(1), 200–222. doi:10.1111/itor.12511

Palau-Saumell, R., Matute, J., Derqui, B., & Meyer, J. H. (2021). The impact of the perceived risk of COVID-19 on consumers' attitude and behavior toward locally produced food. *British Food Journal*, *123*(13), 281–301. doi:10.1108/BFJ-04-2021-0380

Pamucar, D., Deveci, M., Gokasar, I., Tavana, M., & Köppen, M. (2022). A metaverse assessment model for sustainable transportation using ordinal priority approach and Aczel-Alsina norms. *Technological Forecasting and Social Change*, *182*, 121778. doi:10.1016/j.techfore.2022.121778

Pandaily. (2022). *Taobao to launch metaverse shopping for 618 E-commerce festival.* Pandaily. Available at: https://pandaily.com/taobao-to-launch-metaverse-shopping-for-618-ecommerce-festival/

Parton, S. (2018). *The rise of dataism: A threat to freedom or a scientific revolution?* Singularity Hub. Available at: https://singularityhub.com/2018/09/30/the-rise-of-dataism-a-threat-tofreedom-or-a-scientific-revolution/

Passetti, E. E., Battaglia, M., Bianchi, L., & Annesi, N. (2021). Coping with the COVID-19 pandemic: The technical, moral and facilitating role of management control. *Accounting, Auditing & Accountability Journal*, *34*(6), 1430–1444. doi:10.1108/AAAJ-08-2020-4839

Penco, L., Ciacci, A., Benevolo, C., & Torre, T. (2021). Open social innovation for surplus food recovery and aid during COVID-19 crisis: The case of Fondazione Banco Alimentare Onlus. *British Food Journal*. Advance online publication. doi:10.1108/BFJ-02-2021-0116

Peres, R., Schreier, M., Schweidel, D., & Sorescu, A. (2023). On ChatGPT and beyond: How generative artificial intelligence may affect research, teaching, and practice. *International Journal of Research in Marketing*, *40*(2), 269–275.

Periyasami, S., & Periyasamy, A. P. (2022). Metaverse as Future Promising Platform Business Model: Case Study on Fashion Value Chain. *Businesses*, *2*(4), 527–545. doi:10.3390/businesses2040033

Peters, J. (2022). *Meta is reportedly making 'zuck bucks', The Verge*. The Verge. Available at: https://www.theverge.com/2022/4/6/23013896/meta-facebook-zuck-bucks-financefinancial-services-products

Pietro, D. R. (2022). *The metaverse: Technology, privacy and security risks, and the road ahead, The Metaverse: Technology, Privacy and Security Risks*. Available at: https://www.hbku.edu.qa/en/news/CSE-AI-MTPSR

Pine, B. J., & Gilmore, J. H. (1999). *The experience economy*. Harvard Business Press.

Pine, J. B. II, & Gilmore, J. H. (1998). Welcome to the experience economy. *Harvard Business Review*, *76*(4), 97–105. PMID:10181589

Pitta, D. A., & Franzak, F. J. (2008). Foundations for building share of heart in global brands. *Journal of Product and Brand Management*, *17*(2), 64–72. doi:10.1108/10610420810864676

Pladson, K. (2021). *In 2021, Big Tech may have finally gotten too big – DW – 12/28/2021*. Deutsche Welle. Available at: https://www.dw.com/en/in-2021-big-tech-may-have-finallygotten-too-big/a-60211242

Poell, T., Nieborg, D. B., & Duffy, B. E. (2022). Spaces of negotiation: Analyzing platform power in the news industry. *Digital Journalism (Abingdon, England)*, *0*(0), 1–19. doi:10.1080/21670811.2022.2103011

Pournader, M., Kach, A., & Talluri, S. (2020). A review of the existing and emerging topics in the supply chain risk management literature. *Decision Sciences*, *51*(4), 867–919. doi:10.1111/deci.12470 PMID:34234385

Purdy, M. (2022). How the metaverse could change work. *Harvard Business Review*. Available at: https://hbr.org/2022/04/how-the-metaverse-could-change-work

Puri, Agarwal, Kumar, Thandayuthapani, & Baja. (2023). *Analyzing the Retail Supply Chain Attributes for Improving Product Availability to Satisfy Customer Needs & Reducing Expenses*. Academic Press.

PYMNTS. (2022). *Meta opens its metaverse platform to payments, Meta Opens Its Metaverse Platform to Payments*. PYMNTS.com. Available at: https://www.pymnts.com/metaverse/2022/meta-opens-its-metaverse-platform to payments -and-it-doesnt-come-cheap/

Queiroz, M. M., Wamba, S. F., Jabbour, C. J. C., & Machado, M. C. (2022). Supply chain resilience in the UK during the coronavirus pandemic: A resource orchestration perspective. *International Journal of Production Economics*, *245*, 108405. doi:10.1016/j.ijpe.2021.108405 PMID:35002082

Raassens, N., Haans, H., & Mullick, S. (2021). Surviving the hectic early phase of the COVID-19 pandemic: A qualitative study to the supply chain strategies of food service firms in times of a crisis. *International Journal of Logistics Management*. Advance online publication. doi:10.1108/IJLM-01-2021-0013

Raj, A., Mukherjee, A. A., de Sousa Jabbour, A. B. L., & Srivastava, S. K. (2022, March). Supply chain management during and post-COVID-19 pandemic: Mitigation strategies and practical lessons learned. *Journal of Business Research*, *142*, 1125–1139. doi:10.1016/j.jbusres.2022.01.037 PMID:35079190

Ramirez, R., Mukherjee, M., Vezzoli, S., & Kramer, A. M. (2015). Scenarios as a scholarly methodology to produce “interesting research”. *Futures*, *71*, 70–87. doi:10.1016/j.futures.2015.06.006

Ratan, R., & Meshi, D. (2022). The metaverse is money and crypto is king – why you’ll be on a blockchain when you’re virtual-world hopping. *The Conversation*. Available at: https://theconversation.com/the-metaverse-is-money-and-crypto-is-king-why-youll-be on a-blockchain-when-youre-virtual-world-hopping-171659

Remko, V. H. (2020). Research opportunities for a more resilient post-COVID-19 supply chain–closing the gap between research findings and industry practice. *International Journal of Operations & Production Management*, *40*(4), 341–355. doi:10.1108/IJOPM-03-2020-0165

Repko, M. (2021). *Costco brings back purchase limits on toilet paper, cleaning supplies and More*. CNBC.

Rey, J. (2020). *Amazon is banning the sale of N95 and surgical masks to the general public*. Vox.

Rieder, B., Borra, E., Coromina, Ò., & Matamoros-Fernández, A. (2023). Making a Living in the Creator Economy: A Large-Scale Study of Linking on YouTube. *Social Media + Society*, *9*(2). Advance online publication. doi:10.1177/20563051231180628

Rodrigue, J. P. (2016). *The Geography of Transport Systems*. Taylor & Francis. doi:10.4324/9781315618159

Rozhkov, M., Ivanov, D., Blackhurst, J., & Nair, A. (2022). Adapting supply chain operations in anticipation of and during the COVID-19 pandemic. *Omega*, *110*, 102635. doi:10.1016/j.omega.2022.102635 PMID:35291412

Rustagi, P., & Prakash, A. (2022). Review on Consumer'S Attitude & Purchase Behavioral Intention Towards Green Food Products. *International Journal of Health Sciences*, *6*(May), 9257–9273. doi:10.53730/ijhs.v6nS1.7092

Rust, R. T., Zeithaml, V. A., & Lemon, K. N. (2000). *Driving customer equity: How customer lifetime value is reshaping corporate strategy*. Free Press.

Ryan, R. M., & Deci, E. L. (2000). Self-determination theory and the facilitation of intrinsic motivation, social development, and well-being. *The American Psychologist*, *55*(1), 68–78. doi:10.1037/0003-066X.55.1.68 PMID:11392867

Ryufath Soepeno. (2021). *Metaverse A Potential Threat to Humanity and Ethics. GCOM1304: Final-term essay*. Sampoerna University.

Sahay, S., Mahajan, N., Malik, S., & Kaur, J. (2022, August). Metaverse: Research based analysis and impact on economy and business. In *2022 2nd Asian Conference on Innovation in Technology (ASIANCON)* (pp. 1-8). IEEE.

Salaverria, L. (2020). Manufacturers, retailers seek lifting of purchase limits. *Philippine Daily Inquirer*.

Salvietti, G., Ziliani, C., Teller, C., Ieva, M., & Ranfagni, S. (2022). Omnichannel retailing and post-pandemic recovery: Building a research agenda. *International Journal of Retail & Distribution Management*, *50*(8/9), 1156–1181. doi:10.1108/IJRDM-10-2021-0485

Sanci, E., Daskin, M. S., Hong, Y. C., Roesch, S., & Zhang, D. (2021). Mitigation strategies against supply disruption risk: A case study at the Ford Motor Company. *International Journal of Production Research*. Advance online publication. doi:10.1080/00207543.2021.1975058

Sands, S., Campbell, C. L., Plangger, K., & Ferraro, C. (2022). Unreal influence: Leveraging AI in influencer marketing. *European Journal of Marketing*, *56*(6), 1721–1747. doi:10.1108/EJM-12-2019-0949

Sansone, C., & Harackiewicz, J. M. (2000). *Intrinsic and extrinsic motivation: The search for optimal motivation and performance*. Academic Press.

Satish, K., Venkatesh, A., & Manivannan, A. S. R. (2021). Covid-19 is driving fear and greed in consumer behaviour and purchase pattern. *South Asian Journal of Marketing*, *2*(2), 113–129. doi:10.1108/SAJM-03-2021-0028

Schlegelmilch, B. B., Sharma, K., & Garg, S. (2022). Employing machine learning for capturing COVID-19 consumer sentiments from six countries: A methodological illustration. *International Marketing Review*. Advance online publication. doi:10.1108/IMR-06-2021-0194

Schleper, M. C., Gold, S., Trautrims, A., & Baldock, D. (2021). Pandemic-induced knowledge gaps in operations and supply chain management: COVID-19's impacts on retailing. *International Journal of Operations & Production Management*, *41*(3), 193–205. doi:10.1108/IJOPM-12-2020-0837

Schmitt, A. J., Sun, S. A., Snyder, L. V., & Shen, Z. J. M. (2015). Centralization versus decentralization: Risk pooling, risk diversification, and supply chain disruptions. *Omega*, *52*, 201–212. doi:10.1016/j.omega.2014.06.002

Sekhar, C., Patwardhan, M., & Singh, R. K. (2013). A literature review on motivation. *Glob Bus Perspect*, *1*(4), 471–487. doi:10.1007/s40196-013-0028-1

Shankar, V. (2022). How bezos and Amazon changed the world. *The Conversation*. Available at: https://theconversation.com/how-bezos-and-amazon-changed-the-world-154546

Shanker, S. (2020). Digital India empowered by artificial intelligence. *An International Bilingual Peer Reviewed Refereed Research Journal*, *7*(26), 149–154.

Sharma, G. D., Yadav, A., & Chopra, R. (2020). Artificial intelligence and effective governance: A review, critique and research agenda. *Sustainable Futures : An Applied Journal of Technology, Environment and Society*, *2*(2), 100–104. doi:10.1016/j.sftr.2019.100004

Shen, B., Tan, W., Guo, J., Zhao, L., & Qin, P. (2021). How to Promote User Purchase in Metaverse? A Systematic Literature Review on Consumer Behavior Research and Virtual Commerce Application Design. *Applied Sciences (Basel, Switzerland)*, *11*(23), 11087. doi:10.3390/app112311087

Shen, Z. M., & Sun, Y. (2021). Strengthening supply chain resilience during COVID-19: A case study of JD. com. *Journal of Operations Management*. Advance online publication. doi:10.1002/joom.1161

Shih, W. (2022). From Just-In-Time to Just-In-Case: Is Excess and Obsolete Next? *Forbes*.

Shin, D. H. (2010). The effects of trust, security and privacy in social networking: A security-based approach to understand the pattern of adoption. *Interacting with Computers*, *22*(5), 428–438. doi:10.1016/j.intcom.2010.05.001

Shou, B., Xiong, H., & Shen, X. M. (2013). *Consumer panic buying and quota policy under supply disruptions.* Working paper. Hong Kong: City University of Hong Kong.

Siebert, B. (2020). *Coronavirus hoarder tries to return $10,000 worth of goods to Adelaide supermarket.* ABC Radio.

Singh, J. P., Dwivedi, Y. K., Rana, N. P., Kumar, A., & Kapoor, K. K. (2019). Event classification and location prediction from tweets during disasters. *Annals of Operations Research*, *283*(1), 737–757. doi:10.1007/s10479-017-2522-3

Singh, S., Kumar, R., Panchal, R., & Tiwari, M. K. (2021). Impact of COVID-19 on logistics systems and disruptions in food supply chain. *International Journal of Production Research*, *59*(7), 1993–2008. doi:10.1080/00207543.2020.1792000

Smith, R., & Brown, A. (2021). Metaverse Adoption in Retail: Understanding Customer Acceptance. *Journal of Retail Technology*, *17*(4), 321–335.

Smith, S., & Milligan, A. (2002). *Uncommon practice: People who deliver a great brand experience*. Pearson Education.

Srivastava, S. K. (2018). Artificial Intelligence: Way forward for India. *Journal of Information Systems and Technology Management*, *15*, 1–23. doi:10.4301/S1807-1775201815004

Stephenson, N. (1992). *Snow Crash.* Random House Worlds.

Stephenson, N. (2003). *Snow Crash: A Novel.* Random House Publishing Group.

Stiff, R., Johnson, K., & Tourk, K. A. (1975). *Scarcity and hoarding: economic and social explanations and marketing implications.* ACR North American Advances.

Stokel-Walker, C. (2021). Why has Facebook changed its name to Meta and what is the metaverse? *New Scientist*. Available at: https://www.newscientist.com/article/2295438-why-has-facebook-changed-its-name-to-meta-and-what-is-the-metaverse/

Sucky, E. (2009). The bullwhip effect in supply chains—An overestimated problem? *International Journal of Production Economics*, *118*(1), 311–322. doi:10.1016/j.ijpe.2008.08.035

Surendhranatha Reddy, C., & Aradhya, D. G. B. (2020). Driving Forces for the Success of Food Ordering and Delivery Apps: A Descriptive Study. *International Journal of Engineering and Management Research*, *10*(02), 131–134. doi:10.31033/ijemr.10.2.15

Surwade, A. U. (2020). Phishing e-mail is an increasing menace. *International Journal of Information Technology : an Official Journal of Bharati Vidyapeeth's Institute of Computer Applications and Management*, *12*(2), 611–617. doi:10.1007/s41870-019-00407-6

Su, X., & Zhang, F. (2008). Strategic customer behavior, commitment, and supply chain performance. *Management Science*, *54*(10), 1759–1773. doi:10.1287/mnsc.1080.0886

Swalehin, M. (2021). Digital Divide and digital Inclusive policies in India: A sociological study. *International Journal of Trend in Scientific Research and Development*, *2*(1), 232–238.

Swinney, R. (2011). Selling to strategic consumers when product value is uncertain: The value of matching supply and demand. *Management Science*, *57*(10), 1737–1751. doi:10.1287/mnsc.1110.1360

Szymkowiak, A., Melović, B., Dabić, M., Jeganathan, K., & Kundi, G. S. (2021). Information technology and Gen Z: The role of teachers, the internet, and technology in the education of young people. *Technology in Society*, *65*, 1–10. doi:10.1016/j.techsoc.2021.101565

Tafesse, W., & Dayan, M. (2023). Content creators' participation in the creator economy: Examining the effect of creators' content sharing frequency on user engagement behavior on digital platforms. *Journal of Retailing and Consumer Services*, *73*(C).

Tahseen, I. (2011). *Facebook's setting changes confuse users: Study.* Available at: https://www.indiansinkuwait.com/news/Facebook-s-setting-changes-confuseusers-Study

Tai, M. C. (2020). The Impact of Artificial Intelligence on Human Society and Bioethics. *Tzu-Chi Medical Journal*, *32*(4), 339. doi:10.4103/tcmj.tcmj_71_20 PMID:33163378

Talaviya, T., Shah, D. N., Patel, N., Yagnik, H., & Shah, M. (2020). Implementation of artificial intelligence in agriculture for optimisation of irrigation and application of pesticides and herbicides. *Artificial Intelligence in Agriculture, 4*, 58–73. doi:10.1016/j.aiia.2020.04.002

Tandon, A., Kaur, P., Bhatt, Y., Mäntymäki, M., & Dhir, A. (2021). Why do people purchase from food delivery apps? A consumer value perspective. *Journal of Retailing and Consumer Services, 63*(September). doi:10.1016/j.jretconser.2021.102667

Taylor, D., Pritchard, A., Duhan, D., & Mishra, S. (2020). What's behind the empty grocery shelves? *Supply Chain Management Review*, 1–4.

Terazono, E., & Evans, J. (2020). How coronavirus is affecting pasta's complex supply chain. *Financial Times.*

Thomas, L. (2020). *Coronavirus wreaks havoc on retail supply chains globally, even as China's factories come back online*. CNBC.

Thornhill, J. (2022). Reality+ - looking forward to life in the metaverse, subscribe to read, Financial Times. *Financial Times*. Available at: https://www.ft.com/content/e9d4875c06ab-44bc-8d93-4655b80b88b8

Tolk, A., Harper, A., & Mustafee, N. (2021). Hybrid models as transdisciplinary research enablers. *European Journal of Operational Research, 291*(3), 1075–1090. doi:10.1016/j.ejor.2020.10.010 PMID:33078041

Tong, X., & Hawley, J. M. (2009). Measuring customer-based brand equity: Empirical evidence from the sportswear market in China. *Journal of Product and Brand Management, 18*(4), 262–271. doi:10.1108/10610420910972783

Tsao, Y. C., Raj, P., & Raj, P. V. (2019). Product substitution with customer segmentation under panic buying behavior. *Scientia Iranica*. Advance online publication. doi:10.24200/sci.2019.5099.1093

Tsiligianni, C., Tsiligiannis, A., & Tsiliyannis, C. (2022). A stochastic inventory model of COVID-19 and robust, real-time identification of carriers at large and infection rate via asymptotic laws. *European Journal of Operational Research, 304*(1), 42–56. doi:10.1016/j.ejor.2021.12.037 PMID:35035055

Tussyadiah, I., & Park, S. (2018). Consumer Evaluation of Hotel Service Robots' Attributes: The Role of Perceived Risk and Emotional Responses. *International Journal of Hospitality Management, 72*, 47–58.

Tyko, K. (2022). Grocery stores still have empty shelves amid supply chain disruptions,omicron and winter storms. *USA Today.*

Van Oorschot, K. E., Van Wassenhove, L. N., & Jahre, M. (2022). Collaboration–competition dilemma in flattening the COVID-19 curve. *Production and Operations Management*. Advance online publication. doi:10.1111/poms.13709 PMID:35601840

Van Rijmenam, M. (2022). *Step into the metaverse: How the immersive internet will unlock a trillion-dollar social economy*. John Wiley & Sons.

Vázquez, Á., & Manassero, M. A. (2000). Análisis empírico de dos escalas de motivación escolar. *Revista Electrónica de Motivación y Emoción*, *3*, 5–6.

Verma, M. (2018). Artificial intelligence and its scope in different areas with special reference to the field of education. *International Journal of Advanced Educational Research*, *3*(1), 5–10.

Vidal-Tomás, D. (2023). The illusion of the metaverse and meta-economy. *International Review of Financial Analysis*, *86*, 102560. doi:10.1016/j.irfa.2023.102560

Vosinakis, S., & Xenakis, I. (2011). *A Virtual World Installation in an Art Exhibition: Providing a Shared Interaction Space for Local and Remote Visitors*. Academic Press.

Vosinakis, S., & Xenakis, I. (2011). *A Virtual World Installation in an Art Exhibition: Providing a Shared Interaction Space for Local and Remote Visitors. In Step into the metaverse: How the immersive internet will unlock a trillion-dollar social economy*. John Wiley & Sons.

Walker, J., Brewster, C., Fontinha, R., Haak-Saheem, W., Benigni, S., Lamperti, F., & Ribaudo, D. (2022). The unintended consequences of the pandemic on non-pandemic research activities. *Research Policy*, *51*(1), 104369. doi:10.1016/j.respol.2021.104369 PMID:34565926

WEF. (2020). *Read Yuval Harari's blistering warning to Davos in full*. World Economic Forum. Available at: https://www.weforum.org/agenda/2020/01/yuval-hararis-warning-davosspeech-future-predications/

Wenzel, K. R., & Wigfield, A. (Eds.). (2009). *Handbook of motivation at school*. Routledge. doi:10.4324/9780203879498

Williams, M., & Chen, L. (2022). Navigating Virtual Retail: A Study of Consumer Behavior in the Metaverse. *International Journal of Consumer Studies*, *46*(2), 210–225.

Wilson, K. B., Karg, A., & Ghaderi, H. (2022). Prospecting non-fungible tokens in the digital economy: Stakeholders and ecosystem, risk and opportunity. *Business Horizons*, *65*(5), 657–670. doi:10.1016/j.bushor.2021.10.007

Wright, G., Cairns, G., & Bradfield, R. (2013). Scenario methodology: New developments in theory and practice: Introduction to the Special Issue. *Technological Forecasting and Social Change*, *80*(4), 561–565. doi:10.1016/j.techfore.2012.11.011

Yadav, S. (2021). Digital India Programme: An Overview. *International Journal of Creative Research Thoughts*, *9*(2), 15–20.

Yang, B., Yang, S., Lv, Z., Wang, F., & Olofsson, T. (2022). Application of Digital Twins and Meta- verse in the Field of Fluid Machinery Pumps and Fans: A Review. *Sensors (Basel)*, *22*(23), 9294.

Yang, H., & Schrage, L. (2009). Conditions that cause risk pooling to increase inventory. *European Journal of Operational Research*, *192*(3), 837–851. doi:10.1016/j.ejor.2007.10.064

Yang, J., Xie, H., Yu, G., & Liu, M. (2021). Antecedents and consequences of supply chain risk management capabilities: An investigation in the post-coronavirus crisis. *International Journal of Production Research*, *59*(5), 1573–1585. doi:10.1080/00207543.2020.1856958

Ye, F., Liu, K., Li, L., Lai, K. H., Zhan, Y., & Kumar, A. (2022). Digital supply chain management in the COVID-19 crisis: An asset orchestration perspective. *International Journal of Production Economics*, *245*, 108396. doi:10.1016/j.ijpe.2021.108396 PMID:34931109

Yimu, J., & Shangdong, L. (2020). *Threats from botnets*. Computer Security Threats. [Preprint], doi:10.5772/intechopen.88927

Yuan, Y., & Yang, Y. (2022). Embracing the Metaverse: Mechanism and logic of a new digital economy. *Metaverse*, *3*(2), 15. doi:10.54517/m.v3i2.1814

Zarantonello, L., & Schmitt, B. H. (2013). The impact of event marketing on brand equity: The mediating roles of brand experience and brand attitude. *International Journal of Advertising*, *32*(2), 255–280. doi:10.2501/IJA-32-2-255-280

Zhao, Y., Jiang, J., Chen, Y., Liu, R., Yang, Y., Xue, X., & Chen, S. (2022). Metaverse: Perspectives from graphics, interactions and visualization. *Visual Informatics*, *6*(1), 56–67. Advance online publication. doi:10.1016/j.visinf.2022.03.002

Ziady, H. (2020). *Panic buying is forcing supermarkets to ration food and other supplies*. CNN Business.

Zuboff, S. (2015). Big other: Surveillance capitalism and the prospects of an information civilization. *Journal of Information Technology*, *30*(1), 75–89. doi:10.1057/jit.2015.5

Zuboff, S. (2019, January). Surveillance capitalism and the challenge of collective action. *New Labor Forum*, *28*(1), 10–29. doi:10.1177/1095796018819461

Zuboff, S. (2020). *The age of surveillance capitalism: The fight for a human future at the New Frontier of Power*. Public Affairs.

Related References

To continue our tradition of advancing information science and technology research, we have compiled a list of recommended IGI Global readings. These references will provide additional information and guidance to further enrich your knowledge and assist you with your own research and future publications.

Abdul Razak, R., & Mansor, N. A. (2021). Instagram Influencers in Social Media-Induced Tourism: Rethinking Tourist Trust Towards Tourism Destination. In M. Dinis, L. Bonixe, S. Lamy, & Z. Breda (Eds.), *Impact of New Media in Tourism* (pp. 135-144). IGI Global. https://doi.org/10.4018/978-1-7998-7095-1.ch009

Abir, T., & Khan, M. Y. (2022). Importance of ICT Advancement and Culture of Adaptation in the Tourism and Hospitality Industry for Developing Countries. In C. Ramos, S. Quinteiro, & A. Gonçalves (Eds.), *ICT as Innovator Between Tourism and Culture* (pp. 30–41). IGI Global. https://doi.org/10.4018/978-1-7998-8165-0.ch003

Abtahi, M. S., Behboudi, L., & Hasanabad, H. M. (2017). Factors Affecting Internet Advertising Adoption in Ad Agencies. *International Journal of Innovation in the Digital Economy*, *8*(4), 18–29. doi:10.4018/IJIDE.2017100102

Afenyo-Agbe, E., & Mensah, I. (2022). Principles, Benefits, and Barriers to Community-Based Tourism: Implications for Management. In I. Mensah & E. Afenyo-Agbe (Eds.), *Prospects and Challenges of Community-Based Tourism and Changing Demographics* (pp. 1–29). IGI Global. doi:10.4018/978-1-7998-7335-8.ch001

Agbo, V. M. (2022). Distributive Justice Issues in Community-Based Tourism. In I. Mensah & E. Afenyo-Agbe (Eds.), *Prospects and Challenges of Community-Based Tourism and Changing Demographics* (pp. 107–129). IGI Global. https://doi.org/10.4018/978-1-7998-7335-8.ch005

Agrawal, S. (2017). The Impact of Emerging Technologies and Social Media on Different Business(es): Marketing and Management. In O. Rishi & A. Sharma (Eds.), *Maximizing Business Performance and Efficiency Through Intelligent Systems* (pp. 37–49). Hershey, PA: IGI Global. doi:10.4018/978-1-5225-2234-8.ch002

Ahmad, A., & Johari, S. (2022). Georgetown as a Gastronomy Tourism Destination: Visitor Awareness Towards Revisit Intention of Nasi Kandar Restaurant. In M. Valeri (Ed.), *New Governance and Management in Touristic Destinations* (pp. 71–83). IGI Global. https://doi.org/10.4018/978-1-6684-3889-3.ch005

Alkhatib, G., & Bayouq, S. T. (2021). A TAM-Based Model of Technological Factors Affecting Use of E-Tourism. *International Journal of Tourism and Hospitality Management in the Digital Age*, *5*(2), 50–67. https://doi.org/10.4018/IJTHMDA.20210701.oa1

Altinay Ozdemir, M. (2021). Virtual Reality (VR) and Augmented Reality (AR) Technologies for Accessibility and Marketing in the Tourism Industry. In C. Eusébio, L. Teixeira, & M. Carneiro (Eds.), *ICT Tools and Applications for Accessible Tourism* (pp. 277-301). IGI Global. https://doi.org/10.4018/978-1-7998-6428-8.ch013

Anantharaman, R. N., Rajeswari, K. S., Angusamy, A., & Kuppusamy, J. (2017). Role of Self-Efficacy and Collective Efficacy as Moderators of Occupational Stress Among Software Development Professionals. *International Journal of Human Capital and Information Technology Professionals*, *8*(2), 45–58. doi:10.4018/IJHCITP.2017040103

Aninze, F., El-Gohary, H., & Hussain, J. (2018). The Role of Microfinance to Empower Women: The Case of Developing Countries. *International Journal of Customer Relationship Marketing and Management*, *9*(1), 54–78. doi:10.4018/IJCRMM.2018010104

Antosova, G., Sabogal-Salamanca, M., & Krizova, E. (2021). Human Capital in Tourism: A Practical Model of Endogenous and Exogenous Territorial Tourism Planning in Bahía Solano, Colombia. In V. Costa, A. Moura, & M. Mira (Eds.), *Handbook of Research on Human Capital and People Management in the Tourism Industry* (pp. 282–302). IGI Global. https://doi.org/10.4018/978-1-7998-4318-4.ch014

Arsenijević, O. M., Orčić, D., & Kastratović, E. (2017). Development of an Optimization Tool for Intangibles in SMEs: A Case Study from Serbia with a Pilot Research in the Prestige by Milka Company. In M. Vemić (Ed.), *Optimal Management Strategies in Small and Medium Enterprises* (pp. 320–347). Hershey, PA: IGI Global. doi:10.4018/978-1-5225-1949-2.ch015

Aryanto, V. D., Wismantoro, Y., & Widyatmoko, K. (2018). Implementing Eco-Innovation by Utilizing the Internet to Enhance Firm's Marketing Performance: Study of Green Batik Small and Medium Enterprises in Indonesia. *International Journal of E-Business Research, 14*(1), 21–36. doi:10.4018/IJEBR.2018010102

Asero, V., & Billi, S. (2022). New Perspective of Networking in the DMO Model. In M. Valeri (Ed.), *New Governance and Management in Touristic Destinations* (pp. 105–118). IGI Global. https://doi.org/10.4018/978-1-6684-3889-3.ch007

Atiku, S. O., & Fields, Z. (2017). Multicultural Orientations for 21st Century Global Leadership. In N. Baporikar (Ed.), *Management Education for Global Leadership* (pp. 28–51). Hershey, PA: IGI Global. doi:10.4018/978-1-5225-1013-0.ch002

Atiku, S. O., & Fields, Z. (2018). Organisational Learning Dimensions and Talent Retention Strategies for the Service Industries. In N. Baporikar (Ed.), *Global Practices in Knowledge Management for Societal and Organizational Development* (pp. 358–381). Hershey, PA: IGI Global. doi:10.4018/978-1-5225-3009-1.ch017

Atsa'am, D. D., & Kuset Bodur, E. (2021). Pattern Mining on How Organizational Tenure Affects the Psychological Capital of Employees Within the Hospitality and Tourism Industry: Linking Employees' Organizational Tenure With PsyCap. *International Journal of Tourism and Hospitality Management in the Digital Age, 5*(2), 17–28. https://doi.org/10.4018/IJTHMDA.2021070102

Ávila, L., & Teixeira, L. (2018). The Main Concepts Behind the Dematerialization of Business Processes. In M. Khosrow-Pour, D.B.A. (Ed.), Encyclopedia of Information Science and Technology, Fourth Edition (pp. 888-898). Hershey, PA: IGI Global. https://doi.org/ doi:10.4018/978-1-5225-2255-3.ch076

Ayorekire, J., Mugizi, F., Obua, J., & Ampaire, G. (2022). Community-Based Tourism and Local People's Perceptions Towards Conservation: The Case of Queen Elizabeth Conservation Area, Uganda. In I. Mensah & E. Afenyo-Agbe (Eds.), *Prospects and Challenges of Community-Based Tourism and Changing Demographics* (pp. 56–82). IGI Global. https://doi.org/10.4018/978-1-7998-7335-8.ch003

Baleiro, R. (2022). Tourist Literature and the Architecture of Travel in Olga Tokarczuk and Patti Smith. In R. Baleiro & R. Pereira (Eds.), *Global Perspectives on Literary Tourism and Film-Induced Tourism* (pp. 202-216). IGI Global. https://doi.org/10.4018/978-1-7998-8262-6.ch011

Barat, S. (2021). Looking at the Future of Medical Tourism in Asia. *International Journal of Tourism and Hospitality Management in the Digital Age, 5*(1), 19–33. https://doi.org/10.4018/IJTHMDA.2021010102

Barbosa, C. A., Magalhães, M., & Nunes, M. R. (2021). Travel Instagramability: A Way of Choosing a Destination? In M. Dinis, L. Bonixe, S. Lamy, & Z. Breda (Eds.), *Impact of New Media in Tourism* (pp. 173-190). IGI Global. https://doi.org/10.4018/978-1-7998-7095-1.ch011

Bari, M. W., & Khan, Q. (2021). Pakistan as a Destination of Religious Tourism. In E. Alaverdov & M. Bari (Eds.), *Global Development of Religious Tourism* (pp. 1-10). IGI Global. https://doi.org/10.4018/978-1-7998-5792-1.ch001

Bartens, Y., Chunpir, H. I., Schulte, F., & Voß, S. (2017). Business/IT Alignment in Two-Sided Markets: A COBIT 5 Analysis for Media Streaming Business Models. In S. De Haes & W. Van Grembergen (Eds.), *Strategic IT Governance and Alignment in Business Settings* (pp. 82–111). Hershey, PA: IGI Global. doi:10.4018/978-1-5225-0861-8.ch004

Bashayreh, A. M. (2018). Organizational Culture and Organizational Performance. In W. Lee & F. Sabetzadeh (Eds.), *Contemporary Knowledge and Systems Science* (pp. 50–69). Hershey, PA: IGI Global. doi:10.4018/978-1-5225-5655-8.ch003

Bechthold, L., Lude, M., & Prügl, R. (2021). Crisis Favors the Prepared Firm: How Organizational Ambidexterity Relates to Perceptions of Organizational Resilience. In A. Zehrer, G. Glowka, K. Schwaiger, & V. Ranacher-Lackner (Eds.), *Resiliency Models and Addressing Future Risks for Family Firms in the Tourism Industry* (pp. 178–205). IGI Global. https://doi.org/10.4018/978-1-7998-7352-5.ch008

Bedford, D. A. (2018). Sustainable Knowledge Management Strategies: Aligning Business Capabilities and Knowledge Management Goals. In N. Baporikar (Ed.), *Global Practices in Knowledge Management for Societal and Organizational Development* (pp. 46–73). Hershey, PA: IGI Global. doi:10.4018/978-1-5225-3009-1.ch003

Bekjanov, D., & Matyusupov, B. (2021). Influence of Innovative Processes in the Competitiveness of Tourist Destination. In J. Soares (Ed.), *Innovation and Entrepreneurial Opportunities in Community Tourism* (pp. 243–263). IGI Global. https://doi.org/10.4018/978-1-7998-4855-4.ch014

Bharwani, S., & Musunuri, D. (2018). Reflection as a Process From Theory to Practice. In M. Khosrow-Pour, D.B.A. (Ed.), Encyclopedia of Information Science and Technology, Fourth Edition (pp. 1529-1539). Hershey, PA: IGI Global. doi:10.4018/978-1-5225-2255-3.ch132

Bhatt, G. D., Wang, Z., & Rodger, J. A. (2017). Information Systems Capabilities and Their Effects on Competitive Advantages: A Study of Chinese Companies. *Information Resources Management Journal*, *30*(3), 41–57. doi:10.4018/IRMJ.2017070103

Bhushan, M., & Yadav, A. (2017). Concept of Cloud Computing in ESB. In R. Bhadoria, N. Chaudhari, G. Tomar, & S. Singh (Eds.), *Exploring Enterprise Service Bus in the Service-Oriented Architecture Paradigm* (pp. 116–127). Hershey, PA: IGI Global. doi:10.4018/978-1-5225-2157-0.ch008

Bhushan, S. (2017). System Dynamics Base-Model of Humanitarian Supply Chain (HSCM) in Disaster Prone Eco-Communities of India: A Discussion on Simulation and Scenario Results. *International Journal of System Dynamics Applications*, *6*(3), 20–37. doi:10.4018/IJSDA.2017070102

Binder, D., & Miller, J. W. (2021). A Generations' Perspective on Employer Branding in Tourism. In V. Costa, A. Moura, & M. Mira (Eds.), *Handbook of Research on Human Capital and People Management in the Tourism Industry* (pp. 152–174). IGI Global. https://doi.org/10.4018/978-1-7998-4318-4.ch008

Birch Freeman, A. A., Mensah, I., & Antwi, K. B. (2022). Smiling vs. Frowning Faces: Community Participation for Sustainable Tourism in Ghanaian Communities. In I. Mensah & E. Afenyo-Agbe (Eds.), *Prospects and Challenges of Community-Based Tourism and Changing Demographics* (pp. 83–106). IGI Global. https://doi.org/10.4018/978-1-7998-7335-8.ch004

Biswas, A., & De, A. K. (2017). On Development of a Fuzzy Stochastic Programming Model with Its Application to Business Management. In S. Trivedi, S. Dey, A. Kumar, & T. Panda (Eds.), *Handbook of Research on Advanced Data Mining Techniques and Applications for Business Intelligence* (pp. 353–378). Hershey, PA: IGI Global. doi:10.4018/978-1-5225-2031-3.ch021

Boragnio, A., & Faracce Macia, C. (2021). "Taking Care of Yourself at Home": Use of E-Commerce About Food and Care During the COVID-19 Pandemic in the City of Buenos Aires. In M. Korstanje (Ed.), *Socio-Economic Effects and Recovery Efforts for the Rental Industry: Post-COVID-19 Strategies* (pp. 45–71). IGI Global. https://doi.org/10.4018/978-1-7998-7287-0.ch003

Borges, V. D. (2021). Happiness: The Basis for Public Policy in Tourism. In A. Perinotto, V. Mayer, & J. Soares (Eds.), *Rebuilding and Restructuring the Tourism Industry: Infusion of Happiness and Quality of Life* (pp. 1–25). IGI Global. https://doi.org/10.4018/978-1-7998-7239-9.ch001

Bücker, J., & Ernste, K. (2018). Use of Brand Heroes in Strategic Reputation Management: The Case of Bacardi, Adidas, and Daimler. In A. Erdemir (Ed.), *Reputation Management Techniques in Public Relations* (pp. 126–150). Hershey, PA: IGI Global. doi:10.4018/978-1-5225-3619-2.ch007

Buluk Eşitti, B. (2021). COVID-19 and Alternative Tourism: New Destinations and New Tourism Products. In M. Demir, A. Dalgıç, & F. Ergen (Eds.), *Handbook of Research on the Impacts and Implications of COVID-19 on the Tourism Industry* (pp. 786–805). IGI Global. https://doi.org/10.4018/978-1-7998-8231-2.ch038

Bureš, V. (2018). Industry 4.0 From the Systems Engineering Perspective: Alternative Holistic Framework Development. In R. Brunet-Thornton & F. Martinez (Eds.), *Analyzing the Impacts of Industry 4.0 in Modern Business Environments* (pp. 199–223). Hershey, PA: IGI Global. doi:10.4018/978-1-5225-3468-6.ch011

Buzady, Z. (2017). Resolving the Magic Cube of Effective Case Teaching: Benchmarking Case Teaching Practices in Emerging Markets – Insights from the Central European University Business School, Hungary. In D. Latusek (Ed.), *Case Studies as a Teaching Tool in Management Education* (pp. 79–103). Hershey, PA: IGI Global. doi:10.4018/978-1-5225-0770-3.ch005

Camillo, A. (2021). *Legal Matters, Risk Management, and Risk Prevention: From Forming a Business to Legal Representation*. IGI Global. doi:10.4018/978-1-7998-4342-9.ch004

Căpusneanu, S., & Topor, D. I. (2018). Business Ethics and Cost Management in SMEs: Theories of Business Ethics and Cost Management Ethos. In I. Oncioiu (Ed.), *Ethics and Decision-Making for Sustainable Business Practices* (pp. 109–127). Hershey, PA: IGI Global. doi:10.4018/978-1-5225-3773-1.ch007

Chan, R. L., Mo, P. L., & Moon, K. K. (2018). Strategic and Tactical Measures in Managing Enterprise Risks: A Study of the Textile and Apparel Industry. In K. Strang, M. Korstanje, & N. Vajjhala (Eds.), *Research, Practices, and Innovations in Global Risk and Contingency Management* (pp. 1–19). Hershey, PA: IGI Global. doi:10.4018/978-1-5225-4754-9.ch001

Charlier, S. D., Burke-Smalley, L. A., & Fisher, S. L. (2018). Undergraduate Programs in the U.S: A Contextual and Content-Based Analysis. In J. Mendy (Ed.), *Teaching Human Resources and Organizational Behavior at the College Level* (pp. 26–57). Hershey, PA: IGI Global. doi:10.4018/978-1-5225-2820-3.ch002

Chumillas, J., Güell, M., & Quer, P. (2022). The Use of ICT in Tourist and Educational Literary Routes: The Role of the Guide. In C. Ramos, S. Quinteiro, & A. Gonçalves (Eds.), *ICT as Innovator Between Tourism and Culture* (pp. 15–29). IGI Global. https://doi.org/10.4018/978-1-7998-8165-0.ch002

Dahlberg, T., Kivijärvi, H., & Saarinen, T. (2017). IT Investment Consistency and Other Factors Influencing the Success of IT Performance. In S. De Haes & W. Van Grembergen (Eds.), *Strategic IT Governance and Alignment in Business Settings* (pp. 176–208). Hershey, PA: IGI Global. doi:10.4018/978-1-5225-0861-8.ch007

Damnjanović, A. M. (2017). Knowledge Management Optimization through IT and E-Business Utilization: A Qualitative Study on Serbian SMEs. In M. Vemić (Ed.), *Optimal Management Strategies in Small and Medium Enterprises* (pp. 249–267). Hershey, PA: IGI Global. doi:10.4018/978-1-5225-1949-2.ch012

Daneshpour, H. (2017). Integrating Sustainable Development into Project Portfolio Management through Application of Open Innovation. In M. Vemić (Ed.), *Optimal Management Strategies in Small and Medium Enterprises* (pp. 370–387). Hershey, PA: IGI Global. doi:10.4018/978-1-5225-1949-2.ch017

Daniel, A. D., & Reis de Castro, V. (2018). Entrepreneurship Education: How to Measure the Impact on Nascent Entrepreneurs. In A. Carrizo Moreira, J. Guilherme Leitão Dantas, & F. Manuel Valente (Eds.), *Nascent Entrepreneurship and Successful New Venture Creation* (pp. 85–110). Hershey, PA: IGI Global. doi:10.4018/978-1-5225-2936-1.ch004

David, R., Swami, B. N., & Tangirala, S. (2018). Ethics Impact on Knowledge Management in Organizational Development: A Case Study. In N. Baporikar (Ed.), *Global Practices in Knowledge Management for Societal and Organizational Development* (pp. 19–45). Hershey, PA: IGI Global. doi:10.4018/978-1-5225-3009-1.ch002

De Uña-Álvarez, E., & Villarino-Pérez, M. (2022). Fostering Ecocultural Resources, Identity, and Tourism in Inland Territories (Galicia, NW Spain). In G. Fernandes (Ed.), *Challenges and New Opportunities for Tourism in Inland Territories: Ecocultural Resources and Sustainable Initiatives* (pp. 1-16). IGI Global. https://doi.org/10.4018/978-1-7998-7339-6.ch001

Delias, P., & Lakiotaki, K. (2018). Discovering Process Horizontal Boundaries to Facilitate Process Comprehension. *International Journal of Operations Research and Information Systems*, *9*(2), 1–31. doi:10.4018/IJORIS.2018040101

Denholm, J., & Lee-Davies, L. (2018). Success Factors for Games in Business and Project Management. In *Enhancing Education and Training Initiatives Through Serious Games* (pp. 34–68). Hershey, PA: IGI Global. doi:10.4018/978-1-5225-3689-5.ch002

Deshpande, M. (2017). Best Practices in Management Institutions for Global Leadership: Policy Aspects. In N. Baporikar (Ed.), *Management Education for Global Leadership* (pp. 1–27). Hershey, PA: IGI Global. doi:10.4018/978-1-5225-1013-0.ch001

Deshpande, M. (2018). Policy Perspectives for SMEs Knowledge Management. In N. Baporikar (Ed.), *Knowledge Integration Strategies for Entrepreneurship and Sustainability* (pp. 23–46). Hershey, PA: IGI Global. doi:10.4018/978-1-5225-5115-7.ch002

Dezdar, S. (2017). ERP Implementation Projects in Asian Countries: A Comparative Study on Iran and China. *International Journal of Information Technology Project Management, 8*(3), 52–68. doi:10.4018/IJITPM.2017070104

Domingos, D., Respício, A., & Martinho, R. (2017). Reliability of IoT-Aware BPMN Healthcare Processes. In C. Reis & M. Maximiano (Eds.), *Internet of Things and Advanced Application in Healthcare* (pp. 214–248). Hershey, PA: IGI Global. doi:10.4018/978-1-5225-1820-4.ch008

Dosumu, O., Hussain, J., & El-Gohary, H. (2017). An Exploratory Study of the Impact of Government Policies on the Development of Small and Medium Enterprises in Developing Countries: The Case of Nigeria. *International Journal of Customer Relationship Marketing and Management, 8*(4), 51–62. doi:10.4018/IJCRMM.2017100104

Durst, S., Bruns, G., & Edvardsson, I. R. (2017). Retaining Knowledge in Smaller Building and Construction Firms. *International Journal of Knowledge and Systems Science, 8*(3), 1–12. doi:10.4018/IJKSS.2017070101

Edvardsson, I. R., & Durst, S. (2017). Outsourcing, Knowledge, and Learning: A Critical Review. *International Journal of Knowledge-Based Organizations, 7*(2), 13–26. doi:10.4018/IJKBO.2017040102

Edwards, J. S. (2018). Integrating Knowledge Management and Business Processes. In M. Khosrow-Pour, D.B.A. (Ed.), Encyclopedia of Information Science and Technology, Fourth Edition (pp. 5046-5055). Hershey, PA: IGI Global. doi:10.4018/978-1-5225-2255-3.ch437

Eichelberger, S., & Peters, M. (2021). Family Firm Management in Turbulent Times: Opportunities for Responsible Tourism. In A. Zehrer, G. Glowka, K. Schwaiger, & V. Ranacher-Lackner (Eds.), *Resiliency Models and Addressing Future Risks for Family Firms in the Tourism Industry* (pp. 103–124). IGI Global. https://doi.org/10.4018/978-1-7998-7352-5.ch005

Eide, D., Hjalager, A., & Hansen, M. (2022). Innovative Certifications in Adventure Tourism: Attributes and Diffusion. In R. Augusto Costa, F. Brandão, Z. Breda, & C. Costa (Eds.), *Planning and Managing the Experience Economy in Tourism* (pp. 161-175). IGI Global. https://doi.org/10.4018/978-1-7998-8775-1.ch009

Ejiogu, A. O. (2018). Economics of Farm Management. In *Agricultural Finance and Opportunities for Investment and Expansion* (pp. 56–72). Hershey, PA: IGI Global. doi:10.4018/978-1-5225-3059-6.ch003

Ekanem, I., & Abiade, G. E. (2018). Factors Influencing the Use of E-Commerce by Small Enterprises in Nigeria. *International Journal of ICT Research in Africa and the Middle East, 7*(1), 37–53. doi:10.4018/IJICTRAME.2018010103

Ekanem, I., & Alrossais, L. A. (2017). Succession Challenges Facing Family Businesses in Saudi Arabia. In P. Zgheib (Ed.), *Entrepreneurship and Business Innovation in the Middle East* (pp. 122–146). Hershey, PA: IGI Global. doi:10.4018/978-1-5225-2066-5.ch007

El Faquih, L., & Fredj, M. (2017). Ontology-Based Framework for Quality in Configurable Process Models. *Journal of Electronic Commerce in Organizations, 15*(2), 48–60. doi:10.4018/JECO.2017040104

Faisal, M. N., & Talib, F. (2017). Building Ambidextrous Supply Chains in SMEs: How to Tackle the Barriers? *International Journal of Information Systems and Supply Chain Management, 10*(4), 80–100. doi:10.4018/IJISSCM.2017100105

Fernandes, T. M., Gomes, J., & Romão, M. (2017). Investments in E-Government: A Benefit Management Case Study. *International Journal of Electronic Government Research, 13*(3), 1–17. doi:10.4018/IJEGR.2017070101

Figueira, L. M., Honrado, G. R., & Dionísio, M. S. (2021). Human Capital Management in the Tourism Industry in Portugal. In V. Costa, A. Moura, & M. Mira (Eds.), *Handbook of Research on Human Capital and People Management in the Tourism Industry* (pp. 1–19). IGI Global. doi:10.4018/978-1-7998-4318-4.ch001

Gao, S. S., Oreal, S., & Zhang, J. (2018). Contemporary Financial Risk Management Perceptions and Practices of Small-Sized Chinese Businesses. In I. Management Association (Ed.), Global Business Expansion: Concepts, Methodologies, Tools, and Applications (pp. 917-931). Hershey, PA: IGI Global. doi:10.4018/978-1-5225-5481-3.ch041

Garg, R., & Berning, S. C. (2017). Indigenous Chinese Management Philosophies: Key Concepts and Relevance for Modern Chinese Firms. In B. Christiansen & G. Koc (Eds.), *Transcontinental Strategies for Industrial Development and Economic Growth* (pp. 43–57). Hershey, PA: IGI Global. doi:10.4018/978-1-5225-2160-0.ch003

Gencer, Y. G. (2017). Supply Chain Management in Retailing Business. In U. Akkucuk (Ed.), *Ethics and Sustainability in Global Supply Chain Management* (pp. 197–210). Hershey, PA: IGI Global. doi:10.4018/978-1-5225-2036-8.ch011

Gera, R., Arora, S., & Malik, S. (2021). Emotional Labor in the Tourism Industry: Strategies, Antecedents, and Outcomes. In V. Costa, A. Moura, & M. Mira (Eds.), *Handbook of Research on Human Capital and People Management in the Tourism Industry* (pp. 73–91). IGI Global. https://doi.org/10.4018/978-1-7998-4318-4.ch004

Giacosa, E. (2018). The Increasing of the Regional Development Thanks to the Luxury Business Innovation. In L. Carvalho (Ed.), *Handbook of Research on Entrepreneurial Ecosystems and Social Dynamics in a Globalized World* (pp. 260–273). Hershey, PA: IGI Global. doi:10.4018/978-1-5225-3525-6.ch011

Glowka, G., Tusch, M., & Zehrer, A. (2021). The Risk Perception of Family Business Owner-Manager in the Tourism Industry: A Qualitative Comparison of the Intra-Firm Senior and Junior Generation. In A. Zehrer, G. Glowka, K. Schwaiger, & V. Ranacher-Lackner (Eds.), *Resiliency Models and Addressing Future Risks for Family Firms in the Tourism Industry* (pp. 126–153). IGI Global. https://doi.org/10.4018/978-1-7998-7352-5.ch006

Glykas, M., & George, J. (2017). Quality and Process Management Systems in the UAE Maritime Industry. *International Journal of Productivity Management and Assessment Technologies*, *5*(1), 20–39. doi:10.4018/IJPMAT.2017010102

Glykas, M., Valiris, G., Kokkinaki, A., & Koutsoukou, Z. (2018). Banking Business Process Management Implementation. *International Journal of Productivity Management and Assessment Technologies*, *6*(1), 50–69. doi:10.4018/IJPMAT.2018010104

Gomes, J., & Romão, M. (2017). The Balanced Scorecard: Keeping Updated and Aligned with Today's Business Trends. *International Journal of Productivity Management and Assessment Technologies*, *5*(2), 1–15. doi:10.4018/IJPMAT.2017070101

Gomes, J., & Romão, M. (2017). Aligning Information Systems and Technology with Benefit Management and Balanced Scorecard. In S. De Haes & W. Van Grembergen (Eds.), *Strategic IT Governance and Alignment in Business Settings* (pp. 112–131). Hershey, PA: IGI Global. doi:10.4018/978-1-5225-0861-8.ch005

Goyal, A. (2021). Communicating and Building Destination Brands With New Media. In M. Dinis, L. Bonixe, S. Lamy, & Z. Breda (Eds.), *Impact of New Media in Tourism* (pp. 1-20). IGI Global. https://doi.org/10.4018/978-1-7998-7095-1.ch001

Grefen, P., & Turetken, O. (2017). Advanced Business Process Management in Networked E-Business Scenarios. *International Journal of E-Business Research, 13*(4), 70–104. doi:10.4018/IJEBR.2017100105

Guasca, M., Van Broeck, A. M., & Vanneste, D. (2021). Tourism and the Social Reintegration of Colombian Ex-Combatants. In J. da Silva, Z. Breda, & F. Carbone (Eds.), *Role and Impact of Tourism in Peacebuilding and Conflict Transformation* (pp. 66-86). IGI Global. https://doi.org/10.4018/978-1-7998-5053-3.ch005

Haider, A., & Saetang, S. (2017). Strategic IT Alignment in Service Sector. In S. Rozenes & Y. Cohen (Eds.), *Handbook of Research on Strategic Alliances and Value Co-Creation in the Service Industry* (pp. 231–258). Hershey, PA: IGI Global. doi:10.4018/978-1-5225-2084-9.ch012

Hajilari, A. B., Ghadaksaz, M., & Fasghandis, G. S. (2017). Assessing Organizational Readiness for Implementing ERP System Using Fuzzy Expert System Approach. *International Journal of Enterprise Information Systems, 13*(1), 67–85. doi:10.4018/IJEIS.2017010105

Haldorai, A., Ramu, A., & Murugan, S. (2018). Social Aware Cognitive Radio Networks: Effectiveness of Social Networks as a Strategic Tool for Organizational Business Management. In H. Bansal, G. Shrivastava, G. Nguyen, & L. Stanciu (Eds.), *Social Network Analytics for Contemporary Business Organizations* (pp. 188–202). Hershey, PA: IGI Global. doi:10.4018/978-1-5225-5097-6.ch010

Hall, O. P. Jr. (2017). Social Media Driven Management Education. *International Journal of Knowledge-Based Organizations, 7*(2), 43–59. doi:10.4018/IJKBO.2017040104

Hanifah, H., Halim, H. A., Ahmad, N. H., & Vafaei-Zadeh, A. (2017). Innovation Culture as a Mediator Between Specific Human Capital and Innovation Performance Among Bumiputera SMEs in Malaysia. In N. Ahmad, T. Ramayah, H. Halim, & S. Rahman (Eds.), *Handbook of Research on Small and Medium Enterprises in Developing Countries* (pp. 261–279). Hershey, PA: IGI Global. doi:10.4018/978-1-5225-2165-5.ch012

Hartlieb, S., & Silvius, G. (2017). Handling Uncertainty in Project Management and Business Development: Similarities and Differences. In Y. Raydugin (Ed.), *Handbook of Research on Leveraging Risk and Uncertainties for Effective Project Management* (pp. 337–362). Hershey, PA: IGI Global. doi:10.4018/978-1-5225-1790-0.ch016

Hass, K. B. (2017). Living on the Edge: Managing Project Complexity. In Y. Raydugin (Ed.), *Handbook of Research on Leveraging Risk and Uncertainties for Effective Project Management* (pp. 177–201). Hershey, PA: IGI Global. doi:10.4018/978-1-5225-1790-0.ch009

Hawking, P., & Carmine Sellitto, C. (2017). Developing an Effective Strategy for Organizational Business Intelligence. In M. Tavana (Ed.), *Enterprise Information Systems and the Digitalization of Business Functions* (pp. 222–237). Hershey, PA: IGI Global. doi:10.4018/978-1-5225-2382-6.ch010

Hawking, P., & Sellitto, C. (2017). A Fast-Moving Consumer Goods Company and Business Intelligence Strategy Development. *International Journal of Enterprise Information Systems, 13*(2), 22–33. doi:10.4018/IJEIS.2017040102

Hawking, P., & Sellitto, C. (2017). Business Intelligence Strategy: Two Case Studies. *International Journal of Business Intelligence Research, 8*(2), 17–30. doi:10.4018/IJBIR.2017070102

Hee, W. J., Jalleh, G., Lai, H., & Lin, C. (2017). E-Commerce and IT Projects: Evaluation and Management Issues in Australian and Taiwanese Hospitals. *International Journal of Public Health Management and Ethics, 2*(1), 69–90. doi:10.4018/IJPHME.2017010104

Hernandez, A. A. (2018). Exploring the Factors to Green IT Adoption of SMEs in the Philippines. *Journal of Cases on Information Technology, 20*(2), 49–66. doi:10.4018/JCIT.2018040104

Hollman, A., Bickford, S., & Hollman, T. (2017). Cyber InSecurity: A Post-Mortem Attempt to Assess Cyber Problems from IT and Business Management Perspectives. *Journal of Cases on Information Technology, 19*(3), 42–70. doi:10.4018/JCIT.2017070104

Ibrahim, F., & Zainin, N. M. (2021). Exploring the Technological Impacts: The Case of Museums in Brunei Darussalam. *International Journal of Tourism and Hospitality Management in the Digital Age, 5*(1), 1–18. https://doi.org/10.4018/IJTHMDA.2021010101

Igbinakhase, I. (2017). Responsible and Sustainable Management Practices in Developing and Developed Business Environments. In Z. Fields (Ed.), *Collective Creativity for Responsible and Sustainable Business Practice* (pp. 180–207). Hershey, PA: IGI Global. doi:10.4018/978-1-5225-1823-5.ch010

Iwata, J. J., & Hoskins, R. G. (2017). Managing Indigenous Knowledge in Tanzania: A Business Perspective. In P. Jain & N. Mnjama (Eds.), *Managing Knowledge Resources and Records in Modern Organizations* (pp. 198–214). Hershey, PA: IGI Global. doi:10.4018/978-1-5225-1965-2.ch012

Jain, P. (2017). Ethical and Legal Issues in Knowledge Management Life-Cycle in Business. In P. Jain & N. Mnjama (Eds.), *Managing Knowledge Resources and Records in Modern Organizations* (pp. 82–101). Hershey, PA: IGI Global. doi:10.4018/978-1-5225-1965-2.ch006

James, S., & Hauli, E. (2017). Holistic Management Education at Tanzanian Rural Development Planning Institute. In N. Baporikar (Ed.), *Management Education for Global Leadership* (pp. 112–136). Hershey, PA: IGI Global. doi:10.4018/978-1-5225-1013-0.ch006

Janošková, M., Csikósová, A., & Čulková, K. (2018). Measurement of Company Performance as Part of Its Strategic Management. In R. Leon (Ed.), *Managerial Strategies for Business Sustainability During Turbulent Times* (pp. 309–335). Hershey, PA: IGI Global. doi:10.4018/978-1-5225-2716-9.ch017

Jean-Vasile, A., & Alecu, A. (2017). Theoretical and Practical Approaches in Understanding the Influences of Cost-Productivity-Profit Trinomial in Contemporary Enterprises. In A. Jean Vasile & D. Nicolò (Eds.), *Sustainable Entrepreneurship and Investments in the Green Economy* (pp. 28–62). Hershey, PA: IGI Global. doi:10.4018/978-1-5225-2075-7.ch002

Joia, L. A., & Correia, J. C. (2018). CIO Competencies From the IT Professional Perspective: Insights From Brazil. *Journal of Global Information Management, 26*(2), 74–103. doi:10.4018/JGIM.2018040104

Juma, A., & Mzera, N. (2017). Knowledge Management and Records Management and Competitive Advantage in Business. In P. Jain & N. Mnjama (Eds.), *Managing Knowledge Resources and Records in Modern Organizations* (pp. 15–28). Hershey, PA: IGI Global. doi:10.4018/978-1-5225-1965-2.ch002

K., I., & A, V. (2018). Monitoring and Auditing in the Cloud. In K. Munir (Ed.), *Cloud Computing Technologies for Green Enterprises* (pp. 318-350). Hershey, PA: IGI Global. https://doi.org/ doi:10.4018/978-1-5225-3038-1.ch013

Kabra, G., Ghosh, V., & Ramesh, A. (2018). Enterprise Integrated Business Process Management and Business Intelligence Framework for Business Process Sustainability. In A. Paul, D. Bhattacharyya, & S. Anand (Eds.), *Green Initiatives for Business Sustainability and Value Creation* (pp. 228–238). Hershey, PA: IGI Global. doi:10.4018/978-1-5225-2662-9.ch010

Kaoud, M. (2017). Investigation of Customer Knowledge Management: A Case Study Research. *International Journal of Service Science, Management, Engineering, and Technology*, *8*(2), 12–22. doi:10.4018/IJSSMET.2017040102

Katuu, S. (2018). A Comparative Assessment of Enterprise Content Management Maturity Models. In N. Gwangwava & M. Mutingi (Eds.), *E-Manufacturing and E-Service Strategies in Contemporary Organizations* (pp. 93–118). Hershey, PA: IGI Global. doi:10.4018/978-1-5225-3628-4.ch005

Khan, M. Y., & Abir, T. (2022). The Role of Social Media Marketing in the Tourism and Hospitality Industry: A Conceptual Study on Bangladesh. In C. Ramos, S. Quinteiro, & A. Gonçalves (Eds.), *ICT as Innovator Between Tourism and Culture* (pp. 213–229). IGI Global. https://doi.org/10.4018/978-1-7998-8165-0.ch013

Kinnunen, S., Ylä-Kujala, A., Marttonen-Arola, S., Kärri, T., & Baglee, D. (2018). Internet of Things in Asset Management: Insights from Industrial Professionals and Academia. *International Journal of Service Science, Management, Engineering, and Technology*, *9*(2), 104–119. doi:10.4018/IJSSMET.2018040105

Klein, A. Z., Sabino de Freitas, A., Machado, L., Freitas, J. C. Jr, Graziola, P. G. Jr, & Schlemmer, E. (2017). Virtual Worlds Applications for Management Education. In L. Tomei (Ed.), *Exploring the New Era of Technology-Infused Education* (pp. 279–299). Hershey, PA: IGI Global. doi:10.4018/978-1-5225-1709-2.ch017

Kővári, E., Saleh, M., & Steinbachné Hajmásy, G. (2022). The Impact of Corporate Digital Responsibility (CDR) on Internal Stakeholders' Satisfaction in Hungarian Upscale Hotels. In M. Valeri (Ed.), *New Governance and Management in Touristic Destinations* (pp. 35–51). IGI Global. https://doi.org/10.4018/978-1-6684-3889-3.ch003

Kożuch, B., & Jabłoński, A. (2017). Adopting the Concept of Business Models in Public Management. In M. Lewandowski & B. Kożuch (Eds.), *Public Sector Entrepreneurship and the Integration of Innovative Business Models* (pp. 10–46). Hershey, PA: IGI Global. doi:10.4018/978-1-5225-2215-7.ch002

Kumar, J., Adhikary, A., & Jha, A. (2017). Small Active Investors' Perceptions and Preferences Towards Tax Saving Mutual Fund Schemes in Eastern India: An Empirical Note. *International Journal of Asian Business and Information Management*, *8*(2), 35–45. doi:10.4018/IJABIM.2017040103

Latusi, S., & Fissore, M. (2021). Pilgrimage Routes to Happiness: Comparing the Camino de Santiago and Via Francigena. In A. Perinotto, V. Mayer, & J. Soares (Eds.), *Rebuilding and Restructuring the Tourism Industry: Infusion of Happiness and Quality of Life* (pp. 157–182). IGI Global. https://doi.org/10.4018/978-1-7998-7239-9.ch008

Lavassani, K. M., & Movahedi, B. (2017). Applications Driven Information Systems: Beyond Networks toward Business Ecosystems. *International Journal of Innovation in the Digital Economy*, *8*(1), 61–75. doi:10.4018/IJIDE.2017010104

Lazzareschi, V. H., & Brito, M. S. (2017). Strategic Information Management: Proposal of Business Project Model. In G. Jamil, A. Soares, & C. Pessoa (Eds.), *Handbook of Research on Information Management for Effective Logistics and Supply Chains* (pp. 59–88). Hershey, PA: IGI Global. doi:10.4018/978-1-5225-0973-8.ch004

Lechuga Sancho, M. P., & Martín Navarro, A. (2022). Evolution of the Literature on Social Responsibility in the Tourism Sector: A Systematic Literature Review. In G. Fernandes (Ed.), *Challenges and New Opportunities for Tourism in Inland Territories: Ecocultural Resources and Sustainable Initiatives* (pp. 169–186). IGI Global. https://doi.org/10.4018/978-1-7998-7339-6.ch010

Lederer, M., Kurz, M., & Lazarov, P. (2017). Usage and Suitability of Methods for Strategic Business Process Initiatives: A Multi Case Study Research. *International Journal of Productivity Management and Assessment Technologies*, *5*(1), 40–51. doi:10.4018/IJPMAT.2017010103

Lee, I. (2017). A Social Enterprise Business Model and a Case Study of Pacific Community Ventures (PCV). In V. Potocan, M. Üngan, & Z. Nedelko (Eds.), *Handbook of Research on Managerial Solutions in Non-Profit Organizations* (pp. 182–204). Hershey, PA: IGI Global. doi:10.4018/978-1-5225-0731-4.ch009

Leon, L. A., Seal, K. C., Przasnyski, Z. H., & Wiedenman, I. (2017). Skills and Competencies Required for Jobs in Business Analytics: A Content Analysis of Job Advertisements Using Text Mining. *International Journal of Business Intelligence Research*, *8*(1), 1–25. doi:10.4018/IJBIR.2017010101

Levy, C. L., & Elias, N. I. (2017). SOHO Users' Perceptions of Reliability and Continuity of Cloud-Based Services. In M. Moore (Ed.), *Cybersecurity Breaches and Issues Surrounding Online Threat Protection* (pp. 248–287). Hershey, PA: IGI Global. doi:10.4018/978-1-5225-1941-6.ch011

Levy, M. (2018). Change Management Serving Knowledge Management and Organizational Development: Reflections and Review. In N. Baporikar (Ed.), *Global Practices in Knowledge Management for Societal and Organizational Development* (pp. 256–270). Hershey, PA: IGI Global. doi:10.4018/978-1-5225-3009-1.ch012

Lewandowski, M. (2017). Public Organizations and Business Model Innovation: The Role of Public Service Design. In M. Lewandowski & B. Kożuch (Eds.), *Public Sector Entrepreneurship and the Integration of Innovative Business Models* (pp. 47–72). Hershey, PA: IGI Global. doi:10.4018/978-1-5225-2215-7.ch003

Lhannaoui, H., Kabbaj, M. I., & Bakkoury, Z. (2017). A Survey of Risk-Aware Business Process Modelling. *International Journal of Risk and Contingency Management, 6*(3), 14–26. doi:10.4018/IJRCM.2017070102

Li, J., Sun, W., Jiang, W., Yang, H., & Zhang, L. (2017). How the Nature of Exogenous Shocks and Crises Impact Company Performance?: The Effects of Industry Characteristics. *International Journal of Risk and Contingency Management, 6*(4), 40–55. doi:10.4018/IJRCM.2017100103

Lopez-Fernandez, M., Perez-Perez, M., Serrano-Bedia, A., & Cobo-Gonzalez, A. (2021). Small and Medium Tourism Enterprise Survival in Times of Crisis: "El Capricho de Gaudí. In D. Toubes & N. Araújo-Vila (Eds.), *Risk, Crisis, and Disaster Management in Small and Medium-Sized Tourism Enterprises* (pp. 103–129). IGI Global. doi:10.4018/978-1-7998-6996-2.ch005

Mahajan, A., Maidullah, S., & Hossain, M. R. (2022). Experience Toward Smart Tour Guide Apps in Travelling: An Analysis of Users' Reviews on Audio Odigos and Trip My Way. In R. Augusto Costa, F. Brandão, Z. Breda, & C. Costa (Eds.), *Planning and Managing the Experience Economy in Tourism* (pp. 255-273). IGI Global. https://doi.org/10.4018/978-1-7998-8775-1.ch014

Malega, P. (2017). Small and Medium Enterprises in the Slovak Republic: Status and Competitiveness of SMEs in the Global Markets and Possibilities of Optimization. In M. Vemić (Ed.), *Optimal Management Strategies in Small and Medium Enterprises* (pp. 102–124). Hershey, PA: IGI Global. doi:10.4018/978-1-5225-1949-2.ch006

Malewska, K. M. (2017). Intuition in Decision-Making on the Example of a Non-Profit Organization. In V. Potocan, M. Üngan, & Z. Nedelko (Eds.), *Handbook of Research on Managerial Solutions in Non-Profit Organizations* (pp. 378–399). Hershey, PA: IGI Global. doi:10.4018/978-1-5225-0731-4.ch018

Maroofi, F. (2017). Entrepreneurial Orientation and Organizational Learning Ability Analysis for Innovation and Firm Performance. In N. Baporikar (Ed.), *Innovation and Shifting Perspectives in Management Education* (pp. 144–165). Hershey, PA: IGI Global. doi:10.4018/978-1-5225-1019-2.ch007

Marques, M., Moleiro, D., Brito, T. M., & Marques, T. (2021). Customer Relationship Management as an Important Relationship Marketing Tool: The Case of the Hospitality Industry in Estoril Coast. In M. Dinis, L. Bonixe, S. Lamy, & Z. Breda (Eds.), Impact of New Media in Tourism (pp. 39-56). IGI Global. https://doi.org/doi:10.4018/978-1-7998-7095-1.ch003

Martins, P. V., & Zacarias, M. (2017). A Web-based Tool for Business Process Improvement. *International Journal of Web Portals*, *9*(2), 68–84. doi:10.4018/IJWP.2017070104

Matthies, B., & Coners, A. (2017). Exploring the Conceptual Nature of e-Business Projects. *Journal of Electronic Commerce in Organizations*, *15*(3), 33–63. doi:10.4018/JECO.2017070103

Mayer, V. F., Fraga, C. C., & Silva, L. C. (2021). Contributions of Neurosciences to Studies of Well-Being in Tourism. In A. Perinotto, V. Mayer, & J. Soares (Eds.), *Rebuilding and Restructuring the Tourism Industry: Infusion of Happiness and Quality of Life* (pp. 108–128). IGI Global. https://doi.org/10.4018/978-1-7998-7239-9.ch006

McKee, J. (2018). Architecture as a Tool to Solve Business Planning Problems. In M. Khosrow-Pour, D.B.A. (Ed.), Encyclopedia of Information Science and Technology, Fourth Edition (pp. 573-586). Hershey, PA: IGI Global. doi:10.4018/978-1-5225-2255-3.ch050

McMurray, A. J., Cross, J., & Caponecchia, C. (2018). The Risk Management Profession in Australia: Business Continuity Plan Practices. In N. Bajgoric (Ed.), *Always-On Enterprise Information Systems for Modern Organizations* (pp. 112–129). Hershey, PA: IGI Global. doi:10.4018/978-1-5225-3704-5.ch006

Meddah, I. H., & Belkadi, K. (2018). Mining Patterns Using Business Process Management. In R. Hamou (Ed.), *Handbook of Research on Biomimicry in Information Retrieval and Knowledge Management* (pp. 78–89). Hershey, PA: IGI Global. doi:10.4018/978-1-5225-3004-6.ch005

Melian, A. G., & Camprubí, R. (2021). The Accessibility of Museum Websites: The Case of Barcelona. In C. Eusébio, L. Teixeira, & M. Carneiro (Eds.), *ICT Tools and Applications for Accessible Tourism* (pp. 234–255). IGI Global. https://doi.org/10.4018/978-1-7998-6428-8.ch011

Mendes, L. (2017). TQM and Knowledge Management: An Integrated Approach Towards Tacit Knowledge Management. In D. Jaziri-Bouagina & G. Jamil (Eds.), *Handbook of Research on Tacit Knowledge Management for Organizational Success* (pp. 236–263). Hershey, PA: IGI Global. doi:10.4018/978-1-5225-2394-9.ch009

Menezes, V. D., & Cavagnaro, E. (2021). Communicating Sustainable Initiatives in the Hotel Industry: The Case of the Hotel Jakarta Amsterdam. In F. Brandão, Z. Breda, R. Costa, & C. Costa (Eds.), *Handbook of Research on the Role of Tourism in Achieving Sustainable Development Goals* (pp. 224-234). IGI Global. https://doi.org/10.4018/978-1-7998-5691-7.ch013

Menezes, V. D., & Cavagnaro, E. (2021). Communicating Sustainable Initiatives in the Hotel Industry: The Case of the Hotel Jakarta Amsterdam. In F. Brandão, Z. Breda, R. Costa, & C. Costa (Eds.), *Handbook of Research on the Role of Tourism in Achieving Sustainable Development Goals* (pp. 224-234). IGI Global. https://doi.org/10.4018/978-1-7998-5691-7.ch013

Mitas, O., Bastiaansen, M., & Boode, W. (2022). If You're Happy, I'm Happy: Emotion Contagion at a Tourist Information Center. In R. Augusto Costa, F. Brandão, Z. Breda, & C. Costa (Eds.), *Planning and Managing the Experience Economy in Tourism* (pp. 122-140). IGI Global. https://doi.org/10.4018/978-1-7998-8775-1.ch007

Mnjama, N. M. (2017). Preservation of Recorded Information in Public and Private Sector Organizations. In P. Jain & N. Mnjama (Eds.), *Managing Knowledge Resources and Records in Modern Organizations* (pp. 149–167). Hershey, PA: IGI Global. doi:10.4018/978-1-5225-1965-2.ch009

Mokoqama, M., & Fields, Z. (2017). Principles of Responsible Management Education (PRME): Call for Responsible Management Education. In Z. Fields (Ed.), *Collective Creativity for Responsible and Sustainable Business Practice* (pp. 229–241). Hershey, PA: IGI Global. doi:10.4018/978-1-5225-1823-5.ch012

Monteiro, A., Lopes, S., & Carbone, F. (2021). Academic Mobility: Bridging Tourism and Peace Education. In J. da Silva, Z. Breda, & F. Carbone (Eds.), *Role and Impact of Tourism in Peacebuilding and Conflict Transformation* (pp. 275-301). IGI Global. https://doi.org/10.4018/978-1-7998-5053-3.ch016

Muniapan, B. (2017). Philosophy and Management: The Relevance of Vedanta in Management. In P. Ordóñez de Pablos (Ed.), *Managerial Strategies and Solutions for Business Success in Asia* (pp. 124–139). Hershey, PA: IGI Global. doi:10.4018/978-1-5225-1886-0.ch007

Murad, S. E., & Dowaji, S. (2017). Using Value-Based Approach for Managing Cloud-Based Services. In A. Turuk, B. Sahoo, & S. Addya (Eds.), *Resource Management and Efficiency in Cloud Computing Environments* (pp. 33–60). Hershey, PA: IGI Global. doi:10.4018/978-1-5225-1721-4.ch002

Mutahar, A. M., Daud, N. M., Thurasamy, R., Isaac, O., & Abdulsalam, R. (2018). The Mediating of Perceived Usefulness and Perceived Ease of Use: The Case of Mobile Banking in Yemen. *International Journal of Technology Diffusion*, *9*(2), 21–40. doi:10.4018/IJTD.2018040102

Naidoo, V. (2017). E-Learning and Management Education at African Universities. In N. Baporikar (Ed.), *Management Education for Global Leadership* (pp. 181–201). Hershey, PA: IGI Global. doi:10.4018/978-1-5225-1013-0.ch009

Naidoo, V., & Igbinakhase, I. (2018). Opportunities and Challenges of Knowledge Retention in SMEs. In N. Baporikar (Ed.), *Knowledge Integration Strategies for Entrepreneurship and Sustainability* (pp. 70–94). Hershey, PA: IGI Global. doi:10.4018/978-1-5225-5115-7.ch004

Naumov, N., & Costandachi, G. (2021). Creativity and Entrepreneurship: Gastronomic Tourism in Mexico. In J. Soares (Ed.), *Innovation and Entrepreneurial Opportunities in Community Tourism* (pp. 90–108). IGI Global. https://doi.org/10.4018/978-1-7998-4855-4.ch006

Nayak, S., & Prabhu, N. (2017). Paradigm Shift in Management Education: Need for a Cross Functional Perspective. In N. Baporikar (Ed.), *Management Education for Global Leadership* (pp. 241–255). Hershey, PA: IGI Global. doi:10.4018/978-1-5225-1013-0.ch012

Nedelko, Z., & Potocan, V. (2017). Management Solutions in Non-Profit Organizations: Case of Slovenia. In V. Potocan, M. Üngan, & Z. Nedelko (Eds.), *Handbook of Research on Managerial Solutions in Non-Profit Organizations* (pp. 1–22). Hershey, PA: IGI Global. doi:10.4018/978-1-5225-0731-4.ch001

Nedelko, Z., & Potocan, V. (2017). Priority of Management Tools Utilization among Managers: International Comparison. In V. Wang (Ed.), *Encyclopedia of Strategic Leadership and Management* (pp. 1083–1094). Hershey, PA: IGI Global. doi:10.4018/978-1-5225-1049-9.ch075

Nedelko, Z., Raudeliūnienė, J., & Črešnar, R. (2018). Knowledge Dynamics in Supply Chain Management. In N. Baporikar (Ed.), *Knowledge Integration Strategies for Entrepreneurship and Sustainability* (pp. 150–166). Hershey, PA: IGI Global. doi:10.4018/978-1-5225-5115-7.ch008

Nguyen, H. T., & Hipsher, S. A. (2018). Innovation and Creativity Used by Private Sector Firms in a Resources-Constrained Environment. In S. Hipsher (Ed.), *Examining the Private Sector's Role in Wealth Creation and Poverty Reduction* (pp. 219–238). Hershey, PA: IGI Global. doi:10.4018/978-1-5225-3117-3.ch010

Obicci, P. A. (2017). Risk Sharing in a Partnership. In *Risk Management Strategies in Public-Private Partnerships* (pp. 115–152). Hershey, PA: IGI Global. doi:10.4018/978-1-5225-2503-5.ch004

Obidallah, W. J., & Raahemi, B. (2017). Managing Changes in Service Oriented Virtual Organizations: A Structural and Procedural Framework to Facilitate the Process of Change. *Journal of Electronic Commerce in Organizations*, *15*(1), 59–83. doi:10.4018/JECO.2017010104

Ojo, O. (2017). Impact of Innovation on the Entrepreneurial Success in Selected Business Enterprises in South-West Nigeria. *International Journal of Innovation in the Digital Economy*, *8*(2), 29–38. doi:10.4018/IJIDE.2017040103

Okdinawati, L., Simatupang, T. M., & Sunitiyoso, Y. (2017). Multi-Agent Reinforcement Learning for Value Co-Creation of Collaborative Transportation Management (CTM). *International Journal of Information Systems and Supply Chain Management*, *10*(3), 84–95. doi:10.4018/IJISSCM.2017070105

Olivera, V. A., & Carrillo, I. M. (2021). Organizational Culture: A Key Element for the Development of Mexican Micro and Small Tourist Companies. In J. Soares (Ed.), *Innovation and Entrepreneurial Opportunities in Community Tourism* (pp. 227–242). IGI Global. doi:10.4018/978-1-7998-4855-4.ch013

Ossorio, M. (2022). Corporate Museum Experiences in Enogastronomic Tourism. In R. Augusto Costa, F. Brandão, Z. Breda, & C. Costa (Eds.), Planning and Managing the Experience Economy in Tourism (pp. 107-121). IGI Global. https://doi.org/doi:10.4018/978-1-7998-8775-1.ch006

Ossorio, M. (2022). Enogastronomic Tourism in Times of Pandemic. In G. Fernandes (Ed.), *Challenges and New Opportunities for Tourism in Inland Territories: Ecocultural Resources and Sustainable Initiatives* (pp. 241–255). IGI Global. https://doi.org/10.4018/978-1-7998-7339-6.ch014

Özekici, Y. K. (2022). ICT as an Acculturative Agent and Its Role in the Tourism Context: Introduction, Acculturation Theory, Progress of the Acculturation Theory in Extant Literature. In C. Ramos, S. Quinteiro, & A. Gonçalves (Eds.), *ICT as Innovator Between Tourism and Culture* (pp. 42–66). IGI Global. https://doi.org/10.4018/978-1-7998-8165-0.ch004

Pal, K. (2018). Building High Quality Big Data-Based Applications in Supply Chains. In A. Kumar & S. Saurav (Eds.), *Supply Chain Management Strategies and Risk Assessment in Retail Environments* (pp. 1–24). Hershey, PA: IGI Global. doi:10.4018/978-1-5225-3056-5.ch001

Palos-Sanchez, P. R., & Correia, M. B. (2018). Perspectives of the Adoption of Cloud Computing in the Tourism Sector. In J. Rodrigues, C. Ramos, P. Cardoso, & C. Henriques (Eds.), *Handbook of Research on Technological Developments for Cultural Heritage and eTourism Applications* (pp. 377–400). Hershey, PA: IGI Global. doi:10.4018/978-1-5225-2927-9.ch018

Papadopoulou, G. (2021). Promoting Gender Equality and Women Empowerment in the Tourism Sector. In F. Brandão, Z. Breda, R. Costa, & C. Costa (Eds.), Handbook of Research on the Role of Tourism in Achieving Sustainable Development Goals (pp. 152-174). IGI Global. https://doi.org/ doi:10.4018/978-1-7998-5691-7.ch009

Papp-Váry, Á. F., & Tóth, T. Z. (2022). Analysis of Budapest as a Film Tourism Destination. In R. Baleiro & R. Pereira (Eds.), *Global Perspectives on Literary Tourism and Film-Induced Tourism* (pp. 257-279). IGI Global. https://doi.org/10.4018/978-1-7998-8262-6.ch014

Patiño, B. E. (2017). New Generation Management by Convergence and Individual Identity: A Systemic and Human-Oriented Approach. In N. Baporikar (Ed.), *Innovation and Shifting Perspectives in Management Education* (pp. 119–143). Hershey, PA: IGI Global. doi:10.4018/978-1-5225-1019-2.ch006

Patro, C. S. (2021). Digital Tourism: Influence of E-Marketing Technology. In M. Dinis, L. Bonixe, S. Lamy, & Z. Breda (Eds.), *Impact of New Media in Tourism* (pp. 234-254). IGI Global. https://doi.org/10.4018/978-1-7998-7095-1.ch014

Pawliczek, A., & Rössler, M. (2017). Knowledge of Management Tools and Systems in SMEs: Knowledge Transfer in Management. In A. Bencsik (Ed.), *Knowledge Management Initiatives and Strategies in Small and Medium Enterprises* (pp. 180–203). Hershey, PA: IGI Global. doi:10.4018/978-1-5225-1642-2.ch009

Pejic-Bach, M., Omazic, M. A., Aleksic, A., & Zoroja, J. (2018). Knowledge-Based Decision Making: A Multi-Case Analysis. In R. Leon (Ed.), *Managerial Strategies for Business Sustainability During Turbulent Times* (pp. 160–184). Hershey, PA: IGI Global. doi:10.4018/978-1-5225-2716-9.ch009

Perano, M., Hysa, X., & Calabrese, M. (2018). Strategic Planning, Cultural Context, and Business Continuity Management: Business Cases in the City of Shkoder. In A. Presenza & L. Sheehan (Eds.), *Geopolitics and Strategic Management in the Global Economy* (pp. 57–77). Hershey, PA: IGI Global. doi:10.4018/978-1-5225-2673-5.ch004

Pereira, R., Mira da Silva, M., & Lapão, L. V. (2017). IT Governance Maturity Patterns in Portuguese Healthcare. In S. De Haes & W. Van Grembergen (Eds.), *Strategic IT Governance and Alignment in Business Settings* (pp. 24–52). Hershey, PA: IGI Global. doi:10.4018/978-1-5225-0861-8.ch002

Pérez-Uribe, R. I., Torres, D. A., Jurado, S. P., & Prada, D. M. (2018). Cloud Tools for the Development of Project Management in SMEs. In R. Perez-Uribe, C. Salcedo-Perez, & D. Ocampo-Guzman (Eds.), *Handbook of Research on Intrapreneurship and Organizational Sustainability in SMEs* (pp. 95–120). Hershey, PA: IGI Global. doi:10.4018/978-1-5225-3543-0.ch005

Petrisor, I., & Cozmiuc, D. (2017). Global Supply Chain Management Organization at Siemens in the Advent of Industry 4.0. In L. Saglietto & C. Cezanne (Eds.), *Global Intermediation and Logistics Service Providers* (pp. 123–142). Hershey, PA: IGI Global. doi:10.4018/978-1-5225-2133-4.ch007

Pierce, J. M., Velliaris, D. M., & Edwards, J. (2017). A Living Case Study: A Journey Not a Destination. In N. Silton (Ed.), *Exploring the Benefits of Creativity in Education, Media, and the Arts* (pp. 158–178). Hershey, PA: IGI Global. doi:10.4018/978-1-5225-0504-4.ch008

Pipia, S., & Pipia, S. (2021). Challenges of Religious Tourism in the Conflict Region: An Example of Jerusalem. In E. Alaverdov & M. Bari (Eds.), *Global Development of Religious Tourism* (pp. 135-148). IGI Global. https://doi.org/10.4018/978-1-7998-5792-1.ch009

Poulaki, P., Kritikos, A., Vasilakis, N., & Valeri, M. (2022). The Contribution of Female Creativity to the Development of Gastronomic Tourism in Greece: The Case of the Island of Naxos in the South Aegean Region. In M. Valeri (Ed.), *New Governance and Management in Touristic Destinations* (pp. 246–258). IGI Global. https://doi.org/10.4018/978-1-6684-3889-3.ch015

Radosavljevic, M., & Andjelkovic, A. (2017). Multi-Criteria Decision Making Approach for Choosing Business Process for the Improvement: Upgrading of the Six Sigma Methodology. In J. Stanković, P. Delias, S. Marinković, & S. Rochhia (Eds.), *Tools and Techniques for Economic Decision Analysis* (pp. 225–247). Hershey, PA: IGI Global. doi:10.4018/978-1-5225-0959-2.ch011

Radovic, V. M. (2017). Corporate Sustainability and Responsibility and Disaster Risk Reduction: A Serbian Overview. In M. Camilleri (Ed.), *CSR 2.0 and the New Era of Corporate Citizenship* (pp. 147–164). Hershey, PA: IGI Global. doi:10.4018/978-1-5225-1842-6.ch008

Raghunath, K. M., Devi, S. L., & Patro, C. S. (2018). Impact of Risk Assessment Models on Risk Factors: A Holistic Outlook. In K. Strang, M. Korstanje, & N. Vajjhala (Eds.), *Research, Practices, and Innovations in Global Risk and Contingency Management* (pp. 134–153). Hershey, PA: IGI Global. doi:10.4018/978-1-5225-4754-9.ch008

Raman, A., & Goyal, D. P. (2017). Extending IMPLEMENT Framework for Enterprise Information Systems Implementation to Information System Innovation. In M. Tavana (Ed.), *Enterprise Information Systems and the Digitalization of Business Functions* (pp. 137–177). Hershey, PA: IGI Global. doi:10.4018/978-1-5225-2382-6.ch007

Rao, Y., & Zhang, Y. (2017). The Construction and Development of Academic Library Digital Special Subject Databases. In L. Ruan, Q. Zhu, & Y. Ye (Eds.), *Academic Library Development and Administration in China* (pp. 163–183). Hershey, PA: IGI Global. doi:10.4018/978-1-5225-0550-1.ch010

Ravasan, A. Z., Mohammadi, M. M., & Hamidi, H. (2018). An Investigation Into the Critical Success Factors of Implementing Information Technology Service Management Frameworks. In K. Jakobs (Ed.), *Corporate and Global Standardization Initiatives in Contemporary Society* (pp. 200–218). Hershey, PA: IGI Global. doi:10.4018/978-1-5225-5320-5.ch009

Rezaie, S., Mirabedini, S. J., & Abtahi, A. (2018). Designing a Model for Implementation of Business Intelligence in the Banking Industry. *International Journal of Enterprise Information Systems, 14*(1), 77–103. doi:10.4018/IJEIS.2018010105

Richards, V., Matthews, N., Williams, O. J., & Khan, Z. (2021). The Challenges of Accessible Tourism Information Systems for Tourists With Vision Impairment: Sensory Communications Beyond the Screen. In C. Eusébio, L. Teixeira, & M. Carneiro (Eds.), *ICT Tools and Applications for Accessible Tourism* (pp. 26–54). IGI Global. https://doi.org/10.4018/978-1-7998-6428-8.ch002

Rodrigues de Souza Neto, V., & Marques, O. (2021). Rural Tourism Fostering Welfare Through Sustainable Development: A Conceptual Approach. In A. Perinotto, V. Mayer, & J. Soares (Eds.), *Rebuilding and Restructuring the Tourism Industry: Infusion of Happiness and Quality of Life* (pp. 38–57). IGI Global. https://doi.org/10.4018/978-1-7998-7239-9.ch003

Romano, L., Grimaldi, R., & Colasuonno, F. S. (2017). Demand Management as a Success Factor in Project Portfolio Management. In L. Romano (Ed.), *Project Portfolio Management Strategies for Effective Organizational Operations* (pp. 202–219). Hershey, PA: IGI Global. doi:10.4018/978-1-5225-2151-8.ch008

Rubio-Escuderos, L., & García-Andreu, H. (2021). Competitiveness Factors of Accessible Tourism E-Travel Agencies. In C. Eusébio, L. Teixeira, & M. Carneiro (Eds.), *ICT Tools and Applications for Accessible Tourism* (pp. 196–217). IGI Global. https://doi.org/10.4018/978-1-7998-6428-8.ch009

Rucci, A. C., Porto, N., Darcy, S., & Becka, L. (2021). Smart and Accessible Cities?: Not Always – The Case for Accessible Tourism Initiatives in Buenos Aries and Sydney. In C. Eusébio, L. Teixeira, & M. Carneiro (Eds.), *ICT Tools and Applications for Accessible Tourism* (pp. 115–145). IGI Global. https://doi.org/10.4018/978-1-7998-6428-8.ch006

Ruhi, U. (2018). Towards an Interdisciplinary Socio-Technical Definition of Virtual Communities. In M. Khosrow-Pour, D.B.A. (Ed.), Encyclopedia of Information Science and Technology, Fourth Edition (pp. 4278-4295). Hershey, PA: IGI Global. doi:10.4018/978-1-5225-2255-3.ch371

Ryan, L., Catena, M., Ros, P., & Stephens, S. (2021). Designing Entrepreneurial Ecosystems to Support Resource Management in the Tourism Industry. In V. Costa, A. Moura, & M. Mira (Eds.), *Handbook of Research on Human Capital and People Management in the Tourism Industry* (pp. 265–281). IGI Global. https://doi.org/10.4018/978-1-7998-4318-4.ch013

Sabuncu, I. (2021). Understanding Tourist Perceptions and Expectations During Pandemic Through Social Media Big Data. In M. Demir, A. Dalgıç, & F. Ergen (Eds.), *Handbook of Research on the Impacts and Implications of COVID-19 on the Tourism Industry* (pp. 330–350). IGI Global. https://doi.org/10.4018/978-1-7998-8231-2.ch016

Safari, M. R., & Jiang, Q. (2018). The Theory and Practice of IT Governance Maturity and Strategies Alignment: Evidence From Banking Industry. *Journal of Global Information Management, 26*(2), 127–146. doi:10.4018/JGIM.2018040106

Sahoo, J., Pati, B., & Mohanty, B. (2017). Knowledge Management as an Academic Discipline: An Assessment. In B. Gunjal (Ed.), *Managing Knowledge and Scholarly Assets in Academic Libraries* (pp. 99–126). Hershey, PA: IGI Global. doi:10.4018/978-1-5225-1741-2.ch005

Saini, D. (2017). Relevance of Teaching Values and Ethics in Management Education. In N. Baporikar (Ed.), *Management Education for Global Leadership* (pp. 90–111). Hershey, PA: IGI Global. doi:10.4018/978-1-5225-1013-0.ch005

Sambhanthan, A. (2017). Assessing and Benchmarking Sustainability in Organisations: An Integrated Conceptual Model. *International Journal of Systems and Service-Oriented Engineering*, *7*(4), 22–43. doi:10.4018/IJSSOE.2017100102

Sambhanthan, A., & Potdar, V. (2017). A Study of the Parameters Impacting Sustainability in Information Technology Organizations. *International Journal of Knowledge-Based Organizations*, *7*(3), 27–39. doi:10.4018/IJKBO.2017070103

Sánchez-Fernández, M. D., & Manríquez, M. R. (2018). The Entrepreneurial Spirit Based on Social Values: The Digital Generation. In P. Isaias & L. Carvalho (Eds.), *User Innovation and the Entrepreneurship Phenomenon in the Digital Economy* (pp. 173–193). Hershey, PA: IGI Global. doi:10.4018/978-1-5225-2826-5.ch009

Sanchez-Ruiz, L., & Blanco, B. (2017). Process Management for SMEs: Barriers, Enablers, and Benefits. In M. Vemić (Ed.), *Optimal Management Strategies in Small and Medium Enterprises* (pp. 293–319). Hershey, PA: IGI Global. doi:10.4018/978-1-5225-1949-2.ch014

Sanz, L. F., Gómez-Pérez, J., & Castillo-Martinez, A. (2018). Analysis of the European ICT Competence Frameworks. In V. Ahuja & S. Rathore (Eds.), *Multidisciplinary Perspectives on Human Capital and Information Technology Professionals* (pp. 225–245). Hershey, PA: IGI Global. doi:10.4018/978-1-5225-5297-0.ch012

Sarvepalli, A., & Godin, J. (2017). Business Process Management in the Classroom. *Journal of Cases on Information Technology*, *19*(2), 17–28. doi:10.4018/JCIT.2017040102

Saxena, G. G., & Saxena, A. (2021). Host Community Role in Medical Tourism Development. In M. Singh & S. Kumaran (Eds.), *Growth of the Medical Tourism Industry and Its Impact on Society: Emerging Research and Opportunities* (pp. 105–127). IGI Global. https://doi.org/10.4018/978-1-7998-3427-4.ch006

Saygili, E. E., Ozturkoglu, Y., & Kocakulah, M. C. (2017). End Users' Perceptions of Critical Success Factors in ERP Applications. *International Journal of Enterprise Information Systems*, *13*(4), 58–75. doi:10.4018/IJEIS.2017100104

Saygili, E. E., & Saygili, A. T. (2017). Contemporary Issues in Enterprise Information Systems: A Critical Review of CSFs in ERP Implementations. In M. Tavana (Ed.), *Enterprise Information Systems and the Digitalization of Business Functions* (pp. 120–136). Hershey, PA: IGI Global. doi:10.4018/978-1-5225-2382-6.ch006

Schwaiger, K. M., & Zehrer, A. (2021). The COVID-19 Pandemic and Organizational Resilience in Hospitality Family Firms: A Qualitative Approach. In A. Zehrer, G. Glowka, K. Schwaiger, & V. Ranacher-Lackner (Eds.), *Resiliency Models and Addressing Future Risks for Family Firms in the Tourism Industry* (pp. 32–49). IGI Global. https://doi.org/10.4018/978-1-7998-7352-5.ch002

Scott, N., & Campos, A. C. (2022). Cognitive Science of Tourism Experiences. In R. Augusto Costa, F. Brandão, Z. Breda, & C. Costa (Eds.), Planning and Managing the Experience Economy in Tourism (pp. 1-21). IGI Global. https://doi.org/ doi:10.4018/978-1-7998-8775-1.ch001

Seidenstricker, S., & Antonino, A. (2018). Business Model Innovation-Oriented Technology Management for Emergent Technologies. In M. Khosrow-Pour, D.B.A. (Ed.), Encyclopedia of Information Science and Technology, Fourth Edition (pp. 4560-4569). Hershey, PA: IGI Global. doi:10.4018/978-1-5225-2255-3.ch396

Selvi, M. S. (2021). Changes in Tourism Sales and Marketing Post COVID-19. In M. Demir, A. Dalgıç, & F. Ergen (Eds.), *Handbook of Research on the Impacts and Implications of COVID-19 on the Tourism Industry* (pp. 437–460). IGI Global. doi:10.4018/978-1-7998-8231-2.ch021

Senaratne, S., & Gunarathne, A. D. (2017). Excellence Perspective for Management Education from a Global Accountants' Hub in Asia. In N. Baporikar (Ed.), *Management Education for Global Leadership* (pp. 158–180). Hershey, PA: IGI Global. doi:10.4018/978-1-5225-1013-0.ch008

Sensuse, D. I., & Cahyaningsih, E. (2018). Knowledge Management Models: A Summative Review. *International Journal of Information Systems in the Service Sector*, *10*(1), 71–100. doi:10.4018/IJISSS.2018010105

Seth, M., Goyal, D., & Kiran, R. (2017). Diminution of Impediments in Implementation of Supply Chain Management Information System for Enhancing its Effectiveness in Indian Automobile Industry. *Journal of Global Information Management*, *25*(3), 1–20. doi:10.4018/JGIM.2017070101

Seyal, A. H., & Rahman, M. N. (2017). Investigating Impact of Inter-Organizational Factors in Measuring ERP Systems Success: Bruneian Perspectives. In M. Tavana (Ed.), *Enterprise Information Systems and the Digitalization of Business Functions* (pp. 178–204). Hershey, PA: IGI Global. doi:10.4018/978-1-5225-2382-6.ch008

Shaqrah, A. A. (2018). Analyzing Business Intelligence Systems Based on 7s Model of McKinsey. *International Journal of Business Intelligence Research*, *9*(1), 53–63. doi:10.4018/IJBIR.2018010104

Sharma, A. J. (2017). Enhancing Sustainability through Experiential Learning in Management Education. In N. Baporikar (Ed.), *Management Education for Global Leadership* (pp. 256–274). Hershey, PA: IGI Global. doi:10.4018/978-1-5225-1013-0.ch013

Shetty, K. P. (2017). Responsible Global Leadership: Ethical Challenges in Management Education. In N. Baporikar (Ed.), *Innovation and Shifting Perspectives in Management Education* (pp. 194–223). Hershey, PA: IGI Global. doi:10.4018/978-1-5225-1019-2.ch009

Sinthupundaja, J., & Kohda, Y. (2017). Effects of Corporate Social Responsibility and Creating Shared Value on Sustainability. *International Journal of Sustainable Entrepreneurship and Corporate Social Responsibility*, *2*(1), 27–38. doi:10.4018/IJSECSR.2017010103

Škarica, I., & Hrgović, A. V. (2018). Implementation of Total Quality Management Principles in Public Health Institutes in the Republic of Croatia. *International Journal of Productivity Management and Assessment Technologies*, *6*(1), 1–16. doi:10.4018/IJPMAT.2018010101

Skokic, V. (2021). How Small Hotel Owners Practice Resilience: Longitudinal Study Among Small Family Hotels in Croatia. In A. Zehrer, G. Glowka, K. Schwaiger, & V. Ranacher-Lackner (Eds.), *Resiliency Models and Addressing Future Risks for Family Firms in the Tourism Industry* (pp. 50–73). IGI Global. doi:10.4018/978-1-7998-7352-5.ch003

Smuts, H., Kotzé, P., Van der Merwe, A., & Loock, M. (2017). Framework for Managing Shared Knowledge in an Information Systems Outsourcing Context. *International Journal of Knowledge Management*, *13*(4), 1–30. doi:10.4018/IJKM.2017100101

Sousa, M. J., Cruz, R., Dias, I., & Caracol, C. (2017). Information Management Systems in the Supply Chain. In G. Jamil, A. Soares, & C. Pessoa (Eds.), *Handbook of Research on Information Management for Effective Logistics and Supply Chains* (pp. 469–485). Hershey, PA: IGI Global. doi:10.4018/978-1-5225-0973-8.ch025

Spremic, M., Turulja, L., & Bajgoric, N. (2018). Two Approaches in Assessing Business Continuity Management Attitudes in the Organizational Context. In N. Bajgoric (Ed.), *Always-On Enterprise Information Systems for Modern Organizations* (pp. 159–183). Hershey, PA: IGI Global. doi:10.4018/978-1-5225-3704-5.ch008

Steenkamp, A. L. (2018). Some Insights in Computer Science and Information Technology. In *Examining the Changing Role of Supervision in Doctoral Research Projects: Emerging Research and Opportunities* (pp. 113–133). Hershey, PA: IGI Global. doi:10.4018/978-1-5225-2610-0.ch005

Stipanović, C., Rudan, E., & Zubović, V. (2022). Reaching the New Tourist Through Creativity: Sustainable Development Challenges in Croatian Coastal Towns. In M. Valeri (Ed.), *New Governance and Management in Touristic Destinations* (pp. 231–245). IGI Global. https://doi.org/10.4018/978-1-6684-3889-3.ch014

Tabach, A., & Croteau, A. (2017). Configurations of Information Technology Governance Practices and Business Unit Performance. *International Journal of IT/Business Alignment and Governance*, *8*(2), 1–27. doi:10.4018/IJITBAG.2017070101

Talaue, G. M., & Iqbal, T. (2017). Assessment of e-Business Mode of Selected Private Universities in the Philippines and Pakistan. *International Journal of Online Marketing*, *7*(4), 63–77. doi:10.4018/IJOM.2017100105

Tam, G. C. (2017). Project Manager Sustainability Competence. In *Managerial Strategies and Green Solutions for Project Sustainability* (pp. 178–207). Hershey, PA: IGI Global. doi:10.4018/978-1-5225-2371-0.ch008

Tambo, T. (2018). Fashion Retail Innovation: About Context, Antecedents, and Outcome in Technological Change Projects. In I. Management Association (Ed.), Fashion and Textiles: Breakthroughs in Research and Practice (pp. 233-260). Hershey, PA: IGI Global. https://doi.org/ doi:10.4018/978-1-5225-3432-7.ch010

Tantau, A. D., & Frăţilă, L. C. (2018). Information and Management System for Renewable Energy Business. In *Entrepreneurship and Business Development in the Renewable Energy Sector* (pp. 200–244). Hershey, PA: IGI Global. doi:10.4018/978-1-5225-3625-3.ch006

Teixeira, N., Pardal, P. N., & Rafael, B. G. (2018). Internationalization, Financial Performance, and Organizational Challenges: A Success Case in Portugal. In L. Carvalho (Ed.), *Handbook of Research on Entrepreneurial Ecosystems and Social Dynamics in a Globalized World* (pp. 379–423). Hershey, PA: IGI Global. doi:10.4018/978-1-5225-3525-6.ch017

Teixeira, P., Teixeira, L., Eusébio, C., Silva, S., & Teixeira, A. (2021). The Impact of ICTs on Accessible Tourism: Evidence Based on a Systematic Literature Review. In C. Eusébio, L. Teixeira, & M. Carneiro (Eds.), *ICT Tools and Applications for Accessible Tourism* (pp. 1–25). IGI Global. doi:10.4018/978-1-7998-6428-8.ch001

Trad, A., & Kalpić, D. (2018). The Business Transformation Framework, Agile Project and Change Management. In M. Khosrow-Pour, D.B.A. (Ed.), Encyclopedia of Information Science and Technology, Fourth Edition (pp. 620-635). Hershey, PA: IGI Global. https://doi.org/ doi:10.4018/978-1-5225-2255-3.ch054

Trad, A., & Kalpić, D. (2018). The Business Transformation and Enterprise Architecture Framework: The Financial Engineering E-Risk Management and E-Law Integration. In B. Sergi, F. Fidanoski, M. Ziolo, & V. Naumovski (Eds.), *Regaining Global Stability After the Financial Crisis* (pp. 46–65). Hershey, PA: IGI Global. doi:10.4018/978-1-5225-4026-7.ch003

Trengereid, V. (2022). Conditions of Network Engagement: The Quest for a Common Good. In R. Augusto Costa, F. Brandão, Z. Breda, & C. Costa (Eds.), *Planning and Managing the Experience Economy in Tourism* (pp. 69-84). IGI Global. https://doi.org/10.4018/978-1-7998-8775-1.ch004

Turulja, L., & Bajgoric, N. (2018). Business Continuity and Information Systems: A Systematic Literature Review. In N. Bajgoric (Ed.), *Always-On Enterprise Information Systems for Modern Organizations* (pp. 60–87). Hershey, PA: IGI Global. doi:10.4018/978-1-5225-3704-5.ch004

Vargas-Hernández, J. G. (2017). Professional Integrity in Business Management Education. In N. Baporikar (Ed.), *Management Education for Global Leadership* (pp. 70–89). Hershey, PA: IGI Global. doi:10.4018/978-1-5225-1013-0.ch004

Varnacı Uzun, F. (2021). The Destination Preferences of Foreign Tourists During the COVID-19 Pandemic and Attitudes Towards: Marmaris, Turkey. In M. Demir, A. Dalgıç, & F. Ergen (Eds.), *Handbook of Research on the Impacts and Implications of COVID-19 on the Tourism Industry* (pp. 285–306). IGI Global. https://doi.org/10.4018/978-1-7998-8231-2.ch014

Vasista, T. G., & AlAbdullatif, A. M. (2017). Role of Electronic Customer Relationship Management in Demand Chain Management: A Predictive Analytic Approach. *International Journal of Information Systems and Supply Chain Management, 10*(1), 53–67. doi:10.4018/IJISSCM.2017010104

Vieru, D., & Bourdeau, S. (2017). Survival in the Digital Era: A Digital Competence-Based Multi-Case Study in the Canadian SME Clothing Industry. *International Journal of Social and Organizational Dynamics in IT, 6*(1), 17–34. doi:10.4018/IJSODIT.2017010102

Vijayan, G., & Kamarulzaman, N. H. (2017). An Introduction to Sustainable Supply Chain Management and Business Implications. In M. Khan, M. Hussain, & M. Ajmal (Eds.), *Green Supply Chain Management for Sustainable Business Practice* (pp. 27–50). Hershey, PA: IGI Global. doi:10.4018/978-1-5225-0635-5.ch002

Vlachvei, A., & Notta, O. (2017). Firm Competitiveness: Theories, Evidence, and Measurement. In A. Vlachvei, O. Notta, K. Karantininis, & N. Tsounis (Eds.), *Factors Affecting Firm Competitiveness and Performance in the Modern Business World* (pp. 1–42). Hershey, PA: IGI Global. doi:10.4018/978-1-5225-0843-4.ch001

Wang, C., Schofield, M., Li, X., & Ou, X. (2017). Do Chinese Students in Public and Private Higher Education Institutes Perform at Different Level in One of the Leadership Skills: Critical Thinking?: An Exploratory Comparison. In V. Wang (Ed.), *Encyclopedia of Strategic Leadership and Management* (pp. 160–181). Hershey, PA: IGI Global. doi:10.4018/978-1-5225-1049-9.ch013

Wang, J. (2017). Multi-Agent based Production Management Decision System Modelling for the Textile Enterprise. *Journal of Global Information Management, 25*(4), 1–15. doi:10.4018/JGIM.2017100101

Wiedemann, A., & Gewald, H. (2017). Examining Cross-Domain Alignment: The Correlation of Business Strategy, IT Management, and IT Business Value. *International Journal of IT/Business Alignment and Governance, 8*(1), 17–31. doi:10.4018/IJITBAG.2017010102

Wolf, R., & Thiel, M. (2018). Advancing Global Business Ethics in China: Reducing Poverty Through Human and Social Welfare. In S. Hipsher (Ed.), *Examining the Private Sector's Role in Wealth Creation and Poverty Reduction* (pp. 67–84). Hershey, PA: IGI Global. doi:10.4018/978-1-5225-3117-3.ch004

Yablonsky, S. (2018). Innovation Platforms: Data and Analytics Platforms. In *Multi-Sided Platforms (MSPs) and Sharing Strategies in the Digital Economy: Emerging Research and Opportunities* (pp. 72–95). Hershey, PA: IGI Global. doi:10.4018/978-1-5225-5457-8.ch003

Yaşar, B. (2021). The Impact of COVID-19 on Volatility of Tourism Stocks: Evidence From BIST Tourism Index. In M. Demir, A. Dalgıç, & F. Ergen (Eds.), *Handbook of Research on the Impacts and Implications of COVID-19 on the Tourism Industry* (pp. 23–44). IGI Global. https://doi.org/10.4018/978-1-7998-8231-2.ch002

Yusoff, A., Ahmad, N. H., & Halim, H. A. (2017). Agropreneurship among Gen Y in Malaysia: The Role of Academic Institutions. In N. Ahmad, T. Ramayah, H. Halim, & S. Rahman (Eds.), *Handbook of Research on Small and Medium Enterprises in Developing Countries* (pp. 23–47). Hershey, PA: IGI Global. doi:10.4018/978-1-5225-2165-5.ch002

Zacher, D., & Pechlaner, H. (2021). Resilience as an Opportunity Approach: Challenges and Perspectives for Private Sector Participation on a Community Level. In A. Zehrer, G. Glowka, K. Schwaiger, & V. Ranacher-Lackner (Eds.), *Resiliency Models and Addressing Future Risks for Family Firms in the Tourism Industry* (pp. 75–102). IGI Global. https://doi.org/10.4018/978-1-7998-7352-5.ch004

Zanin, F., Comuzzi, E., & Costantini, A. (2018). The Effect of Business Strategy and Stock Market Listing on the Use of Risk Assessment Tools. In *Management Control Systems in Complex Settings: Emerging Research and Opportunities* (pp. 145–168). Hershey, PA: IGI Global. doi:10.4018/978-1-5225-3987-2.ch007

Zgheib, P. W. (2017). Corporate Innovation and Intrapreneurship in the Middle East. In P. Zgheib (Ed.), *Entrepreneurship and Business Innovation in the Middle East* (pp. 37–56). Hershey, PA: IGI Global. doi:10.4018/978-1-5225-2066-5.ch003

About the Contributors

Babita Singla is an Associate Professor at Chitkara Business School, Chitkara University, Punjab, India. She spent a decade pursuing a career in academics, teaching, and research with passion and diligence. She worked as an Assistant Professor at the institute of national repute NIT Jalandhar. She completed an MBA program from RIMT-Mandi Gobindgarh, Punjab, India (2008-2010) in Finance & Marketing, and subsequently earned a doctoral degree from IKGPTU, Jalandhar, India. Her undergraduate studies in Mathematics and Economics from Government Rajindra College, Bathinda. She has cleared the National Eligibility Test (UGC NET) in 2011. She has over twenty research publications in international and national journals, over 11 publications/ presentations in international and national conferences, including 8 Keynote lectures/Invited Talks and ten books to her credit. Her current research interests are in business management, omnichannel retail, marketing management, and managerial economics. She loves to generate new ideas and devise feasible solutions to broadly relevant problems. She enjoys embracing the lessons learned from failure, stands up, and continues to grow.

Kumar Shalender is a Post-Doctoral Fellow of the Global Institute of Flexible Systems Management and a Doctor of Philosophy in Strategic Management. He has more than 14-year experience in the domain of Business Policy, Strategic Management, and Business Model Development and a total of 70 Publications including presentations at international/national conferences and book chapters to his credit. His current research areas include the field of Metaverse, Blockchain Technology, and Sustainable Development with a special focus on sustainable cities and mobility ecosystems in India.

* * *

Juana Maria Anguita-Acero is a PhD in Educational Sciences, MA in the Teaching of Spanish as Foreign Language and in Bilingual Education. Degrees in Translation and Interpreting, in English Studies and in Teaching. Expert in motivation and educational innovation in (non-)bilingual, multicultural and inclusive contexts. Full-time professor at the National University of Distance Education, UNED, Madrid, Spain.

Chandramowleeswaran G. is currently working as Assistant Professor in Department of commerce and business administration, Vel Tech Rangarajan Dr. Sagunthala R&D Institute of Science and Technology (Deemed to be University), Avadi Chennai. He has more than 11 years of experience in industry and 8 months of teaching experience with specialization in HR and Marketing. He Holds a B.Com., M.B.A., M. Phil., and Ph.D. in Management from Bharathidasan University, Trichy. He has contributed to motivating and talented sales & marketing Specialist with 11+ years of experience in business development, Employee Relations, training & development Including Process Development and execution in a consumer durable industry.

Manoj G. is currently working as Associate Professor in Department of Management Studies, VelTech Rangarajan Dr. Sagunthala R&D Institute of Science and Technology (Deemed to be University), Avadi, Chennai. He has more than 10 years of teaching experience with specialization in HR and Marketing. He Holds a B.Sc., M.B.A., M. Phil., and Ph.D. in Management from Bharathidasan University, Trichy.

Reena Gabriel is currently working as Asst. Professor Selection grade in SRMIST, Vadapalani. She was confident and result oriented marketing professional with nearly 20 plus years of distinguished performance in FMCG/ Healthcare/ Dairy Products / Food/ Hospitality industries. Passionate with proven abilities in the field of business management generating quantum growth within a highly competitive and rapidly changing market place. Proactive manager, team builder and tactical planner generating measurable increase in market share, sales and profitability.

Ravishankar Krishnan has more than 13 years of wide-ranging experience in teaching, research, administration and industrial relations. He has worked in Veltech and other reputed institutions. He holds a Master's Degree in Management Studies from Periyar Institute of Management Studies and a Ph.D. from Anna University, Guindy, Chennai. His teaching and research are in the field of Logistics, Supply Chain, Human Resources, and Sustainability. He has published and indexed more than 10 research articles in Scopus and ABDC (B Category).

Utsav Krishan Murari graduated from University of Delhi studied Economics and Political Science in the year 2009. He did Post-Graduation in Mass Communication from Guru Jambeshwar University of Science and Technology, Hisar in the year 2014. In the year 2015 he completed Bachelor of Education from Maharshi Dyanand University, Rohtak. He holds a doctorate degree in Communication and Media Studies from the Central University of Bihar, Gaya, Bihar. He is having 04 year industry experience. His specializations are Development Communication, Rural Communication, Public Relations, Corporate Communication and New Media. He has published 01 edited book, 12 research papers, articles in various International and National Journals. He has also published 08 Book chapters with different themes. He has participated and presented paper in two dozen National and International Seminar and Conferences. He also took part in research Methodology workshop which helps in improving the quality of research in the field of Social Sciences.

Oscar Navarro-Martinez is Associate Professor at the Faculty of Education in Ciudad Real (University of Castilla-La Mancha). He holds a degree in Pedagogy (UNED), Primary School Teacher (UCM) and PhD in Education (UCLM). He has been teaching Primary Education for more than two decades and at the UNED Associated Centre in Alcázar de San Juan. His main lines of research are: Educational Inclusion, attention to students with Specific Educational Support Needs, Cultural Diversity and use of multimedia materials and LMS systems.

Hemlata Parmar is an accomplished scholar and educator with a strong background in computer science and a remarkable research portfolio. She earned her Ph.D. in Computer Science Engineering from Kalinga University in 2021. Prior to her Ph.D., she completed her M.Tech. in Computer Science Engineering at MDU in 2016 and her B.Tech. in Information Technology from the same institution in 2014. Dr. Hemlata's research contributions are extensive, and she has made significant contributions to the field of computer science. Her publications in various renowned journals and conferences showcase her expertise in areas such as encryption algorithms, cryptography, artificial intelligence, blockchain, and cyber security. Her research has been recognized for its innovation and practical applications. Apart from her research endeavors,

Dr. Hemlata is also an enthusiastic educator. She has delivered lectures and participated in various academic programs and workshops, demonstrating her commitment to knowledge dissemination and pedagogical excellence. Her dedication to both research and education underscores her passion for advancing the field of computer science and contributing to its practical applications. Furthermore, Dr. Hemlata has shown her inventiveness through the filing of multiple patents related to AI, blockchain, and medical services. Her commitment to innovation and technology-driven solutions is evident in her patent applications. Dr. Hemlata has delivered guest lectures and participated in various academic programs and workshops, including topics like Artificial Intelligence in Media and Lean Startup & Minimum Viable Product/Business. Dr. Hemlata is an active researcher with several patent applications related to AI, blockchain, and medical services. Her inventions demonstrate a commitment to technology-driven solutions. In addition to her academic and research achievements, Dr. Hemlata has actively engaged in various national and international conferences, seminars, and workshops, further expanding her academic network and contributing to the academic community. Dr. Hemlata's multifaceted contributions to the fields of computer science, research, education, and innovation make her a prominent figure in the academic and technological landscape. Her continued pursuit of excellence and dedication to advancing knowledge are noteworthy attributes that define her career.

Catherine S. is currently working as an Assistant professor in SRM Institute of Science and Technology, Vadapalani, Chennai. She has specialized in Marketing, and has been in to academics for over a decade. She did her Ph. D in Management from Sathyabama Institute of Science and Technology, Chennai. Acting as Research Supervisor in SRMIST, Vadapalani. Published a Patent Office Journal No. 16/2023 in titled as "instigating machine learning methodology to review monetary advisory records in financial sector", in Application No.202341021851 A, 21/04/2023. She had published over 30 research papers in the journals that are indexed in Scopus, Web of Science, ABDC and UGC Care list, and published book chapters in the IGI Global publisher and national publisher.

Francisco Javier Sánchez-Verdejo Pérez is currently an Associate Teacher at Castilla-La Mancha University (Spain). He holds a BA in English Studies, Language and Literature and a PhD in English Literature (unanimous Cum Laude Distinction). Bilingual education, social and cultural aspects in language learning and teaching are his forte. In 2009 he was awarded a scholarship at St. Joseph's College in Dublin. In 2014 he was appointed to participate in the European Program "Pestalozzi", of the European Council.

N.V. Suresh, an accomplished academician from Chennai, Tamil Nadu, completed his BA at D.G.Vaishnav College, Madras University in 2012. He pursued an MBA and PGDM at Bharathiar University, earning a Ph.D. in Management from the University of Madras. Joining IIKM in 2014, he progressed to Head of the Department at Remo International College by 2020. Currently an Associate Professor and Vice-Principal at ASET College of Science and Technology since March 2022, he has authored textbooks, published 30 research papers, and guided Ph.D. scholars. Dr. Suresh has undertaken funded projects, editorial roles, and served in academic capacities, showcasing a diverse and impactful career.

Sanjay Taneja is currently an Associate Professor in Research at Graphic Era University, Dehradun, India. His significant thrust areas are Banking Regulations, Banking and Finance (Fin Tech, Green Finance), Risks, Insurance Management, Green Economics and Management of Innovation in Insurance. He holds a double master's degree (MBA &M.Com.) in management with a specialization in Finance and Marketing. He received his PG degrees in Management (Gold Medalist) from Chaudhary Devi University, Sirsa, India in 2012. He earned his Doctor of Philosophy (Sponsored By ICSSR) in Banking and Finance entitled "An Appraisal of financial performance of Indian Banking Sector: A Comparative study of Public, Private and Foreign banks in 2016 from Chaudhary Devi University, Sirsa, India. He received his Post Doctoral Degree from faculty of Social Sciences, Department of Banking and Insurance, Usak University, Turkey entitled on "Impact of the European Green Deal on Carbon (CO2) Emission in Turkey" in 2023. He has published research papers in reputed SCOPUS/Web of Science/SCI/ABDC/ UGC Care Journals. Prof. Taneja has more than fifty publications in total (Scopus/ABDC/Web of Science- 27).

Kiruthiga Velmurugan is a dedicated and accomplished academic professional with a strong focus on teaching and research. She is working as an Assistant professor in Faculty of Management, SRM Institute of Science and Technology, Vadapalani. She is specialised in both human resource management and marketing. She has published more than 70 research articles in international journals. Dr Kiruthiga V is actively engaged in contributing to the academic community and advancing knowledge in her areas of expertise.

Index

G

H

I

J

L

M

N

O

P

R

S

T

U

V

W

www.ingramcontent.com/pod-product-compliance
Lightning Source LLC
LaVergne TN
LVHW080651011026
849160LV00014B/1387

* 9 7 9 8 3 6 9 3 4 7 3 1 7 *